What People Are Say

T0343799

Temple of Love

Powerful. Fascinating. Inspiring. This book takes you on a wild ride through spirituality and transformation. A terrific book radiating love.
Dr. Joe Vitale, bestselling author of *Zero Limits* and *The Miracle*

Temple of Love touched me personally, blending the author's life experiences with mysticism, guiding me on a transformative journey of self-healing and self-discovery. This book is a great reminder to EVERYONE that inner peace and growth begin within, through self-reflection and spiritual exploration.
Derick Grant, world-renowned speaker and mindset coach

There is a powerful surge in the search for spiritual exploration, transformation, and healing. Most books discuss scientific facts or cover one type of healing modality. This is where *Temple of Love* stands out. This novel deconstructs layers of personal identity by unweaving faulty patterns and beliefs on the narrator's journey into freedom and light. We are drawn in, joining her as she explores numerous healing practices in sacred places of the world and within. Her passionate desire to free herself leaves the reader celebrating her victory as well as nudging us to explore our personal transformation as well.
Dr. Heather Browne, PsyD, LMFT, author of *Speaking with the Heart: Transforming Your Relationship and Communication with Compassion and Connection*

Natalie Glebova has weaved pure magic into her breakout book *Temple of Love*. In this enchanting parable, readers embark on a soul-stirring journey, guided by the wisdom of ancient traditions and the transformative power of self-discovery. Glebova's ability to blend spirituality and personal growth into a captivating narrative makes *Temple of Love* a profound, heart-opening adventure that will redefine your relationship with self-love and the Great Unknown.

Ashley Mansour, international bestselling author, LA-based writing coach and founder of Brands Through Books

Temple of Love

A Pilgrimage to the Heart

Temple of Love

A Pilgrimage to the Heart

Natalie Glebova

BOOKS

London, UK
Washington, DC, USA

CollectiveInk

First published by O-Books, 2025
O-Books is an imprint of Collective Ink Ltd.,
Unit 11, Shepperton House, 89 Shepperton Road, London, N1 3DF
office@collectiveinkbooks.com
www.collectiveinkbooks.com
www.o-books.com

For distributor details and how to order please visit the 'Ordering' section on our website.

A CIP catalogue record for this book is available from the British Library.

Design: Lapiz Digital Services

UK: Printed and bound by CPI Group (UK) Ltd, Croydon, CR0 4YY
Printed in North America by CPI GPS partners

The author of this book does not dispense medical advice or prescribe the use of any technique as a form of treatment for physical, emotional, or medical problems without the advice of a physician, either directly or indirectly. The intent of the author is only to offer information of a general nature to help you in your quest for emotional and spiritual well-being. In the event you use any of the information in this book for yourself, which is your constitutional right, the author and the publisher assume no responsibility for your actions.

We operate a distinctive and ethical publishing philosophy in all areas of our business, from our global network of authors to production and worldwide distribution.

When you come out of the storm you won't be the same person that walked in. That's what the storm is all about.
Haruki Murakami

Contents

Author's note

This is a work of creative non-fiction based on my own experiences with symbolic elements of a parable.

For years I've been asked by people around the world about what I would be doing had I not won the Miss Universe title in the year 2005. And that had me pondering what my life would've looked like had I gone down a different path. I believe that each decision we make ultimately takes us to a place we are destined for, just through different routes. This story is how I imagine my life would've turned out, and it certainly would've been one of the most scenic and colorful routes of all. Although most characters are real, their names and facts have been adjusted to protect their privacy. Each one is an amalgamation of several people from my life who enrich the story and help deliver a more universal message that goes beyond my personal experience.

As a reader, you can use any large North American city as a placeholder for Toronto, where I immigrated to with my family at thirteen and where I'd be living in that timeline of the multiverse.

One of the things that intrigued me most as a child was my consciousness, and this fascination had me constantly questioning who "I" am, and why was "I" chosen to experience this reality. I'd experiment with altered mental states by going into a place of "nothingness," although at the time I didn't understand what meditation was. As I grew up, that curiosity led me to be a spiritual seeker, a psychonaut, and a yogi. All of the practices described within these pages are real and experienced by me first-hand.

Please seek guidance of an expert professional or facilitator for practices involving plant medicines or intense breathwork techniques presented in this book, especially if you have any health concerns.

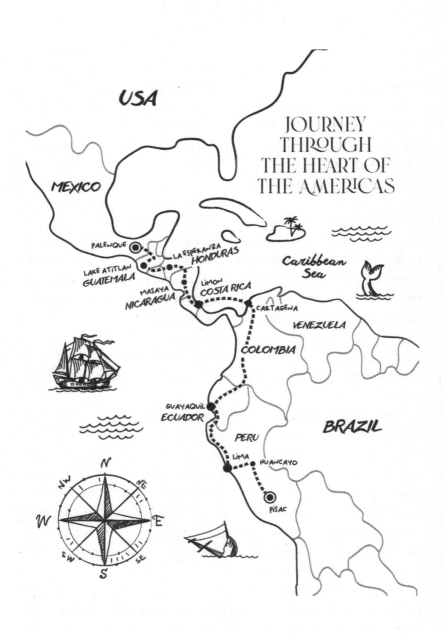

Prologue

A quiver of excitement for the journey ahead spiked the brew of mixed emotions I felt about doing it all on my own.

What am I getting myself into?

I left my work, my life, my responsibilities for something so frivolous and esoteric as a spiritual retreat?

If my parents find out what I am planning to do, I would never hear the end of it!

The airplane pushed off from the gate and proceeded to taxi towards the runway as I sat in the window seat, peering out the small round opening at the people working on the ground. Lost in a downward spiral of thoughts that kept getting darker and increasingly anxious, they seemed to be mirroring the gloomy weather of the late autumn season which was upon us so swiftly after a very short and unsatisfying summer. I looked at the sky and its thick muddy-gray clouds and couldn't help but feel a sense of unease about what was awaiting me on the other side of this flight.

My mind was racing as the airplane gained speed, coming at me from every angle to talk some sense into me in the hopes I would abandon this crazy idea.

There is still time to turn around and go back!

I was already half-way planning to get off the plane in Lima and book my flight back home as soon as we landed. Highly convincing arguments about why this was a bad idea were wildly thrashing in my head. Tears welled up in my eyes as I donned the role of a victim.

If it wasn't for that asshole that ruined my life, I wouldn't have to go on this crazy soul-searching adventure.

He pushed me into this – it's all his fault!

What else am I supposed to do – what are my options?

I can't continue the way I am now – that's just going to land me on anti-depressants.

I guess if anything bad does happen to me, that'll show him! He'll feel so guilty for how he treated me and realize that he is responsible for all of it.

Well, I guess that's the silver lining here...

The tension in my shoulders and jaw was building up as the mind ramped up its agitated monologue. I was restless and uncomfortable, wanting to just get off the plane but it was too late. The plane barreled down the runway and within seconds was airborne, flying through turbulence as it fought against gravity to gain altitude. My eyes were glued to the cloudy sky as if I was headed towards some sort of salvation up there.

I could hear my heart resounding in my ears as they popped with the change in cabin pressure. I felt like I was heading into oblivion – an imminent death. I was seeing dark spots across the sky, which was getting lighter the closer we got to the clouds. The noise of my head was getting progressively louder trying to compete with the hum of the airplane engine, and it all mixed together in a cacophony of madness from which there seemed to be no escape.

I kept watching the sky as though my life depended on it.

No one is going to love you again!

Your boss hates women! And you hate your job!

Time is running out to have children!

What are you doing with your life?

Congratulations, you are having a panic attack!

I was about to go into emergency mode, anticipating an embarrassing scene where I called the flight attendant to help me, when suddenly the plane broke through the clouds and the cabin was flooded with the golden light of the rising sun. At that exact instant, my mind went so quiet it was as if we'd entered a padded recording room.

Silence.

No more pulsating heartbeat in my ears. My breath became deep and slow, and the thoughts stopped for a few moments of complete tranquility. Out of the window I saw a clear ombré sky – oranges and yellows blending into light blue, then brighter blue the higher it went. The panic gave way to a sense of enchantment for the majestic splendor of the infinity and beauty of the open sky in front of me.

Through this quiet mental space, I perceived a faint "knowing" – a message that was coming in – not from my thoughts, but from somewhere deep inside of me.

You are exactly where you need to be. Trust the timing.

I relaxed my entire body, closed my eyes and drifted off into a sleepless hypnotic state of pure bliss. On the screen of my closed eyelids, I saw beautiful colors and shapes that lulled me further into a moment of serenity and comfort.

My peaceful reverie was disrupted by the pilot speaking over the intercom.

"Ladies and gentlemen, welcome aboard. Our flight time to Lima will be 7 hours and 34 minutes. We have clear skies ahead and we expect our arrival to be on time. Enjoy your flight."

34... There's that number again! Okay... Trust the timing.

I think I am on the right path.

Looking out the window again I let the warm rays of the sun kiss my face as the plane dipped to the side to make a course adjustment. There was so much space, stillness, light and beauty as far as the eye could see, and yet it was not visible because of the clouds when we were still on the ground.

I reached for my purse from under the seat and scrambled to find a pen to write down a floating thought. Opening the cover page of *The Alchemist*, which I had brought to read on my trip, I hurriedly scribbled it down...

True happiness is knowing that the sun is always there, even when it's not visible from the ground.

Part 1

The Calling

Chapter 1

Disconnected

I made my way through the crowded streets, dodging people who were in a rush to get somewhere at the end of a work day. With a yoga mat under my right arm and my work backpack slung over my left shoulder, I wanted to get home as soon as possible after a long and extra demanding day. I passed shop windows and ads at practically every step. Everywhere I looked there was someone trying to sell me something: the billboards, front window displays and magazine stands all fighting for my attention. As much as I tried to resist the urge to mentally try on what was displayed, I couldn't help but wonder how that dress or purse would look on me. I purposefully blocked out the thoughts of justifying purchasing that Italian leather computer case and how I really "needed it to look professional at work and to be taken seriously," and pressed on towards my apartment.

I had learned the hard way that no amount of material possessions would fill that gaping hole – the empty feeling inside – throughout most of my twenties when shopping was my favorite pastime whenever I felt lonely, rejected, stressed or anxious. It always seemed like a great idea to buy something new, and it held a great promise of relief from those unfavorable emotions, yet only gave a temporary feeling of wholeness, dissipating swiftly after the thrill of novelty wore off. Soon, I'd start craving that wholeness again, wrongfully associating its satisfaction with more new things. It was a vicious cycle that I managed to keep mostly under control in recent years although the shopping urge was still coming up from time to time.

I kept my gaze down and focused on my cute black Michael Kors combat boots thumping along the pavement.

When was the last time I walked barefoot?

I wistfully flashed back to how nice it was to just walk out of my little bungalow in Ubud to spend the whole day without shoes. Feet actually touching the earth, absorbing pure prana – the energy that is so abundantly present in nature, if we just connect to it and let it flow through us without being blocked by the plastic rubber soles most shoes are made of. My imagination replaced the shop windows and ads with a scenic green landscape of lush rainforests and layered rice paddies.

What a time it had been when I spent nearly a month on the enchanting island of Bali with my best friend, Alejandro [Ah-li-han-droh], a few years back! I had just resigned from a position as an analyst and after getting an offer to work at my current, medium-sized IT company where I headed up the Quality Assurance department as a project manager, I decided to put myself first and accepted the job with the condition that I would start in a month's time. It was three and a half weeks well spent, riding on a small scooter around this tropical mountainous town peppered with Hindu shrines, doing all the typical things that are on free-flow tap for other freedom-seekers like me – daily yoga, breathwork and sound healing workshops, drum circles and as many vegan restaurants as one's heart desires. Being a part-time vegan, I had ambitions to commit to it fully since college, believing it was a higher-conscious goal to aim for. Ultimately, I failed to go through with it, making excuses that good sources of plant protein were not easy to find. At the reasonable advice of my doctor I went back to eating eggs and some meat once in a while.

That's the time when I was really happy. I bet that's the recipe for happiness: nature, yoga, vegan food and no shoes!

How beautiful I had felt all those days when my hair was in its natural messy-curl; a golden tan; the mandala frock or those tie-dye yoga pants I wore almost daily. Oh, and that ankle bracelet I had bought at the local market, which I didn't take off until I came back. Can't wear it in the city with all this restrictive footwear.

Take me back!

Everything just seemed to flow so nicely there, and coincidences and synchronicities were a normal occurrence as I met incredible like-minded people on their own personal discovery journeys who just wanted the same thing I did – to be peaceful and connected to something bigger than us.

That's the last time I felt truly happy! Am I ever going to feel that joy again?

And here in this city, which I loved but was suddenly outgrowing, I was anything but peaceful. I was always preoccupied with pressure to hit my KPIs at work, a packed social calendar, and a gnawing feeling of running against my ticking time-bomb of a biological clock, which I had set at 35 and was approaching faster than I expected. My anxious state was further exacerbated by the fact that I was once again single in a city with millions of people.

Okay, this is not going to help me now – just think of something to be grateful for. Smile and be grateful!

I urged myself to smile and think of my yoga practice which had become my saving grace over the past few weeks after the breakup. Since Ubud, I had managed to establish a semi-regular routine of going to a Hatha flow class after work, which I tried to do at least three times a week if I wasn't completely drained after office hours. It never ceased to amaze me to observe how my outer life reflected the inner balance that yoga gave me. The more regularly I practiced, the better was my mental and emotional well-being.

So why don't I commit to it daily? If I get so much benefit from it, it should be a no-brainer – just do it!

But things always got in the way that seemed to take precedence over my best intentions to stick to this healthy daily habit. For starters, it was the immediate gratification of streaming the latest season of a trending show, or checking social media notifications to see who commented on my latest post and what others were posting. Then, of course, there were the consistently persistent dining invitations with friends, fashion shows, fundraisers that kept my social conscience clear, parties at my favorite hangout spot which never lived up to their expectations but instead just made me lethargic and sluggish the next day, and various family obligations which I begrudgingly attended out of guilt or old habit.

There was always something to do in this city, but most of the things I chose did not provide a feeling of fulfillment and contentment. I wanted the kind of purposeful life that made me spring out of bed each morning, full of energy and eager anticipation to do something meaningful that brought joy not only to myself but to others as well. I often wondered if anyone on this planet actually felt like this or was it just an ephemeral state everyone got a taste of in their post-adolescent idealistic phase before "real life" took over.

Having learned about yoga and mindfulness from my teacher in Bali, Krishnaraj, who was an expert on Vedic and Buddhist philosophies, I remembered the concept of *dukkha* [doo-kuh] – suffering resulting from cravings and general mundanity of human existence.

"We suffer because we resist what is happening and wish it were different," Krishnaraj, who had neatly cropped black hair, and was always clean-shaven and dressed in white clothing, would often say.

I began to ponder if wanting that sense of fulfillment, meaning and purpose was just another dukkha I needed to deal with.

I arrived home – a one-bedroom apartment in a medium high-rise on a narrow street just minutes from the subway. I loved my place. It was homey and a bit eclectic with trinkets and artifacts I'd collected from travels to Asia and the Caribbean. It had a great view of the city from my living room which opened into a small balcony where I often sat down to have my meals, weather permitting. I set up the take-out dinner I had brought home on the balcony table, poured myself a glass of Rioja, my favorite wine region, and took my time to savor the rich oaky dark cherry flavor with a hint of dill and leather. I liked eating alone since it helped me focus more on the food and less on conversation, but today I felt lonely and craved company. Since our separation and moving out of my ex-husband Dave's place and back to my own apartment, I had a sense of discomfort living alone. I missed having a man around the house to help with the hardware of things. But the extra closet and bed space were a welcome change.

The worst thing about going through a divorce was the feeling of failure that accompanied me daily. I felt embarrassed that I couldn't make the relationship work, and that I was somehow letting down all those people who came to our wedding. We had made promises to each other in our vows – to simply love – there was nothing complex about it.

So, what happened? Why did we drift to a place where we treated each other like roommates who don't even like each other very much?

The first year together we had fun, going out for dinners and shows, traveling, exploring each other's bodies and minds. And then, not even two years into our relationship, I started to sense something was wrong. I recalled the first sign of trouble the day we moved into his apartment together. After unpacking a few things, Dave told me he was going to meet someone and left me alone for the whole day, without cable or internet setup. I sat there feeling jilted and bewildered, not sure what to do with myself.

If only I had listened to my intuition back then. It seems so obvious now where it was headed.

But I ignored it and wrote it off as an isolated incident that didn't mean anything.

Things just got worse from there. He wasn't as attentive as he was when we first started dating; the sex dwindled to almost nonexistent; there were no compliments or physical affection. He began spending more time with his friends than with me.

Did he not find me sexy or feminine enough? What did I do wrong?

My desperation and need for intimacy, words of affirmation and to be appreciated for my feminine charm drove me into a two-week fling with a co-worker just a month before the separation. That was the first time I'd ever been unfaithful to a partner and the guilt that I felt right after the affair was haunting me even though I had already given up on the idea of us making it work. The distance between us kept growing and we didn't put any effort into talking about any of our many problems, keeping all the quiet resentment to ourselves.

We didn't even have that much in common! Why did I rush into marrying him so fast? I guess I really wanted to be "settled in" by 30. But now I'll have to celebrate this deadline as a single woman!

The thoughts of the past were starting to unravel me mentally, yet the emotions felt stuck in my gut, like an inflated balloon that was stretching my insides giving me an uncomfortably acidic sensation. I winced at the burning pain and slid down the zipper of my pants to find some relief. It didn't help.

My mind toggled between past and future thoughts, which were becoming more menacing and intense with each passing moment.

He didn't want me anymore!

Maybe I need a nose job, or bigger boobs?

Could I have acted or looked different to keep the fire burning?

I guess I wasn't fit enough for him – he was always such a gym freak.

Wonder if he ever cheated on me... I don't have any proof though...

But I did cheat on him and he never found out...

I want passion – someone who can't keep his hands off me and thinks I'm the most beautiful woman he's ever seen!

I want a partner to build a beautiful life together – I am not a solo act, I'm much better in a couple.

I don't want to be alone – I am a "relationship" person!

With my luck, I'll end up alone, still living here in my forties and beyond.

Why can't anything I do be a success from the first try? First driving test – failed! First job – fired! First marriage – divorced!

I recalled myself as a child, reading fairytales of great love and knowing deep inside that I was destined for it – that one day I would find a person who would love me the way I needed to be loved. My dream man would love me for my quirks and imperfections, for my light as well as my darkness, for my ambitions, values and dreams, and for my soul. And I would love him for the same.

My mental talk was reaching a boiling point that I didn't want to get to, so I launched out of my seat and hurriedly cleared away the dishes, trying to stay centered by focusing on what I was doing in the moment, the way Krishnaraj had taught me.

Breathe. Look at the bubbles of the dish soap. How does it feel on your hands?

Expand your rib cage and breathe three-dimensionally.

Okay, there you go... the power of the present moment. There is no problem in the present moment.

My life is a blessing, there's so much to be grateful for!

I finished the dishes and went to my bedroom where I sat down at my makeup dresser which doubled as an altar. It displayed an assortment of spiritual symbols spanning almost every major religion as well as non-sectarian energy-healing tools and talismans: crystals of different sizes and varieties, a carved wooden Lord Ganesha statue I had brought back from Bali, essential oils and incense sticks sprawled out amidst soy-based candles, a Nepalese mala with 108 sandalwood beads hanging over the mirror corner, a palm-sized copy of the Zohar given to me by a friend who was into Kabbalah, a tiny bronze Buddha statue, and a glass figurine of Saint Michael the Archangel that Alejandro's mother gifted to me.

And there was my most precious piece – a small three-fold orthodox icon of Jesus, Holy Mary with child, and a saint whose name I didn't know, given to me by my maternal grandmother right before we immigrated from Russia, where I was born. I didn't subscribe to the dogma yet the icon simply represented the love for my grandmother and held sentimental meaning for me, connecting me to my roots rather than to a deity.

To say I believe in God would be a much oversimplified statement. The typical understanding of "God" as an external force or entity that could somehow be quantified or conceptualized seemed so strange to me that I didn't even like using that word and cringed internally at the question "do you believe in God?"

For me, the idea of something so incomprehensible and vast, beyond the imagination was contradictory to itself. "God" – to use this word as a placeholder for now – is not of the physical realm, is all-encompassing, unquantifiable and immanent. So, assigning a word to describe this infinite and transcendent energy reduces it to simply another construct of the human mind. That is why none of the religions that dogmatized this unfathomable force appealed to me, but I curiously learned just enough from each one to make up my own understanding. I was not an atheist nor a theist – I was somewhere in the middle, like the Renaissance philosopher Baruch Spinoza. I had read about him in a blog that I loved and followed closely, which talked about Spinoza's concepts of "totality of existence" and "substance" as qualities of God and how he argued that everything in existence, animate or inanimate, is a fundamental part of God's essence.

Just like Spinoza, I associated God and the totality of being to nature, where one could come into contact with the state of beauty and harmony that permeates everything in existence. For that reason, I never prayed to God. The very act of it felt unnatural and futile since I believed that God was not a force outside of myself. No one was responsible for my life and my actions except me, so it was more reasonable to rely on my own strengths and abilities to influence reality.

But that night, alone in my apartment, was one of those rare occasions when I let go of these beliefs, and in a moment of hopelessness and desolation about my life, felt the need to pray. I desperately wished for an unknown force to help me take the pain away. I wanted favorable circumstances to turn in my favor. I surrendered to the idea of something greater than me and found the humility inside to ask for help.

Sitting at my altar, I lit a few candles and incense sticks, and closed my eyes. It felt like the inflated balloon in my gut turned into a heavy stone and was weighing all my emotions down, not letting them up to the surface. That sensation rose up to my throat as I felt it tighten, not allowing any sound to pass through. I fought with it and tried to squeeze out a sentence, a word, or a syllable. But I couldn't make a peep. Praying was such a foreign concept for me and it felt awkward to say out loud what I felt inside. So, I said it internally:

God, I know my perfect love is out there but perhaps out of reach in my current state... and I realize that I need to absolve myself of any dark energies present in me before you bless me with it. I am ready to do the work – whatever is necessary to have access to this love and a person who deserves to share it with me. I don't want to go through life never having experienced it. It is what my heart desires most in life. Thank you, thank you. I believe...

I didn't know what I believed in anymore, but I wanted to believe in *something* – anything that would give me hope and salvation from the infernal suffering I was in. I was ready to let go of any concept I so adamantly defended and to simply accept the mystery – something that I couldn't justify believing in. And to simply place my trust in the unknown vast abyss of nothingness, to be guided, protected, supported and loved. I allowed the stifled emotions to flow out of me like the monsoon rain that suddenly comes over and overpowers all other sounds around. My loud sobs felt cleansing and freeing as I let them shudder through my body originating somewhere so deep inside I didn't think it had a bottom. I gave in to the emotions and let them carry me on a whirlwind journey of my sorrow that was intensifying with each passing moment and climbing up to a crescendo that I hoped would bring some relief. I let it take me over. And when the climax of emotion finally hit, my body, exhausted from the tension, and my mind, not able to handle any more thinking, both released and I fell into a peaceful interlude where I could almost perceive something close to a sense of euphoria, yet couldn't quite grasp it.

Absent-mindedly, I slid over to my bed and fell into a deep dreamless sleep.

Chapter 2

Conditioning

Remember to pay attention to the signs – they are everywhere for you.

Half asleep, I kept repeating this sentence over and over again, fighting to remember it for later. So often, my first morning thoughts, which seemed so profound and important (sometimes even brilliant) in the moment, faded into ether as soon as I woke up.

I finally managed to snap into wakefulness with a startled sigh, and looked around the room. It was late morning by the looks of the light coming through the window. I had stayed up too late the night before and missed my 6 a.m. meditation session, which I had promised myself to get into the habit of daily but kept failing to keep up with it. The effects of the wine I overindulged in made my body heavy and my head hazy.

A faint noise of traffic from the street below wafted into the room – a stark difference to the sounds I had heard waking up each morning in Bali, where I was gently coaxed out of sleep by a choir of chirping jungle birds and wind playfully tussling with the trees. I closed my eyes again for a moment and imagined that I was there, and not in my bedroom, waking up alone, too physically and mentally drained to get out of bed.

What was that thought I just had? I tried hard to grasp the fleeting voice that was still somewhere in the back of my mind.

Was it something about signs being everywhere and needing to pay attention to them? What signs?

Ah, maybe the "Signs from the Universe!"

Although I've always considered myself a practical and straightforward type of person, these mysterious occurrences held a deep symbolic meaning for me, which I always held in great regard my whole life. For example, spotting a lucky penny or animal, a chance meeting with a friend after thinking about her, or seeing the clock display a particular number sequence like 11:11 or 12:34 at a moment of deep reflection. Seeing the angel numbers 1111 felt extra significant for me because my birthday happened to fall on November 11. I interpreted all these seemingly random events as the Universe talking to me. And even though I didn't know what the message was, I simply felt "blessed" in those moments.

Here's what I did know on the subject of synchronicities from one of my psychology classes in college. Synchronicities, which are synonymous with meaningful coincidences, is a term invented by Carl Jung, who described it as two unrelated and acausal events "falling together in time." It explained the internalized importance your mind gives an external event when said event mirrors a thought or a dream without any apparent cause.

I knew the value of paying attention to synchronicities. It facilitated the process Jung called *individuation* – spiritual and psychological development which in the scheme of total human development was at the top of Maslow's hierarchy of needs. It was also used by Jung as a therapeutic practice to help his patients, as in the famous story of the scarab, where a woman of overly rational and analytical mindset was resisting his treatment until he pointed out a beetle outside his office window connecting it to the one she saw in her dream. I believed that assigning importance to signs filled us with hope, a dose of which acted as a kind of placebo effect. So, I chose to create a meaningful connection for every coincidence I've come across with the intention of living a happier life.

I reached out for my phone at the bedside table and looked at the time.

09:34.

Was that a sign? But a sign for what? Maybe Ale will know…

I suddenly remembered that I promised to meet with Alejandro (or Ale [Ah-lei] as he preferred), who had been one of my best friends over the past three years, and I quickly jumped out of bed and into the shower. I was always excited to see him, and today, his lighthearted energy and uplifting aura was just what I needed. I desperately wanted him to help me take my mind off my suffering and advise me what to do next.

Taking extra effort to dress up just a little bit more than my usual weekend clothes, I hastily smudged on enough makeup to look half-way decent for our meeting, and scrambled to find my keys, dropping them from my trembling hands while locking up. I hurried down the street to our favorite vegan brunch spot – Harvest.

Ale, looking as adorable as always – his scruffy chestnut curls framing his face with dimples when he smiled, was already waiting for me when I arrived and waved me over to our table as I weaved my way through the packed restaurant. I plopped down in the seat in front of him.

"Sorry I'm late! I was trying to look beautiful for you," I teased him.

"You could've worn your shower curtain and still looked beautiful!" Ale replied with a big grin, his dark striking almond-shaped eyes doing that thing that always brought on a sensation of butterflies in my belly. I couldn't help but blush and melt inside at hearing his words. There had been a mutual attraction between us ever since we met at a music festival where he played. He was a DJ – amongst other things – and our many similarities and shared taste in music connected us instantly. Despite that, we had never gotten together romantically since one of us was always in a relationship with someone else. Now, for the first time, we were both single, and I couldn't help but wonder if we were destined for romance. But just then Ale interrupted my thoughts by saying he had a date planned later with a woman he just met and he would have to watch the time.

He could tell I had spent the previous night crying, pointing out my puffy eyes.

"Are you still blaming yourself for what happened? C'mon it's time to try to see how this all fits into the big picture! Sure, it hurts now. But I think soon you'll be able to see it as a good thing."

"How can divorce be a good thing? Do you know any happy divorced people?"

I was mentally defeated and had no energy to talk about Dave and our separation, which was still fresh at only three weeks, so I changed the subject.

"Do you remember our time in Bali? My God, it was just perfect! I really don't think I've ever felt so happy in my whole life! I think I want to go back there, or maybe somewhere else this time – not so far away. I just need to be whole again – I'm falling apart here!"

"Do you really think going on the 'hippie trail' again is going to fix you?"

"Look, this city is eating me up. It's like I am in the Matrix movies! This concrete jungle... the walls are starting to close in around me. All this consumerism, all those people chasing power and money and things... It's suffocating!" I exaggerated my tone and then softened it as I dreamily described the scene I was imagining. "I need nature. I need stillness. I want to connect to the elements again. It feels so sterile here. I want my feet on the earth. I want to breathe fresh air. I want to feel the sun on my bare skin. My head is not in the right place – I need an environment that'll help me get back into meditation."

"Do you want me to go with you?"

"No, this time I want to do it alone. It's an independence thing – I've never traveled anywhere on my own. Both my mom and Dave had always told me women shouldn't travel on their own – ugh, what kind of B.S. is that?"

"Alright, say you do go to 'find yourself'– how long is it going to take before you start feeling disconnected again after the trip? Last time it wasn't even two weeks after we got back and you were totally drained again. What you are looking for is not out there to find. Your life is here – *you* are here!"

I was getting slightly annoyed by Ale's unsupportive response. I thought he would be happy to hear that I wanted to work on myself. We were alike in many ways and being sister zodiac signs – him a Taurus and me a Scorpio, which sit directly opposite each other on the astrological wheel – we both were imaginative, stubborn and had the need to discover ourselves beneath the surface.

"So, what do you recommend then, O Great Master?" I asked sarcastically.

Alejandro was someone I looked to for advice on all things about energy and spirituality. Originally from Venezuela, he had spent several years studying at the University of Alchemy in Caracas and belonged to a group called the *Sacred Order of the Rainbow Warriors*, a tribe of people from all over the world. The name of the group was based on an apocryphal ancient Warriors of the Rainbow prophecy of the Hopi and Cree people which, although it had been largely dismissed as "fakelore" by scholars of the Native culture, was a beautiful story that many Indigenous people themselves have claimed to be passed down orally for generations. The legend spoke of a time in a distant future, when the earth would be in great peril and humans would be on a brink of self-destruction, and the spirits of the great chiefs and masters would intervene by inhabiting the bodies of people of different colors and races, making them remember the rituals and wisdom needed to restore health and peace to our planet. These Rainbow Warriors would then bring back the long-forgotten knowledge, teaching humanity how to live in harmony with nature, in unity with one another and in love with the world. A new greater civilization would then come about.

This legend had me rolling my eyes at Ale a few times, and I would tease him about entertaining notions of a future-day utopia. But the idealist in me wanted to believe that one day this prophecy would come to pass.

"When I was studying the Great Work of our teacher in alchemy," Ale replied, "I learned that you cannot run away from your problems. You've got to face them head on and do what it takes to transform yourself."

"What exactly is this alchemy? You never told me much about it."

The only thing I knew on the subject was from one of my favorite books by Paolo Coelho, *The Alchemist*, and that it was an old speculative science of turning base metal into gold, which in the book was extended towards more metaphorical concepts of facilitating personal growth and improvement.

"That's because you never really asked," Ale smirked and then continued, "It is a beautiful, complex and intricate study of energy, which makes up everything around us. For me, this practice has become the process of transmuting dense, dark energies into lighter ones by going through the seven steps of alchemy that turn substances into their pure, untainted versions – their truest essence.

"If alchemy is the science of turning lead into gold, it can be translated into the transformation of self as a spiritual alchemist. It is an individual journey – one that will only work if you walk it alone. It can be lonely on the way and can make you feel separated from your loved ones. But it's a valuable and profound process, provided that you pay attention to the positive changes inside and observe which stage of the seven steps you are in, as you walk this path towards an elevated version of yourself."

"What are the seven stages that you mention?"

Ale proceeded to tell me each stage – calcination, dissolution, separation, conjunction, fermentation, distillation and coagulation – and how they applied to personal transformation, most of which I could only partially grasp, as it sounded much too obscure for my rational "self."

The waiter came by to take our order and we quickly told him what we wanted.

Ale pointed at the pendant with an Egyptian hieroglyphic symbol he always wore on a gold chain around his neck.

"Do you know the ankh?"

"It's ancient Egyptian, isn't it? I heard it is a symbol of life, or something like that."

"Yeah, and it's also known as the key of life but it has many other meanings depending on who you ask. Some people interpret it as the elements required to make life: water, air, and sun. Others see it as the union of heaven and earth. Actually, one of the most common interpretations is that it depicts male and female symbols coming together in union to create life... can you see it? Mostly though, people wear it for protection, good fortune and long life."

"Why do you wear it?" Of course, I had noticed it and had always wanted to ask him about it.

"I see it as the balancing of the masculine and feminine energies which are present in each person. So I wear it as a reminder that we find that balance through our challenges. In alchemy, we can use symbols like this, that have a deep meaning to the person, as a tool for self-transformation and personal power. But you don't need the actual object – you can call upon it."

"Well, I don't really have anything symbolic like that except my ankle bracelet. Remember when I bought it at that market with you? They told us it was blessed by the monks. I should put it back on, maybe it'll bring me better luck in love," I fake-laughed.

Alejandro suddenly seemed to go into a mini-trance as his gaze unfocused, kind of looking right through me. His usual lively tone abruptly became more urgent and commanding.

"These days, everyone is looking for a magic pill – a quick-dissolving, fast-acting, no-assembly-required solution to help them stop the pain they are in. The pain of wanting to matter. The pain of unrequited desires. The pain of the senselessness of life. The pain of not believing we're good enough."

"Yeah," I interjected, "If only someone could just make that pain go away in a snap – how much easier would it be to enjoy life? I'd get so much more things done... maybe I'd finally get that eco business started, write a book, go back to Bali!"

"You and so many others who think they'd start earning more, lose weight and get fitter, or be seen as a role model by their friends and as a 'success' by their parents.

"Oh, if only not for this damn festering pain under all of our great ambition, keeping us at an arm's length – close enough to see it, but just out of reach of our desired lives. And so, we turn away and fall into a subdued despair about this pain, because actually, there *is no* magic pill and we all instinctively know it. We hopelessly grasp at anything that will provide temporary relief, and for a while it seems to work."

I was intrigued by what he was saying but surprised because I had never heard him speak like this. He sounded more like a prophet than his usual sassy self – as though it wasn't really him, but someone else, perhaps an ethereal entity that was using him as a medium. Dressed in a colorful tie-dye shirt and a brown corduroy jacket, his somewhat hipster look contrasted with the wisdom of the universe he seemed to be channeling from another realm.

What does he mean when he says unrequited desires? Is that the pain of wanting to be loved fully and completely?

I didn't want to interrupt this divine connection he seemed to be in, so I let him continue.

"We bury ourselves in work, home chores, and social obligations. We binge on empty calories and mindless TV shows. We pack out the social calendar and dissolve into the social media newsfeed. Sometimes we even turn to those very 'pills,' be it food, alcohol or pharmaceuticals we know aren't good for us but do the trick to numb the pain, yet never heal it.

"We listen to motivational speeches and read inspiring stories of heroes we wish to be like one day, but again, that only gets us as far as the boundary of our comfort zone."

I've been guilty of all of that. Gosh, he's really on point today!

"We clench our jaws, grind our teeth, push and pull at the invisible weight with all our might, in a futile attempt to move it just an inch. We scream into the abyss of the unknown hoping someone out there will hear us and offer a hand, tell us what to do next, and lead us on the right path. But no one is coming..." Ale paused in tandem with my breath as I absorbed the soberness of his words. "And when that help doesn't come, we lose just a little bit more faith each time, and fall deeper into the recesses of our self-loathing caves, moving further and further away from what we as children once believed was so possible."

My eyes went to the ankh pendant on his chest and it appeared to be slightly glowing with a soft golden aura. I blinked twice to clear my eyes and the glowing stopped. Ale was on a roll.

"We stop believing in miracles. We forget about our inner child, inner goddess, and inner warrior. We stop creating and turn to consuming, always wanting things we don't have, and completely terrified to lose the things we do have.

"We continue to live in denial of our great potential, forgetting that we are infinitely powerful beings – able to create and manifest anything we want. We forget that each breath is our opportunity to be that creator and that our imaginations are a fertile soil for growing the seeds of inspiration that we are blessed to receive in abundance... if we stay open to it."

Our food arrived and the waiter wanted to know if there was something else we were planning to order, seeming eager to get us out to get the next customers in. I hastily waved him away keeping my eyes glued on Ale, worried that he would lose the connection and stop speaking. I needed to hear the rest of what he was transmitting. I gently touched his hand as if to nudge him to go ahead.

He looked at me with sadness in his eyes, and in that moment, I felt a pain that he was projecting. I wondered if it could be the collective pain of every human being that has ever lived or will ever live on this planet. He spoke a bit more quietly now, looking straight into my eyes and I felt like he was talking directly to my soul.

"But no one wants to do the real work it takes to change and face up to the truth which can be plain scary and ugly at times. No one wants to look at themselves in the mirror in a moment of an emotional catharsis or a fit of rage. It's tough to face the reality – that you have created your own problems and you are now spinning in a perpetual wheel of your self-imposed limitations, not willing to do the work to get off once and for all."

Well, how the hell do you get off this wheel? I feel like I've tried everything! I do yoga, I meditate... on and off.

"It takes work to find the relief you're looking for." Ale continued as though he felt my inner resistance. "Not the face-contorting, weight-lifter work of pure hard willpower and pain as your mind shouts motivational slogans at you like a maniacal drill sergeant.

"It takes the kind of courageous, intentional and consistent introspection, where you carefully brush away layers of sediment and dust to reveal the gorgeous artifact hidden beneath, like a patient paleontologist discovering the bones of an extinct animal."

"Wow, you sure are getting poetic today," I chuckled mockingly, "but that is so true – I need to do some digging inside. It's just that it's so hard to face some things, you know?"

"As unpleasant as it may be to dissect yourself and inspect the specimens under a microscope, no one is better equipped than you to look inwards, find the stillness, joy, love and great vastness you are composed of. And to recognize the incredible abilities of your true essence."

"So, what's your solution? More meditation?"

Ale wasn't fazed in the slightest by my sarcasm. "What it takes is this: daily rituals, non-negotiable routines, energetic and psychological tools, and simply making the time for yourself to do the inner work needed to achieve real lasting change, healing and transformation you desire."

We sat in silence for a few moments, and I was both in awe and slightly bewildered at his intensity.

"What was THAT?" I inquired, trying to understand what had just happened and how he was able to do what he did. "Where did you go just now? It almost didn't sound like you."

Ale shrugged and said that it was a first for him too, although he felt like it was himself talking. He didn't know where the words came from, but just knew I needed to hear them.

We continued chatting about work and friends, but I was preoccupied with his powerful speech, questioning whether I was that person he was describing, who was eager to find a quick solution to all of my life's problems.

The waiter came over with the bill and our time together was up. I wanted to keep talking to Ale but he had to go.

We walked out onto the street and he gently grabbed me by the shoulders, squaring me off towards him so we were facing each other. He took off his chain with the ankh symbol and put it around my neck.

"No, no, I can't," I tried to protest. "This is your special pendant. You're not Ale without it!"

"I can feel that you're going through something big, and you need it now more than I do. Promise me you won't forget its power and make good use of it, okay?"

Then he gave me a hug, kissed me on both cheeks and softly touching his fingers to my chin to lift up my head like I was a child, said,

"Remember, there is no magic pill. Only magic *you*!"

~

Why do we think the way we do, and why do we believe what we believe?

Who is responsible for the way we view life?

Is it our free will that gives us the permission to construct our own world view – or are we programmed to have a structural flow of thoughts, each one based on some event that caused it to happen?

It was the age-old question of determinism versus free will, which is still argued to this day by philosophers, psychologists and sci-fi nerds, and there doesn't seem to be undisputed proof for either side.

I wanted to believe in free will – it gave me hope that we are free to choose what we decide to do and how we act on our thoughts. Freedom has been my top priority ever since I could remember. As a child, I valued freedom above all else – I wanted to be allowed to let go of my homework obligations and simply enjoy playing and running around outside at my grandparents' house in a small town in southern Russia, where I felt the most liberated because my mother was not there to give me something to study or practice. I would run the length of the tiny living room that connected to a small bedroom and joyously squeal, "FREEDOM!"

Yet the analytical, practical side of me saw very clearly how each of our beliefs had a root cause in some past event in our lives. The determinist in me assumed that the brain was like a computer that was programmed to run code – a sequencing of instructions performed in a specific order in an algorithm.

I wondered how I managed to sway so far from the "freedom-seeking" youngster I once had been, and end up in a corporate system, quietly resenting my boss and the work that I was doing, and plodding along to the tune of my company's slogan which ironically for me, stated, "Developing for freedom of possibilities." I didn't really care about the quarterly output goals and final product quality standards. I did it because I wanted to be taken as a professional and to be able to identify with the respectable title of "software engineer" on my business card. It gave me a sense of pride and I wouldn't dare do anything that would jeopardize the progress I was making towards what society deemed to be successful.

I looked at the people passing me by on the way home from brunch with Alejandro. Everyone appeared like robots on autopilot, with their eyes fixated on their mobile phones and all dressed in monotonous outfits without much color or creativity. They were determined to get to wherever it was they were rushing to, their faces leaden and joyless, probably preoccupied with the next thing they had to do, who they wanted to become, and what they wanted to have. Maybe they were thinking about how their lives could've turned out differently had they done something differently. That was exactly what I was thinking.

What went wrong?

It wasn't supposed to go this way – did I misstep on my perfect plan?

My plan was simple: graduate with a bachelor's degree; get a job which sets me on the fast-track for promotion and a high-paying position so I am making six figures by 40, get an MBA or extra qualifications needed to sling myself over to the higher ranks, get married by 30 and enjoy a few years without kids, travel a few times a year and work our way up to senior-level positions, start a family and move to a nicer neighborhood where we can set up a good base and feel secure, have our mutual savings roll over into a nice retirement package and with any luck of the stock market be F.I.R.E. (Financially Independent Retired Early.)

I always believed that if you have a vision, an action plan, and discipline to see it through, you would reach all of your goals one way or another, even with unplanned detours along the way. But this "life implosion" I seemed to be having lately was not part of my vision. A divorce, with its subsequent total personal meltdown, was shameful and unsavory to the recipe I had concocted in my head about what my ideal life should be. I strongly believed that if you work hard and stay the course, you will be rewarded.

So, did this serve as a punishment for me missing a beat somewhere? Did I take the wrong turn, or get too complacent about being my best self?

I always made choices that would serve the highest good of my vision, and played along to the rules of society, even if it meant giving up on sleep or social life. Every success and small win seemed like rewards from the Universe for the sacrifices I was making. It felt good to make my parents proud and I enjoyed their validation of my accomplishments, basking in the warm glow of their approval. Keeping up with, and at times surpassing, my friends' progress towards that "ideal life" was somehow satisfactory, not in a way of rejoicing for someone else's loss or pain, but as an ego-boosting self-congratulatory way of reaffirming my place in society. I seemed to have it all – a good job and an adequate intellect that afforded me a nice lifestyle, an open and friendly personality, and aesthetically pleasing physical attributes that I leveraged into a brief semi-successful modeling career throughout my early twenties before leaving it for a more serious career in tech. I was well-traveled, well-cultured, played the piano pretty well and spoke three languages.

I knew my worth, but it only extended as far as the abilities I had, the accolades I'd collected, and my physical beauty. Anytime I began falling behind in any of these categories or failed to achieve more qualifications that seemed necessary to be considered successful, my confidence wavered and I desperately tried to get rid of the nasty feeling of not being enough with decisive action to fix myself. I'd up-level my fitness to longer and harder gym sessions, put in extra hours of work to make sure I was the highest performer in my department, posted more on social media to stay relevant and gain more followers, and made sure my personal grooming was impeccable for my boyfriends (eventually my husband) to appreciate me for. I was not a perfectionist by any stretch. I even liked some of my quirks and flaws, and allowed myself the luxury to binge-watch a TV show over the weekend, but my fear of failure kept me from sliding off the discipline wagon. I could not fail at my goals.

That's why this pending divorce hit my ego so hard. Not only was it going to set me back a hefty chunk of time off my planned track, but it also made me revert to the version of myself I thought I had grown out of – the socially and physically awkward, insecure, self-shaming teenager I used to be. It's like I had hopped into a self-image time machine and the emotions it dredged up were dark and debilitating.

Back to self-work – I need to reestablish my self-love again!

If I reconnect to my passions, surely, I'll "find myself" in there.

Okay, but where do I start? Where should I go?

This is exhausting!

My deep despair was draining my energy and I dragged myself back to the apartment to take a nap. Before falling asleep I asked myself again whether or not I believed in free will.

Am I free to make those changes Ale talked about in myself, and actually stick to them?

Or am I pre-programmed to act on my reptilian brain instincts and stay in the same self-sabotaging loop of surviving through life?

I really hoped it was the former, but I didn't have any proof that it really was so. That's when I made a promise to myself to find the confirmation that we, as humans, are in charge of our own happiness.

Chapter 3

Plant Teachers

Sitting in my office at the final hour of the work day, I looked outside the window and watched neighboring office buildings begin to light up as nighttime fell over the city. As far as my eye could see from the twenty-second floor of the building, there was glass, metal and concrete – not a natural element in sight. It was beautiful, nonetheless, in a kind of sterile futuristic sci-fi fantasy novel way. I marveled at the technological advancement of humans – perfect, symmetrical and functional, yet lacking in something that was inherently human – warmth, a sense of interconnectedness and feeling of home.

When I was out in nature, I saw myself reflected in it, with all the asymmetry, imperfections, and a perceived order amidst the chaos of the multitude of life forms that existed there. But here, in the city with millions of human life forms, I felt disconnected from the world and did not see myself in these cold lifeless structures. The pulsing electric energy emitted from power lines, cell towers and LED displays seemed to counteract and cancel out my own energy, and I was constantly fighting to stay ahead of letting it drain me. I hoped that the black tourmaline bracelet I was wearing on my wrist, which has been marketed to block out harmful EMF radiation and soak up negative energy, was doing what it was meant to do. I needed all the help I could get as I often struggled with lethargy and adrenal fatigue, feeling particularly tired in the mornings and late afternoons.

My general health was adequate and I didn't have any serious conditions, but I considered myself as someone who was of "delicate constitution" in terms of physical stamina and immune system. I suffered from frequent headaches, had irregular and very painful periods, and endured bouts of gastritis. Due to persistent and seemingly chronic nasal and throat infections, I had to have my adenoid and tonsil glands extracted in my adolescence. Even then, I still caught colds often. I tried to avoid overly strenuous activities, drinking iced beverages and being in cold temperatures for extended lengths of time, all of which, according to the women in my family, was the culprit of illness. This was the belief that was ingrained in me from a young age.

Suddenly, the lights in the office and outside the building switched off with an audible click, and the background hum of all the electrical equipment powered down. Silence and darkness engulfed the room. It startled me for a moment until I realized it was a power outage. The whole block was affected from what I could see out the window.

A few seconds later, emergency lights flickered on giving the room a faint greenish glow and illuminating the hazy outlines of the furniture and the computer monitor in front of me. I couldn't see much as my eyes hadn't yet adjusted to the darkness, so my attention instantly got drawn to the only source of light in front of me – the computer screen reflecting the emergency lights and... myself.

The person staring back at the monitor looked as miserable as I felt, and it jolted me to my core. I hardly recognized myself in the reflection – tired apathetic eyes, caved in mouth with deep nasal-fold lines that the overhead lights seemed to accentuate, dull skin tone, and drab-colored clothing. This was not an image of the person I wanted to identify with.

Where is that joyful, adventurous, curious, fearless woman with a nice tan, free flowing hair, adorned in bright colors and an ankle bracelet?

I yearned to be her. I didn't want to continue on the path I was currently on because it scared me. I was afraid that if I didn't act on bringing that other "self" back, I would start to slowly wither away into an angry, bitter cynic who hated the world and blamed it for all of her misfortunes. I could already sense that resentment for my job bubbling up, so something would have to change in order to have a shot at true happiness and total wellness.

I knew I had two options: change my attitude and outlook on how I viewed my job, or change the job.

I rarely allowed myself to play the victim and loved taking responsibility for how I was feeling, being proactive in nipping my negative feelings in the bud before they snowballed into something I couldn't handle. But at this moment I wasn't capable of making any life-changing decision or reframing my position into a positive. I was feeling helpless and too emotionally exhausted to try to figure out a solution. It was a very unpleasant feeling of being trapped in a life I didn't want to live – no escape from the pain. My mind felt like a caged animal pacing back and forth in a tight space looking to find some release or comfort, but bumping into walls over and over again.

It was getting unbearable to be alone with my thoughts. I needed to switch my attention to something else. I reached for my phone which always provided instant but temporary relief and opened my email. The first unread email displayed a subject line "Divine Soul Connections" received at 11:34 a.m. I tapped to open it and remembered that I received it because I was subscribed to a mailing list from a group of healers I had met in Bali when I stumbled into one of their sound bath ceremonies by chance. They performed both offline and online energy healing work in their large community of digital nomads.

The heading read: "A heart-opening shamanic Cacao ceremony in a safe, conscious space of soul expression, healing & reconnection on Saturday, November 10." The body of the email revealed some interesting information about cacao as one of the oldest Master plants that was used by the indigenous people of South and Central America as sacred medicine and invited readers to join a virtual cacao meditation session. It was explained that cacao had both physical and neurological healing properties, promoting cardiovascular health, reducing blood clotting, regulating heartbeat and blood pressure, decreasing risks of heart attack and stroke, enhancing the mood, improving PMS symptoms and menstrual cycles, and detoxifying the liver.

This may be just what I need! And what a great way to start a new decade – it's a day before my birthday!

I pulled up the registration form and eagerly signed up for a virtual session that was a couple of weeks away.

The words "Master plants" intrigued me, and I wanted to know more about what other such plants existed. Opening up a new search query on my phone browser, I typed in the key words. The results displayed suggestions related to my search: *master plant dieta, ayahuasca master plant dieta, camalonga dieta, huachuma plant medicine, teacher plants, Amazon plants, plant medicine retreat...*

I didn't recognize most of the words on the list, but I remembered Ale talking about drinking ayahuasca when he studied with the Sacred Order of the Rainbow Warriors. He didn't go into the details about what this drink was made from or what it did exactly, but he did say that it helped the students connect deeper to the wisdom of the writings of their guru and receive faster transformative results of the alchemy practice. I always figured it was just some kind of fermented herbal drink that made them drunk and they imagined "talking to God" or something along those lines. Ale was a bit secretive about his practice and since I wasn't showing much interest in it, he didn't tell me anything more.

I clicked through a few articles and read about the different Master plants that were in use in shamanic circles. There were some I had heard about, like psilocybin mushrooms that grow all over the world in different varieties and produce hallucinogenic effects on those who take them in moderate to strong doses. Then there were others of which I had no prior knowledge like ayahuasca, also referred to as "the vine of souls" – a culturally significant drink amongst the tribes in Peru, Ecuador and other countries along the Amazon basin, used by healers to connect to the "divine" through the energy of the plant and receive messages from ethereal realms. I read that it is concocted by combining pieces of the ayahuasca vine (Banisteriopsis caapi) and leaves from the chacruna shrub (Psychotria viridis), boiling it for several hours, and performing ceremonial chanting in order to activate the potent ingredients that were responsible for the mind-altering effect. What I found interesting was that on its own, the ayahuasca vine doesn't produce the intended result, but instead acts as an enzyme blocker in the digestive tract to allow the psychoactive ingredient, DMT, in the chacruna to reach the brain without being broken down. How the healers knew about combining these two plants hundreds of years ago remained a mystery.

I also read about Huachuma, also known as San Pedro, a mescaline-containing psychedelic cactus that is indigenous to the mountainous regions of the Andes and spread out throughout South America. It was used in a similar way as ayahuasca, as a tea brewed by shamans to heal people physically and energetically, and to connect to nature and to the spirit world.

Another fascinating part about all of these plant medicines for me was the history of their medicinal, spiritual and ceremonial use. I discovered that they'd been around for centuries, in some cases even millennia. Archeologists and historians have traced uses of various types of entheogenic substances as far back as 1500 BC by ancient Greeks, where the initiates of the Eleusinian mysteries ingested a psychoactive secret potion called kykeon, which induced visions and ecstatic states, and is thought to contain an LSD-like fungus, ergot, that grows on rye. Other ancient civilizations, spanning North and South America, have revealed prominent mushroom depictions in stone sculptures and ceramics, providing clear evidence that psychedelic rituals were central features of the Mayan, Aztec and Incan cultures. Chinese traditions recorded the use of hallucinogenic plants, including mushrooms, in herbal manuscripts almost 2,000 years ago. Ancient Egyptian artifacts have also pointed to some kind of religious reverence of hallucinogenic mushrooms with fungiform representations in Egyptian crowns that provide iconic symbols of entheogenic traditions.

The deeper I searched, the more I noticed that there was a growing body of research on therapeutic benefits of plant medicines and chemical psychedelic substances, which includes significant improvements in depressive and anxious states, and overall increase in emotional well-being. According to one study led by Weill Cornell Medicine researchers, the psychedelic drugs LSD and psilocybin activate serotonin receptors on brain cells in a way that reduces the energy needed for the brain to switch between different activity states.

After satisfying my academic curiosity, what I really wanted to know was what the experience of taking any of these substances was like. I needed to find out from people's personal experiences, so I watched a few video reviews of those who dared to participate in these ceremonies of various settings and share it publicly. Some people went to one of the South American countries, the most popular one being Peru, the supposed birthplace of the ayahuasca tradition. These sounded like the most intense experiences that involved lengthy and strict diets (*dietas*) that participants needed to observe for weeks before beginning the actual ceremony. The shamans who facilitated these ceremonies had a whole choreography of chanting, singing, blowing smoke and burning herbs, playing instruments, dancing and talking to the spirit of "Madre Ayahuasca." Other people did it in a retreat or home setting and from what I was reading you could find a shaman in practically every part of the world, however, not all of them were considered authentic or properly trained. No matter what type of setting was chosen, one common thread about each participant's experience was the uncontrollable and sometimes violent vomiting that ensued after ingesting the ayahuasca brew. The hallucinations ranged greatly from person to person. I was stunned to read that some had the experience of "becoming" an animal and seeing everything through its eyes. More surprising still, some went through a process of being in their mother's womb or remembering their birth and being nursed by their mother as a baby.

As I watched and read review after review, a common theme became clear that this was a way of looking deeper into one's subconscious mind to heal past wounds. The more I thought about how much suffering in love I had endured in my life, the more intrigued I became.

Could this be the key to showing me what went wrong with Dave and all the others?

One of the most memorable reviews was from a young woman of approximately my age who said she had met and talked to her inner child who told her about how she'd forgotten to love life and experience it through play. The child was sad and suffering, and the woman made her a promise that she would give more time to enjoying life's little pleasures and be more curious, adventurous and passionate. *I could use some more play in my life!*

There were also some negative reviews and stories of ayahuasca ceremonies that turned into nightmares. One man wrote about how the entire process was about exorcizing a demon that had haunted him for life. Others went through an emotional/energetic cleanse – vomiting out what appeared to them as snakes and maggots! A woman kept dying in her visions over and over again in horrendous ways, one of which was being buried alive! Some had visions of meeting monsters, gargoyles, mythical creatures of the underworld, and the devil himself! This all sounded terrifying, bewildering and exhilarating at the same time. It was as if I had discovered a new planet where our rules didn't apply, and I was excited about exploring all the possibilities and secrets it held.

How is all of this even possible? Do plants really have intelligence and sentient consciousness? Are there really realms beyond our physical one that we cannot perceive until we use these plants?

I was so engrossed in my research and analysis that I hadn't even noticed the power had come back on in the office. Taking in my surroundings again, I decided to continue reading more on the topic at home. I needed to absorb everything I'd read. A walk home in the unusually warm evening was the perfect setting to do that.

I passed by shop after shop on my way, once again trying not to look at the tempting items they were offering. I stopped at an intersection and my eyes went up to an LED billboard above, which displayed some ad for a realtor and the number of properties sold. The number, glowing in red, was 34. It didn't mean anything to me, but I stared at it, hypnotized by the flashing number while waiting for the light to turn green.

As I continued on, I couldn't help but consider the use of psychedelic plants as it related to our spirituality.

These plants are all around us, a segment of the very nature that we, ourselves are a part of. There must be a reason why we respond in such transcendental ways to the chemicals found in them, and why our brains have receptors for these substances in the first place.

I remembered a few articles from my research earlier that evening about the compound DMT that is the psychoactive ingredient in the ayahuasca brew, and that this compound was abundantly present in nature, from animals including toads and frogs, fish and sea sponges, to flowers, trees and spices. Dimethyltryptamine (DMT) belongs to a class of chemical compounds called tryptamines which mainly modulate amounts of serotonin – a neurotransmitter involved in the regulation of mood, appetite, sleep and memory – throughout the central nervous system. I found it fascinating to read that DMT was biosynthesized in the pineal gland in the human brain.

Perhaps these plants are the link between our physical bodies and our spirit? Could they be the key for what most people are seeking when it comes to that divine connection with something bigger than us?

It would then be very easy to see why the church and major religious institutions would not want people to have access to these devices. If people could find that deep connection to "God" by themselves through the use of entheogens, what benefit would the church bring to them?

Arriving home, I decided to take a bath and have a relaxing self-indulgent evening of pampering myself with essential oils, music and imported Italian gianduja chocolate. This was actually the good part of being single – having the freedom to do what I want with my time and focus on self-love just because... I could!

Sitting in the bathtub filled with bubbles and bath salts, candles and a box of chocolates next to me, I turned on my favorite playlist of downtempo delicate beats with subtle background sounds of nature, shamanic chants and tribal voices. In that moment it felt like this was my own ceremony of connecting to the deeper part of myself and I didn't need any healer or substance to do that. I closed my eyes and thought about all the stories I had read earlier of people's journeys into other worlds with ayahuasca. My imagination was actively shuffling pictures of what it could be like one by one.

So fascinating!

I've always been interested in mystical experiences, even as a child. I recalled a time when I was about eight or nine years of age and, together with a group of neighborhood kids, we decided to see if we could reach an altered state of consciousness. Of course, we didn't know what it was and we didn't have a name for it, but someone in the group had heard it from an older sibling and urged us all to try to "lose our consciousness" as a fun experiment.

The process was as follows: squat down low on your haunches, feet grounded; hold your hands around your waist, pressing into your abdomen tightly; start breathing rapidly in and out while restricting your abdomen; hold your breath after a few minutes at an inhale and stay still for a minute; exhale and stand up quickly while shifting your eye gaze upward to the sky.

At this point, inevitably, each one of us practicing this "ritual" would momentarily pass out and fall backwards, being caught in the arms of our friends who protectively stood guard all around. I don't recall much after the loss of consciousness except for seeing some beautiful visual effects of colors and patterns and being completely free of thoughts. I was not aware of my physical body but had complete mental awareness of "being," a kind of presence of myself.

Little did we know, this silly activity was actually very similar to some very effective and beneficial yoga breathwork techniques such as *achaagri, agnisara dhauti* with *uddiyana bandha,* or *bhastrika* – aimed at purifying the body, removing diseases, eradicating illness and arousing the Kundalini energy. I had heard about these and tried a few of them in Bali when Krishnaraj explained the benefits of awakening our Kundalini. He told us that in Vedic philosophy and yogic practices, Kundalini – meaning "coiled snake" in Sanskrit – is the life-force energy symbolically represented by a snake, that lies dormant at the base of the spine and as it awakens, rises up the spinal energy channel towards the third eye, at which point it can cause a shift in consciousness and allow you to tap into a powerful source of internal power. If all the chakras are clear and open, this energy is able to flow easily to the top and one is able to experience a spiritual "awakening."

I loved the theory behind these practices but was still skeptical about its practical application in my daily life. It didn't seem wise to spend time opening up my third eye and experiencing altered states when I had work deadlines and social obligations to juggle. However, I kept myself open to trying new things and was naturally drawn to practicing yoga and breathwork to explore the farther reaches of my internal universe, although I never experienced any of the transcendent effects that Krishnaraj had described.

My phone pinged, switching my attention from thoughts of the past to whoever might be trying to reach me now in the present. I grabbed it to see the incoming message and noticed the time displaying 20:34 on the locked screen background of a beautiful forest in an unknown jungle, lush with greenery. Something about seeing the number 34 for the third time today made my insides spark with a sense of "knowing," fanning the flames of my curiosity.

My apartment number when I was a kid, doing those consciousness experiments, was 34! That's what I told everyone was my favorite number. I remember chanting it over and over again in a sing-song way! This number feels very familiar, somehow...

Now that I was remembering, 34 – and its mirror image, 43 – were accompanying me throughout my whole life. Street numbers I'd lived on, university ID and employee badge numbers. My passports, license plates and phone numbers, all at one point contained this number. It couldn't be just an empty coincidence. It was definitely a case of Jung's synchronicity and it gave me so much meaning, which let in a sliver of hope that perhaps I wasn't lost and all alone – that there were unseen guides and guardian angels who were always with me, gently nudging me along by leaving little clues that I was heading in the right direction.

The universe favors an open mind and tends to reward us with more frequent synchronicities the greater significance we assign to them. So why not believe in a bit of magic? It's in my favor, after all.

I choose to believe. This is definitely a sign. I have to do ayahuasca, if only for the confirmation that there is something beyond our physical reality and that this "energy" I'm always hearing about really does make up everything around and inside of us.

My intuition told me I needed to have this experience, but I couldn't logically justify it. My mind, in its usual repertoire, was coming up with a thousand and one excuses as to why this was a terrible idea. The relentless ramblings of the voice in my head were so loud, it was hard not to pay attention to them.

This is crazy – taking a psychedelic, and a very powerful one at that! Why would I want to risk something as precious as my mind?

What if something goes wrong? I could go crazy while under the influence of it or worse...

This is not for me. Girls like me don't do such reckless things – what would my parents say if they knew about this insane plan?

Mom would go nuts... I've never really traveled anywhere on my own.

Dave would never have allowed this... he would call me a hippie and try to stop me.

I can't leave now – I have so many important things to do here. Maybe when I find some more time... I could always go then.

Don't they have dengue fever mosquitoes in Peru? What about snakes? I'd be out there in the middle of the jungle, and a snake could bite me!

I am surviving as it is – why rock the boat? I'm not THAT unhappy... this could make things so much worse!

How deep is it going to take me? I am not sure I'm ready to face the dark parts of me that this may uncover...

I pushed all of these fearful thoughts aside and typed in a search for an ayahuasca retreat in Peru. The first link that I intuitively chose was a website with a green tropical jungle banner that looked like my phone lock-screen background, and a logo of a woman standing with arms that stretched out to look like tree branches.

Mayari – Home of Ayahuasca. The name of the hotel that was offering the retreat sounded comforting and inviting. Looking at the program timeline, I noted that the next ceremony dates were neatly fitting into a lull in my jam-packed schedule. But I still wasn't sure I should book it. A deep-seated belief that true love was reserved for only the most pure of hearts, just like the princesses I had read about in fairytales as a child, had me convinced that the reason I wasn't lucky in love must have something to do with my inherent internal darkness and the mistakes I've made with past relationships – cheating on Dave with my coworker, for one.

I need to clear whatever is holding me back from receiving the gift of love. It's a sacrifice I need to be brave enough to make. And maybe then I would be deserving of true love and my ideal partner.

My finger hovered above the Register button on the screen, as I hesitated, holding my breath.

It's now or never! What more do I have to lose?

With a sharp inhale, I tapped on the screen and filled out the registration form, confirming my spot at the retreat. Then I got out of the tub and went to find my ankle bracelet which had become a symbol for my ideal self – the free spirit who takes chances and charges into the unknown.

Chapter 4

Holy Trinity

After a short layover in Lima and an easy hour-long flight, I walked out of the airport in Cusco and looked around for a person holding a sign with my name but didn't spot anyone. Next to me was a man in his mid-twenties with a backpack. He appeared to be of Scandinavian descent – tall with blonde hair on his arms and legs, as well as on his head. He had an air of adventure and excitement about him, probably ready to start his own journey of whatever it was that he came here looking for. He was wearing a banana leaf print shirt that was unbuttoned half-way down his chest, gray shorts and white sneakers. His calf muscles were bulging out of the ankle socks he had on. He was athletic and healthy.

I couldn't help but feel jealous of how confident he looked. He was, after all, a man in his prime, strong and able-bodied, comfortable anywhere he went in the world. I didn't think too many people would want to harass or mess with him, as he was bigger and stronger than the average person. And here I was, a woman in her prime, who by default was perceived vulnerable and helpless, maybe even as prey for someone with bad intentions. I wasn't weak and had a healthy muscle mass, but for me, being a woman came with the glaring reality that I could become a victim at any given point in time, or at least that's how I felt when I traveled alone. Being too friendly could be (and had been in the past) mistaken for flirtation. Wearing something too revealing could bring on unwanted attention. Locking eyes with a stranger for a bit too long could lead to an uninvited conversation. I didn't feel secure in my place in the world, and that's why I avoided travel to unfamiliar places by myself.

I imagined what it would be like to be a man and to enjoy a sense of empowerment and freedom that automatically came with it. Freedom to wear as little as I wanted and not worry about being considered provocative. If I were a man, not only would I feel safe to go anywhere I wanted, but it would also come with an unspoken permission to do so. I wouldn't be judged if I decided to backpack through Asia or Europe, sit alone in a bar or restaurant, or drive across the country in my car. I secretly admired those women who did that – such fearless creatures! I was almost looking forward to the day when I got older, when my feminine allure would wane with age and I'd no longer be an object of men's desires. Then I could have a bit more of that freedom I craved.

My mother, who was a very influential force in my life, would always judgingly say about women who traveled alone, "She's looking for an unfortunate adventure to bite her in the ass" (very loose translation from the Russian idiom). When I was younger these words served as cautionary advice and had me convinced that "good girls" never wandered around like they didn't belong anywhere. So, I never did, except when I modeled – but even then, I always had a chaperone on the other side who was responsible for my whereabouts. Otherwise, I'd go with either my parents, Dave or Ale.

I looked up to my mother as a strong woman who was ambitious and resilient, and I loved her greatly. She raised me with an analytical and practical approach by ensuring I had all the necessary tools to be well-educated and accomplished. Her disciplinarian tactics were strict and purposeful, which as an adult I learned to appreciate more than when I was a child. She wasn't open to esotericism and always taught me to follow my head, rather than my heart. Yet deep down I yearned for a female mother-figure in my life who would nurture my spiritual side and be my mentor for matters of the heart.

Being out here in Cusco, a city nearly four thousand miles away from home in the South American continent, which my family and I had very little information about other than what we had seen on the news, I heard a disapproving voice in my head:

Look at you! Roaming around without supervision like a stray cat!

I felt a pang of guilt in my lower abdomen which swiftly ran up my body towards my head and flushed my cheeks slightly red.

Whose voice is that? Sounds a lot like Mom, but how can her voice be in my head? Is that what I really think about myself?

Where is the airport pickup guy? I just want to get out of here before someone gets the wrong idea here.

What if no one shows up? How would I get a taxi and is that even safe?

Kidnappers are a real threat in these parts of the world as I recall from hearing in the news.

My apprehension was heightened when I began to remember the "dark side of ayahuasca tourism" stories I'd managed to dig up online about sexual assault and rape of female solo travelers who fell victims to ill-intentioned shamans. My fear of being raped stemmed from a few incidences in childhood and adolescence when I had seen strange men exposing themselves to my friends and me on the playground and in the stairwell of the building where I lived in Russia. Those terrifying and confusing moments had ingrained a deep sense of caution and was one of the biggest reasons I liked being in a relationship – to feel protected. It had always seemed to me that a woman alone in the world was more vulnerable to attackers and an easier target for sexual predators. That's what I believed, and with that mindset I began imagining scenarios where the shaman of the ceremony I was about to partake in was molesting me while I was unconscious. This was making my anxiety worse, so I pushed these thoughts to the side and focused on finding my driver.

It had been over 20 minutes and still no one from the hotel showed up to pick me up. I spotted a group of men congregating about 50 meters away – probably taxi drivers looking to pick up a fare. They were eyeing me continuously, which made me uncomfortable. I instinctively shifted my shoulder bag over to my front side and hugged it tightly. The growing tension in my bowels was escalating as my nerves were unraveling by the second – I needed a toilet urgently.

Why does this always happen? Fear is my laxative! Am I the only one who experiences it like that?

Before I could analyze my thought, a smiling middle-aged Peruvian man wearing a shirt with the hotel name on it came up to me from the side and pointed to a clipboard with my name written on it. A sense of relief swept over me and I greeted him with an overly eager handshake, as if he was someone who had just rescued me from a deserted island. He helped me with my bag and led me towards the car.

We drove through the city towards the Sacred Valley of the Incas. I could already feel the effects of mild altitude sickness – unsettled stomach, light headache and shortness of breath. I felt totally fine when the plane landed in Lima but now, being at 11,150 feet above sea level in Cusco, all the signature symptoms I had read about in online reviews were showing up right on schedule. Apparently chewing coca leaves was one effective remedy to help people fight off the symptoms, and I made a mental note to ask for some at the hotel.

As we made our way to a slightly lower elevation towards the town of Pisac, 21 miles from the airport, Luis, my driver, told me about the culture and history of the Sacred Valley in broken English. He used Spanish words where he needed and I was surprised at how much I could understand him, as I had picked up quite a bit of it from Ale. He told me that this valley had special energies coming from the ground which made the soil super fertile, and advised me to try as many vegetables and fruits as I could find, since they were very nourishing for the body. He said that the flora and fauna of the region was very diverse, and as soon as he mentioned that my mind immediately went to snakes. I've had a fear of snakes ever since I could remember.

"Are there a lot of snakes out here?" I worriedly probed Luis.

"*Si*, many beautiful snakes – all different kinds! They are very important to our people."

I assumed he was talking about the Quechua people whose population made up about 83 percent of the four million Amazonian Indigenous Peoples that lived in Peru.

Shuddering at the thought of snakes, I partially regretted coming here and putting myself in potential close proximity to one out here in this lush setting, brimming with all varieties of these slithering reptiles. Even a picture of a snake gave me the creepiest feeling I couldn't shake for hours.

I sure hope I won't be meeting one here!

"The Incas believed that snakes were gods," Luis interrupted my thoughts. "Look – the trilogy there – the condor, the puma, and the serpent." He pointed at a stone wall we passed by that had a carving of all three animals on it. "Each one rules over their own world – heaven, earth and the dead."

I made another mental note to buy a small statue or painting of the three animals for my altar at home. I liked the idea of three deities making up a holy trinity, similar to my grandmother's icon displaying three divine figures – everything special came in threes.

I wanted to know more about Incan gods and Luis listed the main ones: *Inti* (God of the sun), *Pachamama* (God of the earth), *Keel* (God of the moon), *Ray* (God of rain and lightning), *Illapa* (God of mountains), and *Wiracocha* (the creator of all).

The scenery along the road to the Sacred Valley of the Incas, which stretched for 100 miles along the Urubamba River, was breathtaking. Luis explained that the river was special to the Inca people who considered it to be a sacred reflection of the Milky Way. The Incan priests used the natural landscape to erect scaling terraces on hillsides to mark the locations of special constellations on the ground as if creating their reflection from the sky. The rolling mountains with scattered snow patches at the peaks looked like they were dressed in green velvet, dipping into deep valleys with clear water streams. The people coming down from the hills and walking alongside the road looked theatrical – men dressed in colorful ponchos and hats with earmuffs and tassels called the *chullo,* and women in wide skirts with multicolored patterns, wool jackets and flat-top hats with chin straps called *monteras.* Many of the women had their young children in slings behind their backs.

We reached the hotel and I was served some herbal tea with ingredients that would help me relieve altitude sickness, then swiftly checked in and escorted to my private room at the far end of the resort facing the towering Andes mountains.

The views from each part of the resort were majestic. The ground landscaping was impeccable – carefully crafted pathways that led to small enclosures containing hidden gardens, perfectly manicured lawns and flower bushes, and straw-roofed structures peeking out amidst the trees. Normally, a setting like that would envelop me in a sense of calm and ease but, remembering that the first ayahuasca ceremony was going to happen tonight, I was in a state of high alert.

I had prepared myself physically and partially mentally for the next week which was going to hold four daily ceremonies and left a few days for travel through the Sacred Valley. Machu Picchu was definitely on my list of ancient ruins I wanted to visit and was located just 45 miles northwest of Pisac but would take over four hours of driving on a 130 miles of narrow winding road through the mountains to reach. I left the planning aside for the time being and ran through the preparation checklist of items that I was instructed to have for the ceremony.

For seven days before traveling, as suggested by the organizers of the retreat, I observed a diet that was free of spices and salt, all animal products for the exception of free-range chicken and wild-caught fish, avocado and oils, dairy products, chocolate and coffee, fermented foods, protein powders and other nutritional supplements, and refined sugars. It was also advised to avoid any alcohol and other recreational substances including cannabis, stimulating activities and any sexual activity for at least two weeks prior to the first ceremony.

Well, definitely no problem with the last one! I thought to myself sarcastically.

It was a lot harder to maintain the plain-tasting diet. But I figured it would serve me well to play full-out and prepare in the best possible way. It was explained in the welcome email I had received that the reason these diets and abstinence practices were observed were for the purposes of detoxifying and purifying the physical and mental space in order to facilitate a greater connection with the spirit world. I took it to mean that we needed a clear "static-free" path of communication with Madre Ayahuasca, as it was often called by the shamans, to be able to download the messages with more clarity and receive the most out of the experience. The science behind these diets warned that consuming foods high in tyramine (found in fermented foods like yogurt, soy sauce, tofu, kombucha, sauerkraut, aged cheese, and partially in chocolate and peanuts) could be dangerous, due to ayahuasca temporarily disabling monoamine oxydase inhibitors (MAOi) in the stomach – enzymes responsible for breaking down tyramine, leading to toxic levels of this amino acid in the body that could result in hypertension, headaches, and possibly death. I didn't want to take any chances and stuck to the diet guidelines precisely to ensure a safe and highly meaningful experience.

Reading several books on the subject before my trip, I found out that plant diets were designed to help a person to connect to the spirit of the plants and to develop new capabilities like healing and extrasensory perceptions. One book explained that not clearing the toxins collected in our daily life would interfere with the process, or even make it harder than necessary because ayahuasca would attack those points first.

As instructed, I went over to the reception area of the hotel at the designated time to meet with our shaman and the other participants. The sun was still up and it was a pleasant temperature of high sixties. I was wearing loose-fitting bohemian-print zouave yoga pants and a white long-sleeved ballet top, to be fully comfortable and warm as the preparation checklist suggested. I brought a blanket and an eye shade mask as well. Despite the warm early evening, I was already shivering with nervousness, expecting something epic to unfold during the first ceremony. The images of all the things I had heard and read about were dancing in my mind and the only question I had was, *Am I going to die tonight?*

I knew that taking ayahuasca was safe, and I didn't have any family history of schizophrenia or bipolar disorder that could potentially cause a dangerous episode. I wasn't on any contraindicative medications like anti-depressants, sleeping pills or amphetamines, so that made it pretty much risk-free for any medical emergencies. Never having taken a psychedelic substance before, I felt the fear of the unknown and that it all could potentially end up as a traumatizing experience. Reading all those reviews and books was not helping my anxiety and I was anticipating intense hallucinations, vomiting (also known as purging) and distorted perceptions of time and space. Basically, I was ready for all hell to unfold and swallow me up – demonic creatures playing with my essence until I was released from my emotional bondage and healed of the diseases that plagued my soul.

I was trembling like the native Peruvian cinchona tree leaves in the gentle wind that were in plentiful abundance all around me.

When I reached the lobby, the receptionist gestured to a small library where a group of about ten people were gathered.

Most of them were quietly introspecting or meditating, so I found a seat and, without disturbing the atmosphere, made silent greeting gestures to those who looked up at me. Some people were talking softly amongst each other, but I was too focused inwards to pay attention to what anyone was saying. I was on tenterhooks, anxiously waiting to know what was going to happen and who would be the shaman leading us on this adventure of a lifetime.

After a few minutes a woman roughly my mother's age, perhaps a bit younger, walked in with two people, who looked like her entourage, carrying bags with supplies. The moment I saw the woman, I felt a sense of ease – she was radiating a nurturing warmth that made me instantly comfortable and relaxed. She had a round full face with squinty black eyes which made her look like she was always smiling.

"Hello, my darlings! I am Nayanna – your shaman!" she said with a hearty rolling laugh, reading the surprised expression in the room.

Chapter 5

Madre

The shaman is a woman?

I had been picturing our shaman to be an older man with a poncho and a feathered hat. This was a surprise, but a pleasant one, because I had always gravitated towards and felt more connected to the feminine energy. Now at least I didn't have to worry about being molested during the ceremony, which helped to relax me slightly.

Nayanna explained that a word for female shaman in Spanish is "curandera," and that both men and women were traditionally allowed to work with plant teachers in ceremonial settings. She introduced herself and gave us her brief bio: she was of mixed culture and heritage – her mother Peruvian and her father Indian, and she was born and raised in India, arriving in Peru at 18 years of age. I hungrily absorbed everything she was saying and loved her energy instantly!

Nayanna had jet black long wavy hair down to her waist, a voluptuous figure with an ample bosom, and beautiful features that reflected both of her ethnicities. She had a warm maternal look and could've been the human incarnation of Madre Ayahuasca herself by the way that she looked and dressed – a floor-length kaftan and a large crystal pendant hanging down to her chest amidst a variety of other handcrafted necklaces. Nayanna went around the room warmly shaking hands with everyone, then asked each of us to say a few words about ourselves and why we were here. I couldn't concentrate on what others were saying because I was busy contemplating my own reason, which I was slightly embarrassed to say out loud.

I'm here to find out if I'm really worthy of true love.

When my turn came, I simply muttered something about looking for a confirmation that the spirit world actually exists.

After everyone was done talking, Nayanna described the process that would make up the next four days and instructed us to walk around the resort and mentally hold the intention we had set for ourselves. We would meet in the main maloca (the circular open-air house with a pointy straw roof I had seen earlier) promptly at eight o'clock to start the ceremony.

My nerves were starting to make me feel exhausted and all I wanted to do was lie down and go to sleep. I wished it was all over with already so I could go back home where I didn't have to subject myself to this kind of self-inflicted psychological torture.

Why am I doing this?

I tried to keep calm by breathing deeply and observing all the natural beauty that I was surrounded by. I walked around and stopped periodically to admire the flowers and enjoy their pleasant aroma. I listened to the unusual sounds of the local birds and insects that intensified their symphony as the night drew near. And I watched the sky with appreciation of all the colors it was playing with as the sun was setting behind the mammoth mountains. It felt like nature was inviting me to relax and enjoy the performance it was putting on for me.

We gathered for the ceremony in the maloca where each of the four ceremonies was to take place. It was prepared for us with cushioned mats and small pillows, purge bowls and glass bottles of water with drinking cups for each person, and arranged in a circular fashion with a special space for the curandera in the middle. There were candles, herbs, oils and musical instruments spread out in front of her seat and I could already smell the scent of white sage in the air that Nayanna had lit before everyone arrived.

We all settled in on our mats and Nayanna called the ceremony open. She spoke some words in Spanish, some in

Sanskrit and some in the language of the local indigenous people – Quechua. She proceeded to invoke the spirit of Madre Ayahuasca with an "icaro" – a shamanic song, then she lit up some Palo Santo wood sticks and walked around each of us to let the smoke circulate to clear any energies (or spirits) that didn't need to be there. After cleansing the space, Nayanna picked up a pack of leaves tied together, called the "shacapa" in Quechua, which I remembered reading about in the books, and started shaking them rhythmically to accompany her singing. Her voice was divinely comforting and pleasing to the ear. It almost made me forget where I was for a moment and gave me the courage for what was about to happen. We were invited one by one to kneel in front of Nayanna and accept a small cup of ayahuasca brew which was already prepared and cleansed by the mapacho (a type of tobacco and another master plant) smoke she was blowing on it.

When it was my turn to come up and drink, I did so without much hesitation. I was there and my decision had been made – all in, no holding back! Grasping the cup between my two trembling hands while sitting in Japanese prayer position, I brought it up to my heart and with closed eyes repeated my intention:

Spirit of the Great Mother Ayahuasca, please grant me access to the love my heart desires... oh, and please don't let me die!

Placing my trust in the unknown, I gulped down the contents of the cup which was not as unpleasant as I had heard and expected it to be. It didn't taste good, but it was bearable – a dark brown, thick and gooey liquid that was like a mixture of dirt and herbal medicine – earthy, bitter, almost yeasty, yet nurturing. Returning back to my mat I sat rigidly in cross-legged position, as was advised earlier by Nayanna to allow the lessons and guidance from the spirits, otherwise known as "downloads," to flow vertically through the top of the head from the sky.

After the last person in the circle had finished drinking the brew, Nayanna blew out all candles except one and we descended into the dark and quiet setting of the night.

I was vigilantly on guard and watching for any changes in my physiological and mental state. Every muscle twitch of my body or sound that I heard made me jump with alertness.

Is it starting? What was that pinch I just felt? Is that the effect?
Am I still all there mentally or am I checking out?
What's that sound?

The wait for something to happen was excruciating. My heart was beating quickly and powerfully. Although I tried to breathe deeply, the fear kept its tight grip around my lower abdomen and I was shifting nervously to try and find some comfort from the growing pressure in my intestines.

A few minutes dragged by, and I couldn't take the suspense any longer. I stretched out on the cushioned mat to get a bit of rest from the tension I felt all over my body. Nayanna began to sing another icaro. It was a relief from the silence and complemented the background hum of insects that seemed to pick up her tune like backup singers. Her voice was buttery smooth with fluctuating peaks and valleys in her pitch. It was all in Quechua language but at times I thought I picked up some Spanish words.

Nothing was happening with me. In the darkness, I heard some people retching into their bowls and some quiet sobs. I was alert but my body was beginning to relax. Serenaded by Nayanna's songs, I started to drift off into a deep meditative state. Now she was singing a Spanish song with a beautiful melody accompanied by her guitar and I could catch a few words I understood:

"Agua de luz, agua de estrellas... Pacha mama... Limpia corazón..."

I was wondering when the purging would begin for me as it seemed that everyone else in the circle was finished with it and had moved on. Some people even got up and were walking around the maloca. My purge never came. In fact, nothing extraordinary which I was expecting to happen was happening. I simply lay there being comforted by the music and knowing that I could relax into myself with the assurance that I will be protected. It was as if I was receiving a telepathic message to have trust, and that there was a safety net underneath, so I won't fall too deep. I had a sensation of being wrapped up in a mother's warm embrace.

Before I knew it, Nayanna called the ceremony to a close. I couldn't believe it!

Didn't we just get started?

What about the visions? I got nothing!

My mind was swarming with questions and doubts about the plant medicine, the curandera and the whole process of this ceremony. I had spent so much time worrying and thinking about this, but it seemed to be for nothing.

As everyone wandered off to their rooms, I hung back to ask Nayanna why I hadn't felt any effect of the ayahuasca. She didn't seem at all surprised and asked if this was my first time with this plant medicine, and whether I followed all the instructions before coming here.

"Yes, of course!" I answered. "And I was expecting I would experience everything that I'd read about – visions, spirits, colorful patterns, downloads and lessons, but this was not at all like I envisioned it to be."

"So, it didn't live up to your expectations then?" Nayanna asked somewhat defensively.

"Well, I guess I was just hoping for a bit more than what I got." I tried to be as courteous as possible, "I am sorry, it's just that with all the time and money investment, I wanted to experience something profound."

Nayanna was quiet for a moment and looked at me as though she was assessing my aura with her gaze, then smiled at me in her warm motherly way and said:

"You see, sometimes the plant spirit wants to get to know you first before giving you what you need. Maybe with all of your expectations, Madre Ayahuasca needed to reassure you that you are in good hands, so you would let go and give it permission to do the healing that needs to happen."

I thanked Nayanna and started to get up, but she stopped me and asked if I practice any form of meditation. I told her that I do, but not regularly enough and that it was very hard to empty the mind of thoughts and just focus on the present moment.

"The purpose of meditation is not to rid yourself of thought. That is impossible to do. You *have* thoughts – *you are not* your thoughts. When you make that distinction and simply observe them as they are, while realizing that they cannot be controlled, you release your attachment to wanting to be in a different state than you are. Just observing and being watchful is enough, and you'll see how thoughts will roll by like waves, one after the other. That's how easy it is to meditate – don't make it more difficult than it needs to be."

With that, she told me to go and get some rest so I will be ready for our second ceremony the next day. I went to my room, looking carefully under my feet to make sure I wouldn't step on a snake. As physically tired as I was, I found it hard to sleep due to the psychoactive ingredients of the brew. I've always been very sensitive to caffeine and some pharmaceutical drugs like decongestants, antihistamines and antibiotics, which affected my ability to sleep, and it seemed no different to ayahuasca.

In the morning I felt that I hadn't slept at all. I groggily made my way to breakfast and forced some bland-tasting food down, which was specially served to the group in accordance with the ayahuasca diet we were meant to observe. The meals consisted of mostly steamed vegetables without any salt or spices and I didn't have much of an appetite for it.

The second ceremony was scheduled to take place earlier than the first. Nayanna decided to start before sunset and gathered us in the maloca at five o'clock. It was still light out and she said it would be a different kind of experience to do it while being able to see everything around us. Just like the first time, she chanted some prayers to activate the plant spirit, cleansed the space and each one of us with the Palo Santo, and gave each of us the mud-like brew to drink. We were allowed to walk around the resort but were asked to come back to the maloca before dark.

It was so beautiful outside and I was happy to be able to enjoy all the sights while waiting for the effect to hopefully come on this time. I went over to the far side of the resort which was bordered by a flowing creek below a meter drop from the edge of the grassy lawn, and sat on a large log that was made into a bench. Looking up at the cinematic sky, I watched an eagle or a condor perhaps, which made up the sacred trilogy my driver mentioned two days before, gracefully soaring and drawing imaginary circles above me. I internally asked the condor for a blessing on my journey tonight since it was considered an Inca deity.

Something close to an hour had passed and I was once again starting to wonder why nothing out of the ordinary was happening. But then I looked down at the grass and noticed it forming into geometric shapes in front of my eyes. I blinked a few times in case it was a temporary glitch in my eyesight, but the shapes kept forming and changing in intricate patterns like a kaleidoscope I loved playing with when I was a kid. I remembered what Nayanna had said to us in the orientation session about ayahuasca acting with the flow of the earth, which is a live intelligent organism, to help a person return "home" and see reality without the "filters" that the ego sees everything through. She said it gently lifts the veil of perception and shows us the truth of what is inside and around us, and we begin to heal those parts that the ego couldn't let go of. Therefore, physical cleansing like sweating, vomiting or diarrhea can occur as the spirit of the plant moves energetic blockages out of the way and the body reacts in these ways.

I felt slight digestive discomfort but no need to vomit or use the toilet. The urge that was coming over me was to get close to the earth and connect to it. I slid off the bench and sat on the grass with legs spread out and arms stretched out in front, palms on the earth. The beauty of the symmetrical patterns kept my eyes glued to the ground. I had a feeling of being "pulled" towards and through the grass, as if my hands were melting right into the soil from where it was growing. I began to lean into it with my head, my face inching closer and closer into the unfolding continuous geometry that I saw in each blade of grass. But just as I was about to lay my head down on the ground, I remembered that we had to make our way back to the maloca before dark. I knew that if I allowed myself to lie down, I would dissolve into the earth and not be able to bring myself out. Gathering the last bit of strength to stand up on wobbling legs trying to keep my balance, I quickly staggered over to the maloca where the rest of the group had already assembled.

Everything that I looked at was appearing as fractalized and pixelated – on point with the description of visuals I had heard psychotropic drugs produce. I was equal parts amazed, nervous and excited.

Finally, we are getting somewhere!

I sat down on my mat and exhaustion washed over me. I couldn't hold my head up so I leaned it on my forearms supported by the knees and instantly, my consciousness left the body. Where it went, I did not know. I was somewhere that could only be described as a dimension of emotion. There was not much thought, just raw emotions. And what I was perceiving here was sorrow, desolation, abandonment and abuse. I began to cry and these emotions continued to swell up and splash out in explosive sobs like waves crashing into a rocky shore, spraying water out in all directions.

A subtle string of thoughts fought their way through from somewhere far away: *Where are these feelings coming from? I don't remember ever feeling like this. I've never been abused or abandoned...*

And as soon as I pondered it, the answer came to me as an acute awareness – these were not my own emotions I was experiencing – I was crying the tears of Mother Earth.

Chapter 6

Vine of the Dead

I was the earth, and the internal sensation I was experiencing was the equivalent of being physically kicked while lying down in pain and left to suffer alone without anyone coming to the rescue.

There were no visuals to explain why, but I could sense the reasons for this feeling – pollution, depletion, exploitation, overpopulation and extinction. Hopelessness of the situation made it that much more difficult to bear. When the flood of emotion reached a critical point that I couldn't take for a moment more, it began to recede as quickly as it had come on. Now I was back in some bodily sensations for a few seconds to realize I needed to lie down, so I stretched out on the mat, and immediately I was off again into dimensions never explored by my consciousness. This time I was in a multidimensional space "seeing" all around me with my eyes closed as though I was wearing virtual reality goggles. There were astonishing colors and shapes unlike any I've seen before, and everything was perpetually moving like parts of some elaborate mechanism. I saw brightly colored bolts and screws some of which reminded me of the spiraling double helix structures of the DNA. It was serene, beautiful and humbling – I was in the presence of something so much greater than me, my life or what I could ever conceive with my mind. A sense of peace and tranquility pervaded my being. It felt like I was home, and I wanted to stay there indefinitely without any intention of ever leaving, but as with the previous state, I was moving on to the next part of my journey.

I must have gone through several different "dimensions," most of which I have no recollection of, but it must have been very healing because I kept sighing with relief audibly and yawning loudly as weight after weight was lifting off from my emotional grid.

When the healing part of the ceremony ceased, I was left in a state of pure bliss. It was not the kind of bodily euphoria I'd imagined and had heard about that comes from street drugs. It was soul-level pleasure of simply being. There was no thought, no emotion, no body. My eyes were open and I was watching the splendor of the surrounding nature. Everything appeared glowing with a magic hue. The bark on tree trunks transformed into animal prints like cheetah, snake, and turtle shell patterns. Flowers took on shapes of alien-like creatures that were performing a dance for me. Each leaf of every plant was "breathing" and bursting with life-like energy. Despite the beauty and divinity of it all, I wasn't emotional in the slightest – I was still, peaceful, present. I was one with all. Everything in my view reflected my own sense of aliveness. Time stopped. Timelessness prevailed.

What brought me out of this dimension was the appearance of Nayanna in her physical form in my line of sight. She gently looked down at me and inquired about how I was doing.

I am doing gloriously! A thought appeared at last.

The great abyss of nothingness was starting to get filled up with thoughts and reactions to those thoughts once again. I joyously expressed to her the gratitude I felt for my life, for my body, for my mind, and a realization of how precious and delicately elusive all of it really was. I began to cry now with the newfound insights and appreciation for life. Nayanna offered a long comforting hug and we stayed in it for a while.

Soon, the effect of the medicine began to wear off and I was instructed by Nayanna's helpers to take it slow and stay in place until I was physically strong enough to walk back to my room. The rest of the night was spent in quiet reflection, and even though my body was relaxed, I couldn't sleep well once again. I was so happy with what had transpired – it was not at all scary or uncomfortable as I had expected. The message I had received during the first ceremony proved to be right – I was protected, held, loved, and I didn't fall too deep. And best of all – there was no purging!

What was I so terrified of? I should've done this years ago!

I woke up the next morning from another restless sleep feeling the fatigue building up in my body. Mentally, however, I felt strong as the impressions of the previous night's ceremony were still with me, and I felt grateful for all the insights I had received.

What is going to happen tonight?

I knew better now than to have expectations, but I was still curiously pondering what the third ceremony would uncover for me. And what happened next was both an answer and a foreshadowing of what would unfold later that night.

Deciding to do some light yoga in a shala outside of my room, I rolled out a yoga mat and began a warm-up sun salutation sequence, keeping my eyes closed in order to connect deeper to the practice. Just as I was about to jump through with my feet towards the top of the mat while in downward-facing dog, I instinctively opened my eyes and saw something unexpected, startling, and… deadly!

A black scorpion had crawled onto my mat right between my palms, inches away from my face!

At first, my mind didn't register the danger and I looked at it as a harmless creature of the earth, alive and vibrating with life force, just like me. I simply looked at it for what must have been only a few milliseconds and didn't react. But it seemed as though time had stopped – the scorpion and I were suspended in an endless moment, and there was no thought or emotion associated to what I was looking at. There was no fear, no disgust, no desire to get away from it. The scorpion was just another living being that held no other meaning.

And then suddenly, my mind came "online" and the brain went into its emergency response. Scanning the database of all the knowledge it had about scorpion bites – danger, poison and potential death – the brain switched on the flight mode. The body followed the signal and I jumped away from the mat to create a safe distance between myself and the scorpion. It took another few seconds for the shock to wear off and for me to be able to react. Picking up the mat by the far corners, I shook it to release the creature into the bushes on the side. I was surprisingly calm and didn't freak out as I normally would've done in a scenario like this. Something about my connection to the earth the day before made me less reactive to insects and arachnids – they were not my enemies but earthly companions. A snake, however, was a different story, and I silently wished that none would appear before me for the rest of my time in Peru.

The remainder of the day was uneventful, and I dedicated it to reading and talking about our experiences with others in the sharing session after lunch. When I shared my somewhat disturbing but insightful experience of meeting a scorpion, Nayanna said it was a good omen for tonight, and explained that an appearance of this animal totem (spirit guide) was symbolic of renewal and healing. Although in some cultures it was a symbol of death and destruction, she proposed to not take it so literally and instead to look for a deeper meaning of what the toxic venom represents, which could be an indication that one must "kill" certain negative aspects of life to realize true potential and growth.

The evening was upon us and we all gathered in the maloca again. Nayanna reminded us that because the plant spirits worked in mysterious ways, Mother Ayahuasca herself determined the intensity, length and depth of the experience for each individual. As the previous two times, the ritual commenced with an icaro, and we all came up to drink the brew.

The taste of it hadn't grown on me, and in fact it was harder and harder to keep it down each time. I drank it all up in one gulp trying not to breathe through my nose. I still hadn't had any purging like most of the others in the group.

Am I holding something back? Is there nothing that needs to be cleansed?

Only Madre Ayahuasca knew that, so I gave in to whatever she had in store for me on this night.

The beginning of my third "trip" was similar in visuals to the last one – a panoramic display of complex, colorful shapes and forms merging in and out of each other in smooth flowing motions. Once again, I was in a space where thoughts and emotions didn't exist.

Suddenly, the abstract patterns began to form a shape of something I recognized and feared so greatly – a snake! It was beautiful, with multi-colored scales of blue, green and purple, and yellow eyes. It appeared to be an Indian cobra with an open hood behind its head made up of repeating images of itself layered in perpetually moving procession. The snake's coloring and pattern was reminiscent of the psychedelic paintings or digital art of spirit animals I had seen before. I was startled slightly but instinctively knew it didn't pose me any threat, so I allowed it to interact with me. It was swaying closer and farther in rhythmic waves, darting its fuchsia double-pronged tongue at me. A word appeared in my awareness – Naga, which I understood to be the snake's name. Strangely, there was a sense of connection and oneness with this mythical-looking creature.

"Open your heart," the snake transmitted telepathically into my consciousness.

The message I was receiving came with a sensation of slight pressure in my chest area. As suddenly as it appeared, Naga dissolved into the fractalized background.

Immediately after, I was transported into a dark gaping space where I saw a small figure of a child, her face hidden from view.

A gut feeling of being in the presence of someone I knew very well began to form in my stomach as I watched an umbilical cord begin growing out of me and extending towards the child. When the cord reached the child, her face was revealed and I was astounded!

She was me, as a five-year-old girl!

The little "self" came over to me, the big self, and clung to my leg just like a child who seeks affection or protection from a parent. Looking into my own innocent eyes I perceived a space there that yearned to be filled with love. The child "self" wanted to be seen, appreciated and validated. The cord that connected the two selves sent a stabbing feeling of pain into my chest area and the pressure that I had felt earlier began to intensify.

Now, I was no longer looking at my young self, but rather through her eyes. I was standing in the infinite blackness, pangs of loneliness and emptiness probing my insides. A low rumbling growl emerged from the darkness. Fear rippled across the surface of my internal space. Multiple pairs of glowing red eyes, then a body of a massive scaly beast fifty times my size with a slightly parted jaw revealing rows of long sword-like teeth slowly came into view. It was a black hybrid beast with characteristics of a demonic creature unlike any I had ever seen before – legs of a reptile, body of a mammal that blended into a thick bearish head with a protruding snout and flaring nostrils, and a bristly mane that ran along its spine towards a tapered lizard-like tail.

All I could do was stare at the monster, unable to bring myself to look away. Even if I could, there was nowhere to run.

"You are worthless!" I heard an androgynous-sounding voice that seemed to be coming from the monster, although its mouth was not moving.

"No one loves you! You are alone! You don't deserve to be happy! Why don't you just die already?"

The verbal attacks were getting louder and more aggressive by the moment. The pressure in my chest kept growing and it was beginning to feel like physical pain in my heart. I was reeling under the gunfire of insults coming from the monster. Then it opened its maw wide and a deafening sound of "I HATE YOU!" gusted out with such force that I thought it would burst my eardrums. Lightning-like flashes illuminated the ghastly beast in all its ferociousness.

Although I was aware that my physical body was lying flat on the mat, I felt that I was internally cowering down helplessly to the ground. When I looked inside the gaping hole of the beast's open jaw, what I saw inside brought another blow to my chest. Once again it was another "self" – this time of my current age, looking back at me, face contorted in disgust and loathing. This was almost too much to handle and I cried out in despair, stretching out my hands in hopes that someone would come to get me out of this hellish place. I felt a hand grasp mine in the physical world, and barely able to pry my eyes open, saw a blurry image of Nayanna standing over me with her arm outstretched towards me, locking on to my gaze for a few brief moments until I was hurled into darkness again.

"I see what you are going through – it's your heart," Nayanna's voice sounded distant but clear. "Don't fight what's happening, let the pain in, it's only going to be harder if you resist!"

"Am I having a heart attack?" I choked out woozily. The pain in my heart was becoming unbearable and I held on to Nayanna's hand, desperately clinging to her as though she was my last connection to life that was rapidly draining from my body. Nayanna didn't confirm my theory and simply told me to hold on and breathe as she tightened her grasp on my hand and began to sing. Her voice was resonant with pure love, but I only caught a few words:

Lluvia, Lluvia, Agua cristalina…
Lluvia, Lluvia, Limpia medicina…

I was scared – laboriously breathing and sweating. The pain was climbing up towards a place I did not want it to reach.

I don't want to die! Please don't let me die!

But there was no stopping and no mercy. Outside, a torrential downpour commenced a percussion of fat raindrops drumming on the ground, leaves and roof, canceling out all other sounds except Nayanna's voice as she continued her comforting tune. The cruel taunts kept pelting down on me and all I could do was buckle under their painful blows. I was cold and shivering now, and my only lifeline was Nayanna's solid warm hand and soothing voice.

Somewhere in the distance I began to perceive a growing faint light amidst the overwhelming darkness and I wanted to get there desperately. The gripping pressure and stabbing pain in my chest was cranked up to a maximum as it swelled up to an epic finale that knocked the wind out of me. The bright light flooded in and I was released from the agony. It took a few seconds to realize that what I had to do was breathe in, so I inhaled sharply and audibly as my body contorted under the decompression.

When I opened my eyes, Nayanna was sitting next to me gazing down with a smile.

"Welcome to the first day of your new life!"

Part 2

The Journey

Chapter 7

Happily Ever After

When I awoke the next morning, even before opening my eyes, the first thought was,

Which reality am I in?

String theory in theoretical physics tells us there are multiple, possibly infinite, numbers of realities, and our time on earth falls under just one of the realities in this grand scope of dimensional perspectives of the ten proposed dimensions. I had always been curious about the theory that we live in a multiverse, and had read that dimensions beyond our physical world contain all possible futures and all possible pasts, including realities with a completely different set of laws of physics than those we've come to know in ours. I certainly felt like I had a glimpse into some of these multiverses in my ayahuasca journey.

Are time and space really just illusions created in our physical world to help us navigate through the human experience we are having on this planet, in this particular galaxy, at this stage of evolution?

The events of the previous night were still vivid and I remembered all the details of what had transpired with my "near death" episode.

Or was it not so "near," and I am actually dead right now?

I wiggled my toes, then fingers to bring a physical awareness to my body, confirming that I was very much alive and breathing. I scanned the body for pain or discomfort and noticed that everything was in working order. Everything around me, in and outside the room appeared as though I was seeing and hearing for the first time, like a newborn. There was a freshness to it all – rays of the early morning sun sifting through the linen curtains, the way the wood floors and furniture absorbed the light and gave a homey feel to the room, the vibrant colors of the rich vegetation and playful sounds of birds welcoming a brand-new day outside.

I felt a renewed sense of peace and presence, the kind that I had experienced in the second ceremony but being fully aware of my physical senses. There was also a very palpable sensation of a huge empty space that was created inside my chest cavity – the kind of feeling you have after you've had a good cleansing cry. It was a sense of lightness and emptiness, but not of something that needed to be filled – just a boundless space that felt expansive and freeing. I placed a hand on my chest and tuned into that spaciousness, grateful and content with it.

Today was meant to be the last ceremony, but I instinctively felt that my work with this medicine was finished for now, and what I wanted to do was go home to live my new life with this new-found appreciation for all the gifts I'm blessed with. But first, I needed a debrief with Nayanna, so I got up to get ready for the sharing session, which was scheduled after breakfast.

Integration after each ceremony was an essential part of the growth and healing that would ensue in the weeks and months after, as we were told by Nayanna. I found it very helpful to have someone to talk about the insights that were received in each session, and to get clarity on how to apply them in daily life. The group gathered in the library and each person got a chance to speak about their experience for a few minutes.

"How about that epic storm last night?" someone in the group exclaimed. Everyone started sharing their moments during that part of the night. I clearly remembered the rain but didn't recall it being something out of the ordinary.

"That thunder was deafening!" someone else chimed in.

At once, I realized that when I had heard the monster shouting "I hate you!" it must have been the sound of thunder that felt like it was going to burst my eardrums. And the blinding flashes that illuminated the beast was the lightning. My turn came to share and I talked about my meeting with the snake, the inner child, the demonic creature and the heart attack that gave me a new perspective on life.

Nayanna listened intently and then asked if anyone else had visions of themselves dying. A few people raised their hands.

"A spiritual death – or ego death, as it is sometimes called – is a way that the sacred medicine helps us to wipe out that part of the personality that ceased to be useful. The ego is neither something one must rid herself of, nor is it something bad. It is the shadow part of our essence that is as essential as the body that we need to live in the human form. But as we evolve, parts of it – the ones that hold old structures, old conditioning or old patterns that don't serve you, need to be dismantled so that new routes can be carved out in their place."

I considered what Nayanna was saying about the ego playing an important role, flashing back on how my mind, as the byproduct of the ego, reacted in detecting and analyzing danger upon spotting the scorpion. I also remembered what I had read about psychedelic substances having a positive effect on neuro-plasticity – the ability of the brain to form new pathways and rewire connections between the synapses. I discovered that there is a whole world of new and exciting research in this space, and that scientists are eagerly studying these effects to apply their findings towards treatment for addiction, depression and other neurological disorders.

Nayanna continued, "Our formative years from birth until about the age of seven, when the ego hasn't fully developed yet, is the prime time for conditioning to take place. And it settles in easily as the brain absorbs all information as hard facts, and results in our individual programming stemming from the unique combination of our environment, culture, upbringing and political climate at the time. This conditioning forms the base of our belief systems which in turn drive our daily thoughts, emotions and behavior. But these systems are not our own – they are an amalgamation of opinions and attitudes of other people and of the collective societal norms that have been around for years. The ego attaches itself to these beliefs as though they are their own and fights to protect them at all costs, fearing most of all the disintegration of these mental constructs that constitute and validate its very existence."

Everyone in the group had their eyes on Nayanna as she spoke, and what she was saying was so profound, honest, and seemed to resonate with me on an intuitive level.

"After the age of seven when the programming has been complete, world-views formed, and the subconscious turns on the default mode of operation, we begin to drift further and further from the truths that our eternal souls know, and we forget who we are at our essence. Limiting beliefs set in, perfectionism and unworthiness reign supreme, definitions of happiness and success get jumbled up by misguided notions of what it actually means to be happy and successful. We separate each other on the basis of race, nationality, gender, and anything else that forms the ego's identity. And we dismiss and condemn those who don't live up to our standards, morals and values that the ego holds in such high regard, ready to fight, and sometimes die, in the name of justice, religion or principle."

I scanned the room, observing the faces of the people in our group, and wondered whether our differences were greater than our similarities, or the other way around.

If I could look beyond what my mind thinks about each person here, I'd probably see just another version of "me."

Nayanna kept speaking,

"We are hypnotized and we don't even know it. We go about our daily lives on autopilot and hardly ever do we stop to become aware of the repeating loops in our minds that play incessantly like the gramophone needle skipping on a vinyl disk. The ego gains power over us, instead of us being in charge of it. And because of the way our brains have evolved to ensure survival, the reptilian part of the brain zeroes in on any potential danger to keep us safe. This keeps us in survival mode with a very narrow focus on getting through the day, always fixating on the negative, eating up the scary news that's continuously fed to us, and constantly projecting all of these phantom threats into our future."

Spot on again! Maybe that conditioning and looping thoughts are why I haven't left my job to start my own business? I'm so terrified to fail and disappoint my parents.

"We also separate ourselves from nature and other living beings, most of the time living in fear of things we don't understand and deem dangerous. All of this separation disconnects us from the spiritual aspect of ourselves, creates dysfunction, mental distress and physical illness. And when others don't live up to our unrealistic expectations, we put up walls to protect ourselves from being hurt and place conditions on love. That's when the high vibrational frequency with which we once vibrated when we were children gets polluted with resentments and unhealed pain. We pass that pain on to our children, and they in turn pass it on to their children. And on it goes – from generation to generation."

There was a long pause and the room fell silent as each of us quietly absorbed the words Nayanna had spoken.

"The good news is that it doesn't have to keep going – it can stop with *you*! Right here, right now, if you so intend." Nayanna concluded her sermon with a wink, as to dilute the serious atmosphere that had accumulated in the room.

We continued sharing a bit longer, and then the session came to an end. As everyone was leaving, Nayanna asked me to stay back a bit to speak privately.

When we were alone, I started to tell her that I thought my work with ayahuasca was complete and how I was planning to change my flight to go home earlier, but Nayanna didn't try to convince me to stay, like I thought she would try to do. Instead, she asked me if I had any peculiar sensitivities to foods or herbs. I told her that I couldn't drink or eat anything that contained high amounts of caffeine as it gave me anxiety and nervous tremors, and that smoking or consuming cannabis with THC usually caused a panicky feeling even at very low doses, unlike most people who found it relaxed them. I also mentioned how certain pharmaceutical drugs affected me negatively and my overall susceptibility to getting ill.

"This is because you are very 'open,'" Nayanna explained.

"Open?" I was surprised by that description because I wasn't overly extraverted and it took a while for me to get comfortable with strangers.

"Your energy field is very receptive towards the ethereal realms that most people don't perceive."

"Do you mean like extrasensory perceptions? Psychic powers?"

"Yes, precisely."

"But I've never received any voices or visions, other than with these ayahuasca sessions. Don't you have to hear or see something to be considered psychic?"

"Not necessarily. There are several ways the higher self or spirits can communicate with us. Those who receive visions are clairvoyant; those who hear messages are clairaudient; those who perceive feelings are clairsentient; and those who download messages into their consciousness and have a kind of inner 'knowing' – are claircognizant."

The last definition resonated with me and I remembered the experience of "knowing," which came from a deep place inside of me that wasn't my mind. Looking back on my life, I've always had these inner convictions about situations or people, but I hardly ever paid any attention to them.

Perhaps I AM psychic, but I just didn't know it? Wait... that seems contradictory!

"Is there a way of strengthening this ability?" I was curious to know whether there were some exercises I could do to sharpen this sixth sense.

"Yes, it's all about listening to your intuition and learning how to trust it. It's different for everyone, and you have to find your own way of honing it, because only you will know how it chooses to communicate with you. Is that something you'd like to explore?"

"I'm not sure, I have so much going on back home. Work is already piling up at the office and I may be up for a promotion. It doesn't feel like the right time to think about this. Plus, I have to go back and deal with the divorce."

She asked if I wanted to talk about it and I told her briefly about my woes in love that I was beginning to realize were a repeating pattern throughout my life. I seemed to be "pushing" the men away, or rather, they were running from me. I expressed my frustration to Nayanna about how each relationship started like a fairytale but always ended with heartbreak – sometimes it was my heart that got broken, other times I broke the man's heart.

"It switches every time, but it's either I lose interest, or he does! Am I doing something to attract these kinds of relationships?"

"Do you know about divine and wounded masculine feminine energies?"

"I've heard something about that. I think I'm pretty balanced in both – I'm independent and make my own way in life, but I value having a relationship."

"There's a lot to say on this subject, but from what you've told me it seems like you are switching between wounded masculine and wounded feminine energies. Your most recent relationship sounds like you've swung over to the wounded feminine side too far, and your husband, being a masculine type, found it too emotionally draining to be around you."

I scanned my memory bank of past relationships and a pattern began to emerge, revealing my tendency of flipping back and forth between embodying the two polarities, which in turn usually attracted men of opposing polarities to mine. When I was living in the overly feminine, the men coming into my life were dominating, unemotional, and egotistic. It often resulted in me wanting more emotional connection, not getting it and eventually giving up on the relationship in frustration and disappointment. That was the case with Dave.

Other times I would overcompensate and start living in my empowered independent woman state – the overly masculine. That's when the men coming into my life were needy and too emotional for my liking, which quickly made me lose attraction towards them. It was the story of my life – always swinging between independence and dependence, but never being fully content on either side of the pendulum.

"You've told me you are prone to adrenal gland burnout and you are often exhausted – both are signs of wounded masculinity, and when you fall into that state you get sick and burnt out often. Let me ask you – do you have a distrust or dislike of men? And do you feel vulnerable around them?"

There was no denying I had that, remembering my paranoia at the airport in Cusco. I nodded "yes."

"That's a sign of wounded feminine. Do you hold resentment and anger towards your exes, and keep walls up around your heart to guard it?"

I didn't answer, but Nayanna read my expression, "Judging from your 'heart operation' last night, I'd say that's true," she said.

"You see how you keep toggling between the two wounded polarities to the extreme? The key to balancing your energy is to live in the divine feminine and divine masculine, because each of us have both sides present, regardless of which gender we identify as."

I was intrigued and was about to ask Nayanna how to go about living in divine balance of the two polarities, but she interrupted my thought by asking what my astrological sign was and reacted strangely excited when I told her I was a Scorpio.

"Do you believe in signs? Synchronicities?" Nayanna asked with a mysterious smile.

I told her I did and that lately they seemed to be coming with increased frequency in all forms.

"I would like to ask you to extend your trip and stay back to travel with me to an ancient Mayan temple in Mexico near the border of Guatemala. Before you answer, take the night off – you are not required to attend the last plant medicine ceremony tonight. Rest and watch for a sign that'll be your confirmation to put a hold on your work and all other plans back home and take a leap of faith."

I was surprised at her request but said that I'll think about it and let her know the next day.

"Just for your information," Nayanna called out as I was leaving the library, "this temple I am talking about, holds a legend that anyone who reaches it by land and sea, passing through the heart of the Americas, will be rewarded with the gift of 'true love' – and I personally know a few people who pilgrimed there and are now living their 'happily ever after'!"

Chapter 8

Background Noise

The roar of the air conditioner compressor unit, which was periodically turning on and off outside of my bungalow, powered off again, suddenly making me aware of the noise disturbing the silence in the room, although just moments before I was not aware of it at all.

I had been lying on the bed, quietly reflecting on the events of the past few days, indulgently tuning into the expansive space in my chest that has become part of my current internal state. I hadn't felt the need to entertain my mind with checking email, reading or even listening to music. I was content with simply being in the moment and enjoying the sensation of stillness, vastness and timelessness that I now had easy access to after the massive "cleaning out" I had received in the last ceremony. As the AC buzzing cranked on again and launched me into contemplation of my next move, it was no longer possible to not pay attention to the noises in and outside of my head.

I was glad that Nayanna gave me the option to enjoy a night off to recharge and catch up on sleep while the rest of the group were doing the final ceremony. Not only did I feel that this part of the journey was over for me, I didn't want to subject myself to any more spiritual deaths. As cleansing as it was, I didn't want to repeat this process anytime soon.

One ego death is enough to keep me going for a while... until perhaps the next life crisis.

I was certainly intrigued by Nayanna's proposed adventure and the prospect of going off the grid for a while, traveling to all of these exciting new destinations where I had never been before.

It would be no less than three weeks before I'd get back home. That's a lot of time to take off work!

I took out my phone and opened a map to see the path Nayanna told me we would need to take. From where we were currently located, we would travel north through Ecuador towards Colombia by land. Then we'd make our way through Central America, which was composed of seven countries: Belize, Guatemala, El Salvador, Honduras, Nicaragua, Costa Rica, and Panama.

This is probably what she meant by the "heart" of the Americas.

Then we would cross over to Mexico, and I'd be back in North America as we reached the temple in a jungle near the border with Guatemala. I would fly home directly from an airport in either Tabasco or Chiapas provinces. It seemed doable enough, and I wouldn't have to travel alone. Nayanna would accompany me – a great relief considering how I felt about roaming around solo.

I'd never do this journey on my own!

A woman alone wandering through Latin America – what a disgrace!

Is it I who really believes this? Or is it an outside opinion that I adopted as my own?

I couldn't tell whether that belief was mine or my mother's – her voice in my mind had become my own over time, and it was difficult to discern between the two. Once again, I heard that voice disapprovingly telling me that the idea of going on a search for a temple that promised true love was immature and impractical. I couldn't logically justify the choice of taking the trip. I remembered how my mother used to judgmentally say to me to "stop goofing around and do something useful" when I entertained the notion of switching my university major to philosophy, or when I wanted to go and work abroad with a non-profit.

Going on this trip with Nayanna was absolutely ridiculous from the left – logical side of my brain. But I was beginning to realize that all the reasons I had for not going, were coming from that background noise that I had gotten so used to over time, and it wasn't even self-created – it was someone else's noise. Just like that background hum of the AC – once you recognize it is there, makes it very hard to ignore – the awareness of my thoughts became clear and in stark contrast to what my heart truly wanted and yearned for.

What now became apparent as the truth was that most of the time that voice in your head is *not yours, not true,* and *totally contradictory* of what YOU truly want. It is usually the voice of a parent or mentor, a teacher, politician, or someone you were greatly influenced by growing up. It was becoming more and more obvious to me that I had mistaken those voices for my own, completely forgetting to check in with what truly mattered to me.

The pragmatist in me still wanted more information so before I could make this decision, I needed to do some digging about what I was getting into.

I went into research mode, looking up the Maya civilization, which dated as far back as 2600 BC. I read about the temples which the Mayans built to pay respect to their gods. The temples were scattered all over southern Mexico, including the Yucatán Peninsula, and parts of northern Central America, and they were shaped like pyramids. This shape was sacred to their religious practices and represented ascension of the soul to the afterlife, that's why they used these spaces for rituals and celebrations. The Maya people also used the temples for human sacrifice ceremonies.

Now I just need a sign that Nayanna had told me to watch for.

How long should I wait for it? And how will I know when I receive it?

Ahhh… I should just stop goofing around and get back to work. I'm not a child anymore – I need to take my life more seriously.

Suddenly, I began to perceive another type of "background hum," which could be best described as an internal sensation (not a feeling, but energetic acuity) of trying to hold up a really heavy weight above my head, or perhaps that of trying to push a heavy rock up a hill. It was a vague mental image of myself gritting my teeth, turning red in the face, straining and struggling under the crushing weight. Intuitively, I sensed what this was about. Thinking about going back home and diving back into work, fighting for my promotion and clawing my way to the top in the company, desperately trying to secure my future and the potential financial freedom it promised, certainly was that weight that was pushing down on me. Once I became aware of the connection, it was as if a lightbulb switched on in my head, illuminating the timeline of the past few years that were spent working towards my goal of a C-level position in the tech industry. The practical, reasonable voice was urging me to stay the course, encouraging me to push harder day in and day out, meanwhile this internal sensation of resistance against it was growing inside me and humming in the background.

I realized that for years I've had this hum of dissatisfaction unconsciously annoying me, and now that it hit my conscious awareness, it was both a shock and a relief. Shock, because it had taken me such a long time to "hear" it. Relief, because I was no longer a prisoner to it. I was free to choose whether I wanted to keep this hum going or to turn it off.

The question is… how do I turn it off?

I decided to consult Nayanna in the morning, but first I needed to get some rest.

I swiftly fell asleep, and dreamt of a snake, but it was not Naga from my ayahuasca vision – it was a garden snake, not the poisonous kind. The greenish snake was slithering along a grassy path winding through a jungle and my dream "self" was following it from behind. When we came to a clearing, a pyramid rose high up into the sky in front of me and I followed the snake inside. It was mostly an empty space with writings on inner walls in a language I didn't understand and didn't recognize the origin of.

In the center, I saw a figure dressed in red, sitting in a meditation pose. By his posture and clothing, this person looked like a Tibetan monk wrapped in a maroon robe with a shaved head. He was still like a statue, spine perfectly erect, head slightly tilted forward, eyes closed and a soft smile on his lips. Then I noticed two people who had appeared to either side of the monk – a man to his left and a woman to his right, sitting on the floor, facing towards him. They began to meditate together with the monk, and the room was suddenly filled with a brilliant light that was streaming like sunbeams reflected off glass from the top of the pyramid, as well as from its four inner corners at the base. The iridescent rays were flowing towards the center of the room, where the monk was sitting, illuminating his body from within so he looked almost transparent. He began to chant something in a language I couldn't identify but strangely, I understood what he was saying.

As I listened to the sacred song, an understanding came into my consciousness about the meaning of each line. It sounded like a prayer:

From the earth to the heavens, and back down,

The divine water flows and blesses me with life.

I allow the water to cleanse me of all that needn't be there.

As it passes through the gates of every portal that connects me to my source,

My body is pure, so is my mind.

I know myself to be the pure love,

Like a drop of light that comes from the one that IS.

I am a fragment of the same, but its truest essence nonetheless.

I honor the divine wisdom and place my trust in it,

And by default, I place that same trust in myself.

Let me prove to the divine source that I am worthy of the blessings,

And that I am the miracle I have been waiting for.

As the monk finished his chanting, the figures of the man and the woman turned into snakes and rapidly slithered towards his glowing frame to merge with him. The two snakes spiraled upwards in opposite directions through the monk's body interlacing each other as they climbed higher up towards his head. When they reached the top, a bright flash of light emanated from the center of his forehead and washed over everything in its path. When the blinding flash receded, the monk's body, which was already transparent, appeared to be vibrating with crystals of different colors ranging from red at the bottom, all the way up to a purplish hue at the top, in a rainbow spectrum running vertically up his body.

He had a book in his hands and held it out closer to allow me to see the cover, which displayed symbols resembling carvings found on ancient artifacts of the Mayan empire I had seen in my research about the temples. He opened the book and pointed to a number at the bottom middle of the page. The number was 34. Above it, there was a Mayan illustration of two entwined snakes.

He didn't speak, but the information I was receiving from the monk, which he was transferring into my consciousness, was to trust in and follow the signs that were coming my way. When the message was received, the monk, his book and the temple all faded into the infinite background of my subconscious, dissolving into a dreamy canvas of clouds spray-painted across a brilliant blue sky.

Before I knew it, it was morning, and after a deep and restful sleep, I was ready to meet up with Nayanna and tell her my decision to go to Mexico with her. The dream message I had downloaded was as clear a sign as could be that this journey needed to happen. The choice felt right in both my heart and mind. There was no feeling of heaviness, pressure or resistance and the space in my chest was pleasantly vibrating with ease and lightness.

I found Nayanna in the library after she finished the last integration session with the group, and after she said her goodbyes to everyone, I excitedly announced my decision. I told her about my new-found heart space, which seemed to be my intuition opening up and showing me the way.

"This is going to be a great trip with you, I can feel it!" I giddily blurted out.

"I am glad you are comfortable with this decision and that it feels 'right' to you, but to fully own your intuition requires a lot more than that. Intuition lies in here," Nayanna placed her hands over her lower abdomen, "that's why they call it a 'gut' instinct. Your heart is what you use to listen to that instinct. You've cleared out some junk from there, and made it easier to hear, but the work is far from over."

Nayanna's tone dialed down to serious, "You've managed to just crack the door slightly open, but in order to burst it wide open you will have to pass some more tests, so don't take it too lightly!

"You see, most people live their lives operating in the lower chakras, which is a low-vibrational frequency. It's all about survival at this level. To get up to the heart chakra and live from that higher frequency is challenging – it takes courage and willingness to go through the discomfort. The lower frequencies are the emotions of fear, insecurity, lust, guilt, shame, competition, judgment, anger, sadness, doubt, and worry. Living out of these emotions won't let you move into the higher states of consciousness. If you don't work through the emotional blockages that build up and prevent the prana from flowing freely up your main energy channel, the heart stays closed and you focus on simply living day to day without realizing the harm this is causing to yourself."

What Nayanna was saying hit home, especially when I thought about all of those negative, low-vibrating emotions I've had over the past few months. I've let lust, insecurity and anger lead me into infidelity, which I knew was wrong, but wasn't strong enough to stop. And that led me into feeling guilt, self-judgment, and doubt about my worthiness of true love. I told Nayanna how terrible I've been feeling about myself.

"The darkness that can overcome you doesn't make you a bad person. We are all susceptible to it in times of weakness or desperation. Think of it as a way of being tested by it, to be deemed worthy of the light of love. You always have a choice of what you want to do – stay in the darkness, or let the light of love in. Move towards what feels good – move away from what feels bad. It's quite simple.

"When you act upon lower vibrational frequencies to satisfy your heavy, dark energies of lust, greed, gluttony, jealousy, or other negative emotions, the act itself becomes the expression of that energy and you let the dark side win. If you transmute the energy into that of love, you let the light win."

"So, does that mean I have to resist everything that is considered a 'vice' and strive to be as pure as possible? This sounds a lot like religious teachings – 'thou shalt not sin' type of thing. I'm not the religious type."

"You don't have to be. All religions and spiritual teachings essentially point to the same truth but are expressed in different ways. And no, it doesn't mean you have to abstain from life's pleasures. Quite the opposite. Your body, which was given to you by the Great creative power, was designed to receive pleasure for a reason. You cannot deny that part of yourself. It's about how you choose to use your body, and in what frequency, that makes the difference. Enjoying food is not a 'sin,' but using food to escape your emotions or satisfy your gluttony would be the expression of that dark, low energy emotion. Same with sex – if you are using it to satisfy lust, ego or selfish desire, then you are allowing the dark energy to rule you. Sex in its pure form is a beautiful expression of love – of the light. Your body is built with the capacity to enjoy sex, whether alone or with a partner, and when you use it in a light vibration, it becomes simply your sacred right to use it and to connect to your own divinity through the sensations of your body."

"Alright, the next question is then, how do you know when you are operating from the dark energies? Sometimes the 'bad' things feel so right."

"You will know you are in the low frequency emotions because they always take you out of the present moment, and you begin to think about past or future, neglecting the moment you are currently in. Darkness can be tricky and may make you believe it feels good, but when you become aware, you see that it always comes with a host of negative emotions. That's why so many people confuse lust with love. Lust makes you yearn and crave certain emotions or sensations and takes you into the future through anticipation. Or into the past through memories. Love, on the other hand, is present and doesn't require any thoughts, and can even transcend time and space."

"I want to open myself to love! I'm ready, Nayanna, tell me how to earn it."

Nayanna chuckled at my eagerness and told me to be patient, as there was still much to be learned and uncovered first.

"Think of the main energy channel that runs along your spine as a flowing river. If a tree trunk falls into the river and rocks pile up, the water cannot get through easily, and begins to stagnate. That's what happens if you don't clear up those jams of low-vibrational energies – it keeps the heart closed and even begins to manifest as physical illness. Look at how many people are suffering in the world! So many ailments that could be cured with proper mindfulness and psyche adjustments. Yet most people just want a quick-fix solution, a pill for this or that to simply alleviate the symptoms, but not heal the root cause of the problem."

I flashed back on what Ale had said to me before about the "magic pill," noting the coincidence of hearing this again.

"I see it all the time," Nayanna continued, "especially in men, who let their pride, unchecked ego, and unwillingness to show emotion or change their ways build up and turn into heart disease, cancer, and stroke."

I recalled reading about the average life expectancy of Russian men to be 66. And from growing up with and knowing many Russian men throughout my life, I knew how difficult it was for them to express their emotions – at least for the older generation. My own grandfather died of prostate cancer and I asked Nayanna how that could've been related to emotional blockages.

"It is not always easy to explain how it all works. We have three interconnected parts: physical, mental, and energetic, and the way they interact is different for every person. But there is definitely some kind of link between certain emotions and the corresponding organs they affect. Have you heard about cellular memory?" Nayanna asked me. I hadn't.

"Did you know that the cells in our bodies have memory? Kind of like they have their own brain. Our organs retain those memories if they haven't been released subconsciously. That's when disease can develop in those organs based on the trauma or stress the person has been exposed to. Grief usually manifests as problems with the lungs or heart, as it is the emotion of the heart chakra. Ulcers and digestive problems can be the result of unchecked anger, which comes from the solar plexus chakra blockage. Joints and bones problems are a root chakra problem and can be caused by underlying safety or insecurity issues."

"And if you remove these subconscious blocks, you can heal yourself from any illness just like that?" I was a bit skeptical about this without having done my own research and made a mental note to look into this in more detail later.

"Not only do you heal yourself, but you can also heal your ancestors and ensure it doesn't pass on to your descendants! Our pain and trauma linger on for generations, and when we pass away, the energy doesn't just disappear – it continues to live onward in our children and grandchildren, until it is released. In fact, Native Americans believed that when you heal yourself in these metaphysical ways you heal seven generations back and forward!"

"So how does one go about releasing this old pain and heal it once and for all?"

Nayanna paused for a moment, then answered with a question of her own,

"Do you know that feeling of relief you get when an annoying persistent noise from some machine – a refrigerator or an air conditioner, for instance, which you didn't even realize was bothering you, suddenly turns off and a sense of peace takes over?"

I couldn't believe Nayanna was using the very same analogy for something that I had just been contemplating about in the morning on becoming aware of the background hum of my own mind.

Another coincidence?

"I think I know what you are saying!" I enthusiastically answered. "I just realized this morning about that hum of dissatisfaction when I think about my work and the state my life is in at the moment."

"Well, that's great!" Nayanna looked very pleased. "Now that you've noticed it, you've actually taken the first step in the process of self-transformation. This step is – *Awareness* and is something that everyone needs to go through before seeing a positive change in their lives. It is the most important element of initiating the process. Now that you've agreed to go on this trip with me, I will be teaching you the *Four Pillars of Self-transformation*, one by one.

"I will also teach you the *Three Cornerstones of Self-Love*, and the first one, which you just uncovered is *Self-Awareness*. But I don't want to get ahead of myself here. We have a long way to travel and there's a lot I want to share with you. For now, remember this first step as you begin to become more and more aware of things you've never noticed about yourself before. Self-discovery is a thing of beauty!"

I agreed to pay close attention to how I am feeling and what I am thinking with careful introspection and acute awareness. Then Nayanna showed me the roadmap of our 20-day passage towards the fabled temple.

We decided to set off at dawn the next day towards Guayaquil, Ecuador, which would be our first rest stop. After that we would head north to the coastal part of Colombia, and from there we would cross the Caribbean Sea by ferry to Costa Rica. Once there, we'd decide on the best route towards Guatemala, passing through several of the Central American countries to eventually cross over into Mexico – our final destination.

The anticipation of this tantalizing quest was already playing drumrolls in my stomach. The call of adventure, the excitement of the unknown, the promise of discovery, and a vast ocean of possibilities, all of which would normally come with a hefty dose of anxious nervousness, were balanced out by the increasingly comforting knowing that I was exactly where I needed to be.

There was only one more unanswered question still lingering on my mind, so I asked Nayanna in order to gain clarity about this incredible courtesy she was extending by taking me on this trip.

"Why are you helping me with this? It's such a long way... I'm sure you have much more important things to do than go on this pilgrimage with me."

Nayanna didn't hesitate at all and answered in a very matter-of-fact way,

"It is part of my own healing journey to accompany you and make sure that you get there safely. Madre Ayahuasca told me herself that one day I will lead a heart-guarding, highly sensitive and curious 'water sign' woman to the sacred temple. Your appearance here in the retreat was *my* sign, and I choose to follow it!"

Chapter 9

Fear

Can you really trust your mind?

Science says that we have about six thousand thoughts per day, although I've also heard it could be as high as seventy thousand.

Can all of them be true – or even necessary?

Nayanna and I took a bus to Huancayo, a small city in the central highlands of Peru. From there we would hop on the Lima-bound Tren de Sierra on the trans-Andean Ferrocarril Central Andino – the second highest train route in the world, which lost that title to the Qingzang railway that was built in Tibet in 1984.

I was trying to stay present and grounded but was getting lost in thoughts for the majority of the 17-hour drive through the mountainous area, regurgitating all of the events of the past few days in my head. By the time we got on the train, I was mentally exhausted.

An unobserved, untrained mind is a tricky entity.

For one, it never shuts up! It needs to narrate every detail of every damn second we're awake – and sometimes even when we are sleeping, although we may not even be aware of it.

For two, it cannot keep focused on anything for long – it always moves from one thing to another, like a monkey swinging from branch to branch. Just follow your thoughts for a while and observe how swiftly they'll get on a completely different topic, far off from where they had originally started.

One moment I'd notice an annoying mosquito that was circling around my face, the next thing you know I'm worried about the diseases it may carry, and then on my friend who nearly died of malaria on her trip to Myanmar a few years back.

Pretty soon I was picturing myself feverishly fighting for my life in a dodgy hospital in some remote village.

Gosh, all this mental chatter sure does drain your energy!

The "real me" – the awareness inside, notices and observes the mosquito. The "ego me" is the one that piles on all that other stuff about what the mosquito means and what can happen.

The good news was that I was becoming aware of these thought patterns. As Nayanna had said at the retreat, meditation really is all about noticing and observing, rather than trying to quiet your thoughts down or emptying your mind.

Wow, what a leap forward already and I had just started!

Krishnaraj would be proud to see how well I am doing. I am just crushing this mindfulness stuff!

Oh wait, is it okay to think like that? I sound so full of myself... that's not very mindful. Is that my ego getting all puffed up?

Hmm... I am being aware of how I'm proud of myself for being aware... this doesn't seem to have an end point.

How do the monks do it? When do I finally find that inner stillness?

Ahhh... this is so hard and unproductive! Ugh, this mosquito won't let me focus!

Now on the train, I couldn't find internal peace until I stopped trying to figure it out and turned my attention to the hypnotic sounds. Listening to the click clack of train wheels on the tracks and the low rumbling of the engine, the incessant chatter in my head subdued, and I enjoyed the scenery unfolding in front of my eyes like a pop-up picture book showcasing the best landscapes Peru had to offer. The 14-hour journey through towns, tunnels and mines was impressive. But once we got to the coastline, my heart felt like it unlocked ever so slightly at the sight of the open ocean.

Being a water sign I've always been drawn to the calming cool palette, fresh invigorating scent and soothing rhythmic wave sounds of oceans and seas. Having grown on the shores of the Black Sea, my best childhood memories came from daily summer visits to the beach. I'd walk with my grandmother, and sometimes grandfather, the length of half the town to the public beach. Those hot summer days were the perfect time to cannon-ball into the inviting cool water off the wave breaker platforms after an hour-long walk from my grandparents' house. I still remembered the smell of tar (creosote) on the sizzling hot surface of the train tracks running above and along the coast, which we had to cross to find a nice spot on the pebble beach below. And now that we were at the train station in Lima, that smell, however harmful it is to our health, brought back pleasant memories: the sweet anticipation of jumping into the water; slight burning feeling on my feet on hot flat rocks as I ran towards the sea; splashing and squealing with joy in the cool water.

It was a strange association that my brain had made, but isn't it always the case with brains? A bell activating salivary glands, à la Pavlov's experiments. A sight of a clown bringing on a panic attack in the most rational adults. Or how I always got sweaty palms watching someone risking their life at a great height in movies or live performances. Not to forget my loosening bowels at the slightest perception of danger.

So is everything we think and do just a byproduct of our programmed brain?

I wondered about the concept of determinism versus free will once again.

We stopped at a hotel to rest for the night after almost two days on the road. Nayanna hadn't talked much on the bus and looked very content to stay in silence for long periods of time. At breakfast the next morning, however, sitting together at the hotel restaurant that opened into a small garden, Nayanna was chatty and full of insights, which she was happy to share with me. I had many questions about the places we'd be stopping by and modes of transport we'd be taking. Nayanna could read my anxious curiosity and asked me what I was worried about the most so she could quell my discomfort.

"Do you mean what is my biggest fear about what lies ahead?" I reconfirmed her question.

"Yes, if you could pinpoint exactly what it is that scares you the most, knowing how far we have yet to go, what do you think that is?"

"Being kidnapped, I guess. It happens a lot in this part of the world, doesn't it?"

"Actually, it's not as common as the media and movies would have you believe. Statistically, none of the countries we're traveling to are even in the top twenty on the list with most abductions in the world. It is unlikely that either one of us would make a good kidnapping target – they usually look for business professionals – someone high profile."

"Then I would say it's the fear of the unknown – the mystery of it all. Are we going to make it to the temple? And what exactly is going to happen after we get there?"

"You cannot be afraid of something that you don't know. The 'unknown' is not an object of the fear. If you really tune into your awareness here, you'll see that what you are really afraid of is not getting what you want. You have a hope that getting to the temple is going to give you the true love you wish for. The fear is in the way of your dream and threatens that hope. If you are not careful, hope can turn into expectation, and the fear will grow, because you'll be afraid to lose the thing that you don't even have yet.

"But the thing to remember here is that fear is not a physical obstacle. It is simply a projection – or a phantom of the mind. It has no substance – it is ephemeral. You need to learn how to deal with it. Let me show you an exercise that will help you see fear for what it really is."

Nayanna asked me to close my eyes and to breathe, placing awareness on my physical body.

"Pay attention to how the breath *feels* in your nose, throat, lungs, and abdomen. Tune into the sensations of each inhale and each exhale, and how you perceive each breath with your senses. Ground yourself in the body."

I was noticing how my rib cage expanded and stomach inflated on an inhale, and how it all constricted on the exhale. I could feel the tightening and loosening of clothing around my mid-section and chest as I observed the sensations on my skin with each breath. I also noticed an ever-subtle expansion and contraction of my nostrils, and a slight difference in air temperature as it flowed in and out of my nose, remembering the Vipassana meditation technique which I learned from Krishnaraj in Bali.

"Now, visualize yourself standing at the start of a long winding path through a beautiful landscape. See the road ahead as it leads you towards a distant place which is your ultimate destination – up ahead but not yet visible from where you are. Begin walking on the path and observe the details of your surroundings. Take in the beauty and feel your feet firm on the ground with each step."

I did what Nayanna asked of me and imagined a narrow fine-gravel path that ran through a plush green field with wildflowers. It meandered through rolling hills towards towering peaks and disappeared into the dark green creases of the mountains. It was sunny but not too bright and everything was bathed in a golden glow of the setting sun that was hanging just above the mountains. Nayanna continued the guided visualization.

"Up ahead, a few meters away, you notice a dense cloud or glob of thick vapor floating right where you are about to pass. You know you need to go right through it if you are to make it to your destination. See the shape and size of the cloud. Is it bigger than you? Is it the same size or smaller than you? What color and density is it? Feel free to share verbally with me if you wish."

"It's a dark brown, a dirty kind of smog – thick and toxic-looking. It's big – definitely bigger than me, perhaps the size of a camper van. I can barely see through it but it's not totally opaque."

"Do you have a sense of where this smog came from? Do you feel that it was placed by someone in your way, or is it self-created? Who is responsible for this smog cloud? Don't think about it too much, just speak the first words that come to you. The first impulse is usually the right one."

"It's definitely mine – I am responsible for it. I can sense some familiarity with it, as if I'd seen it before."

"It's great to acknowledge this. Now, answer with the first thing that comes through – what do you sense this cloud is associated with? What is it all about?"

"Loneliness," I blurted out without much hesitation. "It's the fear of living and possibly dying alone. This dark, heavy cloud is my fear of never being fully loved by a man for who I am. At the same time, it's a fear of never being able to fully love another person and ending up old and alone. I'm always afraid that I'm not going to be enough, and that he will get bored or lose interest with me over time. But there's also the worry that I will get bored or lose interest in him – no matter how 'perfect' he may be. I've been through six serious relationships and it always ended in one of these scenarios."

"Okay, you are getting some clarity on your fear – good. Just for a moment, allow the emotion of this fear to make its appearance as a physical sensation and acknowledge it. Perhaps notice its presence in your body. Where and how do you feel it?"

I quickly scanned my body for signs of discomfort or pain and noticed a familiar tightness in my lower intestines – the same squeezing pain I felt every time I perceived danger. I wondered why the fear of being alone was being expressed in the same way as a fear for my physical safety. I told everything I was experiencing and thinking to Nayanna.

"Somehow your ego began to associate loneliness with death. Perhaps you think that without a partner who loves you, there is no 'you.' That's why this emotion feels so visceral in your body. That's okay... don't fight it, don't try to suppress it. Allow the emotion to play out and face up to it, like a brave warrior facing a mythical beast and stand your ground.

"Now, start walking towards and through the cloud. Notice how this thing you've created yourself is nothing more than air. It may be dirty or toxic, but it cannot physically harm you if you just keep moving forward. Watch yourself bravely charging ahead, walking through the smog and emerging on the other side, completely intact, unharmed and safe. Turn back to see this useless entity lose its strength and begin to disintegrate bit by bit, dissolving into the air. Watch it shrink down to a small patch that you can simply blow away into oblivion. Poof!

"Breathe out all the remnants of the smog out through your mouth. Now return back to your physical body and scan it from top to bottom. Is there any difference from how you felt in it before this exercise?"

I felt like I had been given a vitamin booster shot – the energy was flowing through me with ease and there was a sense of lightness in the body. The pressure in my bowels, which I had experienced earlier when Nayanna asked to pinpoint the physical sensation of my emotion, was gone. This lightness extended up towards my chest and I could feel my beautiful deep space that ayahuasca helped me to create, even stronger now.

"This is a type of energy healing that's part of the *quantum realm visualization* method I had developed to help people who come to me for inner work. It can be used for anything from changing harmful habits to building more confidence, and for healing an illness or a relationship. It is also a powerful manifestation tool for attracting what you want to happen in your life."

I was impressed. It was so simple yet effective, and didn't require much investment of time, money or energy.

"The mind is an incredibly useful thing indeed, but only if used properly. How objective is it though? Not much, I can tell you." Nayanna gestured at a neatly-trimmed bush in the garden about fifty feet away:

"Take a look at the bird sitting on that bush. What do you think of when you see the bird?"

"I don't know... it's a living creature, it's beautiful and it has the ability to fly, which would be nice to have too."

"Alright, good. Now let's move closer and see what we can see," Nayanna got up and invited me to follow her outside towards the bush.

As we came closer, my perspective changed as the details came into my view to transform it into something else – it was not a bird! Now I saw that it was a dry leaf that had likely fallen from the tree above and landed in a way that made it look like a brown bird from the table. Nayanna smiled at my surprised look and explained:

"The object was always the same – a leaf – but your perception of it changed with your vantage point. First, you were convinced it is a bird, then you changed your opinion to a leaf. When you thought it was a bird, you had certain feelings about it, right? How nice it is to have wildlife in the garden and how beautiful this creature is. But after you discovered that it is just a leaf, it no longer held the meaning of a beautiful or precious thing for you – it became just a useless piece of debris to be discarded."

Nayanna picked up the leaf from the bush and tossed it to the side.

"It's like that with fears and other beliefs. The mind constantly imagines things and convinces us that it is 'reality.' Until it is challenged or shown otherwise, it will fixate on its position and won't budge. It will protect its point of view as if life depended on it. When we get more information, a better understanding or a clearer view about the object, person or situation, then we take on the new perspective and begin to believe in that new 'reality.'

"We cannot trust our own mind! It is the ego in all of us and it is a two-faced bitch! It shifts its conviction to whatever it believes is closest to being right. It hates being wrong."

Once again, it was coincidental and surprising that Nayanna was talking about something that I had been pondering just hours earlier on the train ride here. I wondered if we were kindred spirits, perhaps sister-souls from many lives past.

"So, if I understand you correctly, it's not about the object of the fear at all, but about the meaning my mind assigns to it that makes a difference in how I feel about it. And it's up to me to choose what I want to believe!

"Does that mean we have free will?"

"I will leave it up to you to decide," Nayanna winked at me.

~

Going back to my room after breakfast, I decided to call my parents to tell them I wasn't coming back home as planned and that I was extending my trip for a few weeks, so they wouldn't worry. I knew this was going to be a tough sell to get their approval of me going on this journey on a whim. My mother answered the phone and wanted to know who was accompanying me, and what I was planning to do about my job. I told her I was taking unpaid leave, to which she disapprovingly sighed and tsked. My father cautioned me about the kidnappers he had heard about from the news and told me not to tell anyone I meet any personal information or trip details. Although they were both shocked and worried about my unexpected detour, they seemed to calm down when I reassured them I was in good company and promised to check in with them every few days.

After ending the conversation, doubts and fears started to come up again.

Have I made a huge mistake? Am I going to regret this?

I should have consulted with them before so they'd talk some sense into me.

Hopefully their fears won't be proven right and I'll get home safely.

Should I just go back now?

I needed to talk to someone who'd understand my "insanity," (to use the exact words my mother had used during our talk) so I called Alejandro. He was happy to hear from me and wanted to know everything that had happened so far. I told him about the ayahuasca sessions and the ego death, Nayanna and her teachings, my visions and dreams, and my decision to go in search of the legendary temple.

"Look at you being all bad-ass in doing the hard inner work," he teasingly congratulated me. "Good to see you are not running away the moment things get difficult."

"Well, I'm not done with this work yet – I'm just beginning, so hold off on your praise for now… I may turn up at your door in a few days, tail between my legs," I joked back then paused and switched to a more serious tone, "I feel that there's a battle of dark versus light going on inside of me, and I'm doing my best not to let the dark side win. There are all of these negative emotions that keep coming up, over and over again. I thought I · got rid of them in the ceremonies, but I still feel their presence within. I want to learn how to let the light win, but I'm scared what will happen if I fail."

"There are no guarantees, of course," Ale suggested, "and sometimes you just have to go on pure faith. But just so you know, I see your light and it's stronger than any shadows that you feel inside. I'm not worried about losing you to the darkness!"

A sense of warmth spread out through my chest for Ale, feeling the familiar tickling of my insides, which definitely felt more than platonic. Yet I didn't know if he felt the same way about me, so I just smiled and blew a kiss to the camera, which he playfully received and sent one right back.

"Nayanna has explained that a lot of these negative energies come from our programmed subconscious beliefs, and that once you become aware of them, they can simply go away... through self-work, of course. But what about new fears and negative emotions that keep coming up even with my ability to stay aware? Where do they come from?"

"They are just there – the same way light energies are. It's the duality of life. The darkness seeks out weakened hosts and attaches itself to them. In moments of stress or destabilized mindset, for example. The same way a virus can attack a weakened body if you don't take care of your physical health. You've got to maintain good habits of energetic hygiene to keep your energy body strong and vibrating high daily. That's why we do the alchemy practice – to keep ourselves shielded from these dark energies."

"I'm starting to have a new-found appreciation for all of this spiritual alchemy you've been practicing. But what are these energetic hygiene habits?"

"I have a feeling you will find out soon enough. Nayanna sounds fantastic at what she does! Trust her. By the way, do you remember the seven stages of alchemy I mentioned to you before?"

I struggled to remember the words and what it all meant as it applied to spiritual transformation, so Ale proceeded to remind me the stages and said that he thinks I'm now in the first one – *calcination*.

"In traditional alchemical science as a form of practical philosophy, this stage is when the 'prima materia' is burnt into ash. Look at it as breaking out of your identification with the physical world and seeing beyond the matter, into the energy or spirit of things. You've seen for yourself how attachment to material things, status and prestige never fulfilled that emptiness inside, no matter how much of it you've accumulated, right? And you also know that things that inflate your ego and its identity can totally consume you if you let it. The ego death you've had was the break that you needed to pass through the first stage. It initiated your journey into the true self, so be patient and keep your feet grounded on the path forward."

I thanked Ale for sharing his knowledge with me and as much as I wanted to express this fuzzy warm feeling I had for him, the words were stuck in my throat.

"I love you," Ale, who certainly never had a problem verbalizing what he felt for his friends, said to me.

"Love, love," I winked and winced internally for my inability to say these three simple words out loud back to him. I had always reserved these words for people I was in serious relationships with.

Before saying goodbye, he had one more thing to add,

"You don't have to try to fight with the darkness – it cannot be fought against or forced away. Just let the light of love in and it will dissipate the darkness. Transmute the dense energies with love, and the darkness doesn't stand a chance."

Chapter 10

Inner Warrior

We spent the day doing touristy things in Lima. The hotel had organized a sightseeing tour for us and a few other guests. There was a group of young Australian backpackers, an elderly couple and a mother-daughter duo from the UK who joined us on a minibus that took us around the city.

From the moment I met Faye and Libby, I noticed a familiar dynamic between parent and child, which reminded me of how my father used to raise me. Faye didn't miss any opportunity to caution her four-year-old daughter of the grisly consequences of her actions, no matter how harmless they seemed to me. Anytime Libby had ventured off on her own even slightly, her mother would pull her back saying she was in danger of being kidnapped or run over by a car. If Libby climbed on something, she received a warning that it could lead to a fall, broken bones, and imminent hospitalization. Faye was constantly lecturing Libby about touching things and picking up germs on her hands, that would give her tummy bugs for which she'd have to take worm medicine. It was a continuous stream of "don'ts" and "no's" that was followed by a tale of a seriously grave outcome of Libby's actions, which in my view were quite normal for a child of her age. I could sense that this fearmongering was affecting the young girl, because I was beginning to realize that my own insecurity in the world stemmed from my overly-protective upbringing.

My father worked as a radio communications officer on a merchant ship when I was a child growing up in the Russian part of the USSR. He'd be away for months at a time on distant voyages and come back home for the same length of time. I got to enjoy his presence for only half the time, spending the rest of it living between my mother's two-bedroom apartment in a Soviet era housing block, and my grandparents' house across the small town of about eighty thousand people. It was the late eighties and early nineties when I can recall my childhood memories the most, and in those days, Russia was quite a scary place. The economy was in shambles preceding the fall of communism and restructuring of the political system. There were food shortages, high crime rates with gangs roaming the streets, and an overall sense of deprivation you could feel in the atmosphere, which made people angry and hostile. I remembered walking home with my mother in a near-jog pace through the dark alleys from my grandparents', trying to make it home as fast as possible. Then, walking into a pitch-black lobby of our apartment building, bracing for someone to attack us in the stairwell. Every day I'd hear news on television and radio about someone getting murdered. There were many incidences of rape and assault on local women that I kept hearing about from my friends' parents and from my own. Women, in general, were not treated with much respect in those days and I had seen domestic abuse when I visited my friends' homes. These images were emblazoned in my memories and stayed with me for years after, even into my adulthood. There were sexual predators, "maniacs" as my mother had called them, everywhere, and I was constantly living in fear of them, especially after I had seen some creepy men exposing their genitals to me and my friends in the playground.

Not having my father around for half the time made me feel insecure and unsafe with these "freaks" on the loose. Two vulnerable women alone in the apartment, my mom and I, against all the risks and dangers of the world. We had no protector, or a man of the house, who'd stand up to these guys.

Yet when he came back home to us, his over-protective nature was exacerbating my biggest fears. I'd hear the same stories over and over again about how that one girl – a daughter of his friend I'd never met – was abducted and no one ever saw her again. Or how a neighbor's kid was climbing the roof of a car garage, fell off and had to spend his life in a wheelchair. When we went to the beach in the summers, I'd hear about his childhood friend who drowned because he didn't listen to his parents.

It's no wonder I'm so tense all the time, especially when I don't have a man by my side!

I began to become aware of how I always imagined the worst-case scenario – getting hurt or robbed or possibly dying. I couldn't relax and was always on high alert, assuming the worst about others who looked in the slightest way dubious or out of the ordinary. I could see where all of this insecurity was coming from.

As I witnessed Libby, with her playful nature, being reprimanded for being herself and getting likely traumatized by her restrictive mother, I felt a tinge of empathy for the girl. I told Nayanna my observation and insights about how my experiences growing up in an unsafe environment were clearly the catalyst to my distrust and irrational fear of strange men.

"That's a great self-analysis about your fears and insecurities, but as you do that, don't forget to stay aware of other feelings that surface in these revelations. Just now you felt sorry for that girl – that's a low vibrational frequency, not much better than the frequency of fear. It is not useful to you – or to her for that matter. I can tell you more about empathy versus compassion later.

"First, let's talk about your root chakra blockages. I'm going to show you some exercises to activate your first chakra. Fear, apprehension, insecurity and feeling unsafe in the world are related to the first chakra – *muladhara*, and it is represented by the earth element. These emotions, just like any others, can be felt both psychologically and physically. I've already shared with you the quantum realm energy healing visualization for overcoming fears, which you can continue to practice when you notice anxious thoughts arising. There are also physical exercises I am going to teach you that are part of the spiritual alchemy I've adapted into my own way of teaching. Do you know about alchemy?"

I was happy to announce that I knew a bit about it from Alejandro, and how he was using its values for his spiritual work.

"That's great! In contemporary alchemy practices, which New Age healers like myself are using in their work, there's a principle of transmutation for our spiritual growth – turning fear and many other low-vibrating emotions into love, for example. I'm going to show you some of these rituals that involve chakra work. How much do you know about chakras?"

I knew enough about chakras from books and mindfulness work with Krishnaraj in Bali to understand the basics of how these energy centers of our energy body work and how they affect our physical body. But I wasn't aware that there were physical healing exercises for each of the chakras, other than some yoga poses.

Nayanna promised to show me the *Warrior One* move, which would activate my masculine pole and help me adjust my root chakra from under-active to optimal level, upon our return to the hotel. She asked me to perform this exercise every morning as part of my personal morning alchemy practice.

~

Warrior One Morning Alchemy Practice as taught to me by Nayanna

This active pose is different from the typical yoga asana of the same name and is intended for expressing your power through movement and charging ahead, which are divine masculine energy characteristics.

Start by standing in the mountain pose, feet firmly grounded, tailbone slightly tucked in to a straight spine, arms down your sides with palms facing forward. Engage your legs and glutes and breathe deeply towards your belly for a few rounds.

Bend your arms at elbow height with palms facing down. Find a spot ahead of you where you want to send your energy and keep your gaze on it.

Now take a big step forward with your right leg, bending it at the knee as you step with stability and firmness, and at the same time extend your left arm forward like you are about to punch a wall with your palm, retracting your right arm slightly back.

This will look a bit like a karate move. Do this with intention on sending your energy out and forward as if you want to project it into the spot you are looking at. Step back to initial position.

Repeat this move on the left side with alternate leg and arm.

As an added bonus, you can try the step forward with a forceful exhale through your mouth or even with an audible sound – Haaahhh!

The intensity and duration of this move and sound is up to you. You can do it a few times on one side and the same number of times on the other. Or you can alternate between sides on each step.

~

Lying in bed that night before continuing our road trip to Ecuador the next morning, I reflected on everything I've learned from Nayanna and on what I've realized through my own deep introspection.

Living with fear is no way to live well.

Being a rational, mature and level-headed adult was enough to ensure my survival and minimize any unnecessary risk. But giving myself over to phantom projections of the mind, most of which are not true, necessary or even logical, was certainly going to block me from experiencing life with joy and freedom. I placed my trust in the process of re-wiring my old thought patterns, which Nayanna had introduced me to, and feeling very secure and safe in my bed began to drift off into a sweet slumber.

As I entered the dream world, which had become very vivid and lifelike in the days since the ayahuasca ceremonies, I dissolved into a vortex of earthy visuals consisting of every type of plant life imaginable. Everything was shaded with warm reddish hues: trees of all kinds of shapes and sizes, grass blades, vines, roots, flowers, cacti, moss, shrubs, corals and sea plants, and the soil that birthed it all into existence. It was all alive and moving, breathing with life. Then I was treated to a parade of land animals, reptiles and insects, each appearing so clearly and in so much detail I could practically count the whiskers of the lions and pumas. The abundance of life forms and the intricacy of their distinct constitution was mind-blowing, and I continued to take it all in with awe and gratitude.

Suddenly, the snake that had appeared in my ayahuasca vision came into my field of view in all of her spectacular colors. *Naga!*

I remembered the snake's name, and how she felt like a female presence to me on our first meeting.

Naga, swaying from side to side, as though she was dancing, seemed to be a ubiquitous and benevolent spirit that meant to serve as my guide – my spirit animal. I could sense she was here to assist me in my journey and support my progress as I shed the parasitic microbes and old stagnant cells off my energetic body – much like the snake sheds its skin. She telepathically informed me that the first stage of my healing had been successfully completed and that she had a gift for me to reward my efforts.

With that, a beautiful red jewel – the most beautiful precious crystal, manifested in front of me, symbolically representing my root chakra alignment. I accepted the gift with gratitude and affection for my friendly guide.

There seemed to be a sororal-like connection between us. We stayed together, sweetly relishing each other's presence, and then she was off. And I was left in a peaceful state of everything being in its right place and time.

In the morning, when I told Nayanna about the appearance of the snake in my dream and her name, she excitedly explained that Nagas are a semi-divine race of serpents in Hindu mythology that have traditionally been depicted as either cobras or a hybrid form of human-serpents in iconography.

When I researched the Nagas on my own later that day, I found more information about them in Hindu and Buddhist religions, where they were described as powerful demi-gods who resided and ruled over the netherworld filled with gems, precious metals and earthly treasures called Naga-loka. They were considered guardians of treasure and were often associated with water. Despite their power and venom that could be harmful to humans, they were not deemed evil and assumed a positive role in folklore.

I was honored to have been touched by this semi-divine energy in my visions and to be the recipient of the precious Naga-loka in the form of a gemstone, and hoped I'd meet Naga, my dream snake, again as I passed further stages of healing.

Chapter 11

Guilt

Pondering the entirety of my relationship with Dave and zooming in on moments where I could find clues about the cause of its malfunction, had become my favorite pastime. And here, on the bus to Guayaquil, Ecuador, I had plenty of time to get into it.

What is my love language?

By now the five love languages had become part of our modern culture and everyone knew about them. It was a common question that friends and partners asked each other: What is your love language? The concept was introduced in a 1992 best-selling book by Gary Chapman and divulged the five ways in which we need to experience and express love: quality time, acts of service, words of affirmation, physical touch and gift giving.

I had given this matter a lot of thought since my divorce, to try and figure out where I may have gone wrong in showing my love, and to understand what it was that I really needed that Dave failed to give to me.

Quality time! He didn't want to spend his precious time with me! I tried to give him as much of my time as I could. Perhaps he needed something else from me?

We had met through a mutual friend, who talked about him as "this great guy – slightly older than you, but looks ten years younger than he really is," which actually turned out to be a fifteen year age difference between us. He was well established in his career as an investment broker, owner of a small yacht and a fabulous downtown condo where he loved to entertain his friends with lavish parties. She invited me to one of his soirees in the hopes of a coupling of her two friends, saying that she wanted to get credit for her match-making service in our wedding speeches. Upon introduction, I remembered that I had actually already seen Dave a few times. The first time was when he tried to pick me up with the typical "when I saw you, I just had to come over and meet you" lines on the train one evening after I was coming home from work. I was impervious to these pick-up strategies, and even though I thought he was good looking, an inkling that he was probably using this line on every pretty young girl was a massive turn-off.

Who does this line work on, anyway?

Dave routinely attended the fashion shows I was walking, always sitting in the front row, dressed impeccably in a designer suit and shoes, and attentively admiring the models. He was certainly not there for the fashion. He didn't have a bad reputation amongst the female population in my social circle, but I sensed a bit of a playboy flair from him, that's why I never considered even throwing a glance in his direction.

Let him entertain himself on meaningless flings, I had thought back then, *I don't have time for these types.* I wanted a committed and loyal partner.

Dave was the epitome of the "perfect-on-paper" man – he ticked all the boxes. He was fifth-generation Italian – the only son and youngest child of a big family who were in the restaurant business. His parents were always busy with work, and he had been mostly raised by his aunt on his mother's side who had her own seven children. Tall and nicely toned, with a full head of ash brown hair that he wore as a clean mid-length cut parted in the middle, and two rows of much-too-perfect porcelain veneers, Dave was handsome in a classic way. He was athletic and looked after his appearance. Always immaculately groomed, his eye for detail extended to his home, which was as organized as he was.

After observing him with his friends and seeing how generous and caring he was, I decided to give him a chance. We began dating and he was quick to introduce me to his family, dropping hints that I was making a great impression on them as a potential daughter-in-law. My mother loved him immediately after I introduced him. She said that he was a "smart choice" and that I would have to be "crazy not to consider him as husband material." My father didn't say much, as he was never very opinionated about my boyfriends, and I took his lack of objections as a good sign too. My mother had placed a big importance on marrying a financially stable man, and she would always inquire about every one of my boyfriend's job statuses and what he did for a living. She believed that the beauty and youth of a woman was a fair exchange for an ample bank account, and that I shouldn't ever settle for anything less than I deserved.

And what I deserved was the world, according to her. Being influenced by this idea of financial security as a solid criterion for a "happy marriage" and judging Dave for his outer characteristics was a big reason why I had decided to accept his proposal just six months into our relationship.

There was certainly some hesitation, especially on the day of the wedding. Unnerved by the stress of planning and executing a twelve-hundred-people reception (mostly his side of the "big fat Italian" family), I remember crying together with my mother in the back of the limo on the way to the beauty salon the day of the wedding. These were not tears of happiness but of unease and anxiety, which we both dismissed as simply wedding jitters.

To make things extra complicated, the fact that he had asked me to sign a prenup just weeks before the wedding was weighing heavily on us. My mother was in complete disarray and wanted me to cancel the wedding, but I talked her into agreement, saying that it was the norm these days, and that I admired Dave's prudence and analytical approach, much like her own. After some intense negotiations between our lawyers, we had come to a middle ground which satisfied everyone involved, and the wedding plans resumed. It did, however, leave a sour taste with a hint of doubt about our relationship, which I couldn't shake off for the whole duration of our marriage.

Personally, I didn't feel that asking for a prenup was grounds for a breakup. Although I was only just starting my career as a software engineer, I had made good money from international modeling contracts, and I owned my one-bedroom apartment, debt-free. I understood Dave's need to protect his wealth and wanted to prove to him that I wasn't marrying him for his money. In a way, I was proud that I was a woman who could stand on her own two feet and was independent enough to rely on myself. And having Dave as a husband only added to my self-image of a successful "she-has-it-all" woman. I liked the idea of us together and it neatly fit into my plan that I had meticulously constructed for my perfect future.

Yet here I was, three years after the wedding, feeling like a failure, asking myself where I had gone wrong.

How do we develop a love language, anyway? What is it that makes someone want to experience love by receiving gifts, while others need it by words of affirmation?

I wondered if our upbringing had something to do with it. As Nayanna explained to us in one of the group integration sessions at the retreat, we form the majority of our beliefs in childhood before the age of seven. Everything that we had seen, heard and experienced in that precious time when our minds are super susceptible to programming as the brain develops, becomes part of our ego's identity later on.

I thought back on my early childhood and retrieved some memories about how I received love from my parents and grandparents. The female side of my family certainly didn't hold back with their physical affection. I received plenty of hugs, kisses and cuddles. I also remembered how my mother would put me to sleep and wake me up in the morning by softly massaging my back or my feet. I loved getting massages and having my skin or hair stroked, and often asked my grandmother to do the same for me when I slept over at her house.

Perhaps my love language is actually physical touch? I definitely enjoyed receiving love in this way!

Massage was not the only way my mother expressed her love for me. She truly went above and beyond to make sure I never had to do any house chores – everything was done for me. Food was always served, dishes cleaned, laundry folded, floors swept by my mother, and she purposefully wouldn't let me get involved in housekeeping the entirety of my childhood and even adolescence. When I'd asked why she never wanted me to help her out around the house, she would answer that my job was to study hard and be a kid, and that I'd have plenty of time to clean when I grow up and have a family of my own. Besides, I had a jam-packed schedule which left no time for chores – piano lessons, gymnastics training and a substantial amount of schoolwork to be done daily. I didn't have much spare time and my mother believed that I didn't need housekeeping skills to make a good life for myself.

When I got a bit older and my father was permanently living with us, no longer traveling for work, he was also very supportive and helpful. He would drive me wherever I needed to go and hold the car door open for me, setting an example of what a true gentleman is. I could always come to him for any financial support, and he was there to help me set things up in my apartment when I first moved in and then again after the separation. My mother would point out how good he was to me and how her biggest wish was that I'd eventually find a partner who will treat me in the same way – like a queen!

Maybe my love language is acts of service? Dave certainly was chivalrous – making sure he always treated me like a lady. But he probably needed me to be more of a "mother" to him, as he didn't have much of a relationship with his parents. I never cooked and cleaned for him.

I messed up!

I began to feel intense guilt for not being the kind of woman I thought Dave deserved.

There is so much I could've done differently! If I had taken more care of him, and been more feminine, he wouldn't have lost his attraction. I wonder if we'd still be together?

We crossed the border to Ecuador and were heading towards our next stop, the city of Guayaquil. Nayanna mentioned that the full moon was coming up in two days' time and informed me that this was a very special time when the earth was under massive influence from the energy of its sister planet. She explained that in this once-a-month happening, the sun's rays fully illuminate the surface of the moon, which doesn't have a light of its own, and it reflects the maximum light and energy from its surface towards the earth. That's why many people around the world and throughout history have reported sleepless nights, agitation, changes in mood and other strange occurrences that seemed to coincide with the full moon. It was prime time for over-thinking and anxiety, so Nayanna asked me to be extra vigilant in observing my thoughts.

"Pay attention to your innermost desires and fears over the next few days," she advised. "The full moon is a ripe opportunity to reveal these to you."

I told Nayanna about my guilt surrounding Dave and the love languages that we failed to communicate to each other. I joked that it must be the moon that was making me over-analyze my failed relationship.

"Yes, there certainly seems to be a problem with communication, but I don't think your biggest issue was how you expressed or didn't express love to one another. All of these love languages you mention are not something to look for from outside yourself. It's okay to crave for these things from others – we are human beings with needs, after all. But if you get attached to these expressions of love that you want to be fulfilled by another person, that leaves you in a co-dependent state, relying on someone else to give you what you need to give to yourself first. If you are not a self-contained person, then you are definitely not equipped to give that love to anyone else."

"How does one become self-contained?"

"You find your own love language, but this language is for communicating with yourself!"

"The language of self-love! Of course, that's so spot on! But how do I know what that language is?"

"Only you can know the answer. Perhaps it's the physical touch and acts of service, as you mentioned. Don't try to find these things externally – give them to yourself! Express love to yourself in these ways. And Dave has to do the same for himself too. You are only responsible for your individual needs and not for making the other person feel whole.

"The guilt and self-pity you are experiencing lives in your second chakra – *svadisthana* chakra. It represents the element of water, as I'm sure you already know, and it governs your emotions, sexuality and creativity. May I ask, is your menstrual cycle synchronized to the moon cycle?"

"Do you mean does my period come on the full moon or new moon?"

"Not necessarily on those points, but is your cycle regular and does it come every 28 days or so?"

"It's all over the place! Super irregular and quite painful. Ever since my first period when I was thirteen, I had horrendous cramps and missed periods for up to three months. Sometimes the pain would get so bad that I'd throw up and almost pass out. My doctor diagnosed me with endometriosis and put me on birth control pills at fifteen. I'm off of them now, but I still have problems in that area."

"Right. There is a big connection here from your emotional front to your physical one. Emotions are vibrations in our body created by our nervous system. When we repress our emotions, they settle somewhere in the body, and over time we lose the ability to sense them and process them. That's why it's so important to observe what you are feeling at any given point in time and understand where it may be coming from. Emotions fuel our actions, and if we don't use them in the right way, they can be destructive. But they also can be our greatest superpower! I think it's time I teach you some more exercises for your quantum realm energy healing practice."

We agreed to meet for the healing session after checking into the hotel and getting freshened up after a day-long bus ride.

After a nice dinner at a local restaurant in Guayaquil, we went to Nayanna's room. Once again, she invited me to sit upright with eyes closed and bring attention to my breath and physical senses. After connecting to my breath, she guided me to become aware of each body part from the feet up towards the head, and I experienced a sense of aliveness and vibration all over. I felt particularly strong sensations in my hands as I could feel the pulsating energy and warmth in the palms and fingers of each hand. This sensorial body scan made me feel grounded and present.

"Offer some love to your body first," Nayanna prompted. "Silently say the following words: I am healthy; I am strong; I feel good in my body."

I proceeded to repeat the words internally.

"Keep saying these words and give yourself some physical affection. Wrap your arms around yourself, like a hug. Massage your neck and shoulders, then your arms up and down, giving yourself a squeeze here and there. Rub your feet and tune into the sensations everywhere you touch. Spend a few minutes expressing love for your body."

At first, it felt a bit strange to be massaging myself in such a hedonistic way. But I quickly tuned out the thoughts of guilt and discomfort and tuned into the present moment with body and breath awareness.

"Now that you're grounded and feel secure in your body, ask yourself: What am I feeling now? What emotions are present now? You don't need to label the emotion or try to find words to describe it. Simply acknowledge that it's there and that you are experiencing it."

I was feeling something along the lines of repression and stagnation, although I couldn't quite place an exact word on it. Something needed to be released, and the pressure of whatever it was that was being held down was starting to become obvious on an emotional level.

"Remind yourself that this is a transient state – no feeling is permanent. Feel free to open yourself up to it without fear of being overcome by it and being stuck there forever. Don't react to it and don't judge yourself for having it. The more you resist or try to force yourself to not feel it, the more it will persist. Just continue to breathe deeply with physical and emotional awareness. Sit with it. Let it pass through you, even if you don't like how it feels. If you don't allow it to be, it'll get stuck, and no fresh energy can get in.

"Remember what I said about emotions being vibrations? Can you sense anything now in your physical body? Try to feel these subtle vibrations and pinpoint where they may be located. If it were an object, what do you think it is – or how does it appear to feel to you? As always, the first answer is always correct. Don't think about it too much and just say whatever comes to you first."

"It kind of feels like a rock in my lower abdomen. A heavy sensation – it's pressing down on my internal organs. There's restriction there, like things are not flowing but stagnant."

"What kind of rock is it? I want you to visualize it and see its shape, color and size – the more detail the better. Don't think, just let it come through."

"It is a large gray rock that fits into my two hands and it's an oval shape."

"Is it heavy and dense, or light and porous?"

"Definitely heavy and dense."

"Is it smooth or rough on the surface?"

"It has a smooth texture."

"Is it hot or cool to the touch?"

"It's warm and heating up."

"Okay, stay with the sensation and the image of this rock and let it come up to the surface, as if it's floating out of your body so you can see it in front of you. Does this rock belong to you, or was it placed inside of you by someone? Who is responsible for this rock being here?"

"It's not mine, I know that for sure. I think it's been placed there by someone I have forgotten because it was a long time ago. Perhaps when I was around six years of age. I see my hometown where I went to school, and my mother is picking me up from the first day of school. But it's not her that's tied to the rock. I can't quite place who it is..."

"Alright, no problem if you don't know who it is. It may come to you within days or weeks if you continue doing this exercise. For now, you can give this rock to your mother and ask her to keep it, as she is responsible for you in that timeline as a child. When the rightful owner appears, you can ask your mother to give it to them. Imagine yourself, as best as you can, passing the rock over to your mother and her taking it far away from you. Feel the newfound space in your lower abdomen and the associated sensation of the weight lifting off."

I used my best visualization powers to do as Nayanna had asked and felt slightly lighter after a few minutes. Then with her guidance, I came back into the body in the current space and time and opened my eyes.

"Welcome back, my dear," Nayanna said softly. "These quantum realm healing experiences are powerful, but it can take time to work through deep-rooted emotions, especially if you've become skilled at burying them whenever they surfaced.

Anytime you use an activity to escape your emotions instead of meeting them head on, you are ignoring them and they stick around. Anytime you try to bypass the emotions with gratitude, you are simply suppressing them instead of processing them. It's a common mistake people make, to try and reframe an emotion into what suits them better in the current situation. Of course, gratitude is a high vibration and it can help you tune into the right frequency, but not if you overlay it on top of a low vibrational frequency which you don't like and judge yourself for."

"But what about when I feel ashamed or guilty of my negative thoughts? Do I just let them have free rein? That seems counter-intuitive," I protested.

"Extending judgment on this natural process of your mind is futile, and only keeps you trapped in lower frequencies. You don't need to do much with these self-deprecating thoughts, except become aware of them, and the moment you do that, they will disappear on their own. It's the deep-seated emotions that you can sense in your body as discomfort, or even pain, that require more work and longer time to dislodge."

"Right. Awareness is definitely the key to our healing and transformation. Is this the only way we can heal the sacral chakra?"

"No. We can also align it by tuning into our sexuality."

I was surprised to hear this and asked Nayanna to elaborate.

"While some schools of thought connect sexuality to the root chakra, I believe that together with emotions, sensuality and creativity, it is connected to the sacral chakra. Creativity and sexuality are one and the same in terms of energetic vibration. We use sexuality to express our desires and passion for a person in the same way we use creativity to express passion for life. The act of sex is a creative flow itself – we can create life with our reproductive organs. And when we create art, dance, or music, and whenever we are creating through cooking, writing, sewing or gardening, we are simply extending svadisthana energy through the different points in the energy body. For example, when you sing, the sacral energy is expressed through the throat chakra. When you sculpt or paint, that energy is being expressed through your hands, which have minor chakras in the palms that are energetically linked to the heart chakra. Everything in the energetic body is connected, that's why it's so important to engage yourself in creative activities."

"What if I am not a creative type? I've always thought of myself as analytical and logical. I work with code – I've been trained to use the left side of the brain. And I certainly never created anything in my life."

"It's correct when you say you've been 'trained' to use the left side of the brain. That doesn't mean your right side is not functioning. You speak three languages and play the piano – those are skills related to the right, creative side. Don't dismiss yourself as a non-creative just yet."

Nayanna said it was getting late and suggested we get some rest before continuing our pilgrimage early the next day. I went to my room and ran through the visuals of the heavy rock that I had extracted from my energetic body tonight.

Who planted that rock there?

I set an intention on finding out.

Chapter 12

Inner Goddess

It was finally here – the full moon. And its arrival was rumbling in my insides like a giant mass of emotions bubbling up under the surface, ready to burst through the hatch that was perilously holding it all down. It felt urgent and imminent.

What is happening to me? Is it more of those nagging anxieties that I haven't yet become aware of?

I scanned myself up and down, searching for both physical and emotional signs of fears lurking in my subconscious, but I couldn't find any. It didn't feel visceral and raw like my fears about traveling alone or being stared at by strange men, which rocked my entire body with adrenaline. This was a softer vibration, more fluid, and it concentrated in the area just under my bellybutton.

We had arrived in Cartagena, Colombia, early in the day. The city had a festive atmosphere with locals dressed in colorful traditional clothing and music being played on the streets. They were celebrating the Independence Day of Cartagena, which became the first Colombian city to gain independence from Spain on November 11, 1811. This was a national holiday that spanned the first two weeks of November and culminated in a carnival-type parade with a beauty pageant and dancing in the streets.

It was a perfect time and place to welcome in the next decade of my life. Nayanna suggested we head to Plaza de la Trinidad – the ending point of the parade, where we could join in the celebration to absorb a bit of the culture and history, as this was the location where independence was declared. There was a joyous energy that emanated from everyone we met, from the staff at the hotel to street vendors, and everyone was smiling and greeting us warmly. The booming salsa music was coming from every direction, and it was igniting a sense of playfulness in me that I hadn't felt in years. I wanted to move to the beats although I didn't know the right steps. Locals were dressed in flamboyant costumes – some women were wearing traditional ruffled tops and skirts with colorful stripes; others were in fantasy outfits with feathered wings and head gear. The men were also adorned in bright colors and many of them had faces painted in tribal designs.

I was mesmerized by the way the women danced! They had so much feminine allure and sensuality, and the way they moved their hips was hypnotic. I wished I could dance with such uninhibitedness and abandon, but I was on guard, unable to let myself loose.

Nayanna was totally in her element. She was twirling and shimmying her way into the crowd, interacting with strangers and being totally comfortable with men who invited her to dance with them. I, on the other hand, was stiff and insecure of myself. I wasn't worried about my safety, because everyone exuded warmth and hospitality, but I was locked in my body, feeling self-conscious about my inability to move like the local women. There were cheers, laughter and singing all around me, and I felt the urge to sing on top of my lungs, but nothing was coming out. I felt "blocked."

Suddenly, I was swept up into a swarm of dancing young women who had been watching me standing by myself, not participating in the festivities. One of them, a tall dark-skinned goddess dressed in a hot pink sequined bikini with tassels hanging from her hips and bra cups, grabbed me under the arm and led me to the center of the crowd with others following behind and cheering me on. I found myself in the epicenter of the fiesta, which was pulsating with brilliant energy. It was light and carefree, and I wanted to be part of it. But something inside me was still resisting, and I was starting to get frustrated with myself. I noticed Nayanna a few feet away from me and squeezed my way through the crowd towards her.

"I need to talk to you!" I shouted over the booming music.

Sensing the awkwardness which my aura must've been emitting, Nayanna took my hand and led me out of the crowd to the side of the wall which encircled the plaza.

"Is it getting too rowdy for you? Do you want to go back to the hotel?"

"No, that's the thing, I want to be here. I want to celebrate and dance and sing! But I feel like there's this invisible force holding me back. I can't seem to break through it."

"Find your inner goddess, she's inside of you and she obviously wants to come out and play. Connect to your divine feminine energy and let yourself be guided by it."

Nayanna placed my hands on her hips, covering them up with her own and asked me to close my eyes.

"Feel the beat of the music, find its rhythm and let it guide your movements. I know you know how to keep the rhythm. Just try it."

She swayed her hips, keeping my hands there until I fell into the rhythm myself, then took my hands into hers and let me move on my own.

"Listen to the melody and the different instruments... how they draw you in to this dimension of sound, instructing you how to move your body. Each note, each pitch wants to express itself through your dance movements. There's no limit and no rules on how and where you can move. Let it flow through you."

The music switched from salsa to something more Caribbean – Cumbia – the most famous and popular type of music in this part of the country. It was a unique fusion of African drumbeats, Indigenous tribes' musical instruments like flutes, maracas and percussion, and European influences of the accordion. I felt a stir of excitement coming from deep inside me. It was hard not to move to this kind of music, and I slowly began to relax into it.

The individual sounds of each instrument seemed to be communicating with me, sending a signal to my brain which in turn began interpreting it into movement. I allowed my body to follow along, using every part of it to express the messages the music was sending to me. Little by little, my guard was coming down and I could sense my inner goddess awakening. Nayanna picked up on my new unencumbered energy and joined in with her own inner goddess.

"That's it! She's here, let her play and feel her in every part of your body!" Nayanna was coaxing my inner goddess out as she led me back to the dance space. Then she pointed to an extravagant float decorated with papier-mâché flowers and animals that had just arrived from the parade.

"Get on it! I want you to experience this to the fullest!"

We made our way through the crowd and the people on the float helped me climb up. There were beautiful men and women, dancing, playing drums and other instruments. Someone handed me a handheld drum that could be hung around the neck. I had never played one in my life! A young man with curly black hair and a wide infectious smile urged me to give it a try. I cautiously hit the drum. He laughed and said something to me in Spanish. Then he demonstrated how to hit the drum using his palms and knuckles and invited me to copy him. I began to get into the groove, catching up with the beat of the music and even finding a complementary rhythm of my own creation.

"This is so liberating! I am actually creating the music!" I squeaked with delight as I jammed out on the drum.

I had never imagined being able to do this. Even though I played the piano, I've never been able to compose a tune on my own. The teachers in my music school in Russia discouraged it, making us focus on learning the technique and playing only the classical pieces that were approved by the school board. In fact, originality was something so foreign to us as children who were growing up in a very strict communist regime that it left little room for exploring our own creative desires. And here I was, in a place oozing with joie de vivre out of every single person who was here, and I was blending in quite naturally. A far cry from the studious little girl who was great at following rules, never daring to question authority for the fear of being called out as a rebel or an anti-party troublemaker to be shamed and put on display.

We danced and played into the late hours of the night. The moon hung in the sky like a bright golden medal. I was feeling alive and untamed.

I noticed Nayanna waving up to me from the ground below the float. Saying brief goodbyes and receiving kisses on the cheek from every person on board, I climbed down to reunite with her to continue dancing and exploring the plaza.

Another hour later, still buzzing with festive energy, we made our way back to the hotel. Nayanna noted the orangish color of the moon and explained that it was a "Harvest moon," which symbolized purity and goodness.

"Your inner goddess needs to be called on from time to time. She is the expression of your divine feminine energy. When you are in your divine feminine you are playful, humorous and fun. That's what gives life more joy, and it attracts the divine masculine energy, which is more serious and disciplined. That's how a nice balanced relationship works when each partner is embodying their leading divine energy."

"I can see why some of my relationships became unbalanced. Sometimes I forget to have fun and become quite rigid – too focused on work and achieving goals."

"That's right. To coax out your inner goddess, bring in the element of fun, humor and playfulness to your daily activities. There's a dancer, a painter, singer and artist in all of us. We can feel the rhythm of the earth in our heartbeat. Don't be afraid to embody the essence of your divine feminine. Have you tried ecstatic dance before?"

"I've heard of it, and seen it promoted in Bali and even back home, but I never went."

"You see how good it felt to move your body tonight to the music without inhibition and self-judgment? You can make this type of dance as part of your morning alchemy practice. Just put on any music you like and go wild – do it for a few minutes or as long as you can. The key is to not sensor yourself and let the music flow through you. When we get back to the hotel, I'll show you the *Warrior Two* active pose that activates your feminine energy and tunes you into the creative flow."

I loved going dancing with my friends, but it always felt so constrained and limiting when we went to clubs, even at salsa nights, with all the controlled steps and proper tactics to observe. Ecstatic dance, as Nayanna explained, was much more free-form and expressive, and people could pretty much forget the rules that society binds us with when we dance in public. I asked her to take me to one of these dances on one of the stops towards our final destination and she promised to do that.

~

Warrior Two Morning Alchemy Practice as taught to me by Nayanna

As with Warrior One, this is not the pose of the same name in yoga, but an active exercise intended to express your creative energy through fluid motions while moving around the space, instead of out and forward. This activates your divine feminine energy.

Start by standing in the mountain pose (neutral energy), feet firmly grounded, tailbone slightly tucked in to a straight spine, arms down your sides with palms facing forward. Engage your legs and glutes and breathe deeply towards your belly for a few rounds.

Soften into your spine and keep your knees and elbows soft. Begin moving your arms one at a time while swaying your hips side to side. Make any movements that feel natural, following your intuition. Imagine yourself fluid, like water. Use all parts of your body and all the space that's available to you. Touch your body and feel the sensuality of each movement.

Duration and intensity depend on you. It can be performed with music if you wish.

~

We said goodnight and I went to my room. The connection to my inner goddess was still strong and I didn't want to go to sleep. I put on some sensual music and danced around the room, moving freely and intuitively. It was as if I was channeling Saraswati herself – goddess of knowledge, wisdom, music, the arts and learning, whom I had heard about from Krishnaraj when he talked about Hindu deities in his lectures.

Finally, when I indulged her enough, I laid down on the bed and began my quantum realm visualization to see if my heavy rock from the last session was still there. I scanned the body and felt the heavy sensation again in the lower belly.

A scene from my first day of school came up as a vivid memory. I was in art class and our teacher had asked us to draw a picture using colored pencils. I watched myself diligently drawing a house with a chimney and a person next to it – possibly myself. The girl next to the house looked larger than the house. The teacher came over and proceeded to verbally tear down my effort for the improper use of proportions in my drawing. The girl couldn't be bigger than the house, I was told. Because of this "mistake" I received a poor grade, equivalent to a C. I felt so guilty for having to disappoint my mother, who placed a very high importance on grades and expected me to be a straight A student. When my mother came to pick me up after school, I cried because I felt I had let her down, but instead of comfort and reassurance, she sided with the teacher. My drawing wasn't good enough for an A. I could tell my mother was upset with me. Since then, I became convinced that my work wouldn't measure up to the teacher's standards and stopped drawing from my imagination. A big part of my creative energy was stifled since that day.

That's who placed that rock in my energetic body!

It was so clear to me now, recalling how this teacher burdened the entire class with her harsh military-like discipline. I despised school because of her, and associated learning with some kind of torture. Since an early age, I began to believe that I was not creative and didn't have what it takes to make art.

The moment I realized who had been responsible for this toxic conditioning, a gush of lightness washed over my lower abdomen. Visualizing as best as I could, I handed the heavy gray rock to my first-grade teacher and asked her to take it with her because it didn't serve my highest good to keep it. I watched her walking away with it, leaving me in a state of purity and ease. I had emptied out the unnecessary junk that didn't belong there. Now with all this creative energy pouring in through my sacral space, I was in touch with my inner goddess who was connecting me to other goddesses of the svadisthana chakra.

The energy was concentrating at the mid-point of my physical self like a tight ball of cosmic mass. Instinctively, my hands slid down towards the area of an enticing throbbing sensation inside the deepest part of me that was begging to be explored. I began gently circulating my fingertips around the epicenter of pleasure. Letting my breath guide me, I tuned into the current running up and down my main energy channel up towards my throat chakra. The possibilities for playing with this energy seemed endless. Using my body as a vehicle, which was a strong and beautiful home for my inner goddess, I explored various erotic possibilities. Imbued by this divine power, I began to move my hips in rhythmic motions, as if dancing with an invisible force. It swept me up into a sensual rumba, leading me like an expert ballroom dancer. I savored each moment, completely content to be physically alone, but connected to something so much greater; not trying to achieve anything or be somewhere, but simply being there in the full expression of my divine feminine. The colossal amount of power being channeled through me in that moment was astonishing! I could've continued this dance without getting tired for hours. I caressed every part of myself, bending into elaborate dance poses, and communicating with divine Love through my inner goddess. I could sense her joyously laughing and playing, and I felt alive like never before.

The pressure continued to intensify, threatening to implode. I sped up the tempo until it drove me over the edge, passing the threshold of maximum pleasure. It released into a cascade of tremors that reverberated out from the epicenter to every inch of my body and shot me out into the great abyss of the unknown.

I indulged in the aftershocks that kept going for some time. There wasn't any feeling of guilt I'd normally feel in the past, believing that it was improper or "dirty" to explore myself this way. Instead, I felt honored to serve my inner goddess.

Shortly after, I sank into a deep state of presence and relaxation, suspended in a space between sleep and wakefulness. Vivid visuals flooded in, colored in brilliant orange tones – a generous rainfall, gushing rivers and deep bodies of water that reflected a perfectly round moon I had seen earlier tonight.

An acutely perceptible female energy materialized from the water and enveloped me in her soft nurturing presence. Naga, my beautiful dream spirit guide, appeared holding a sparkling orange crystal, offering it to me as a gift. I thanked her and took the stone, appreciating its value and what it represented – a healing of my sacral chakra.

Naga dissipated into the space from which she had appeared, and before falling asleep, I heard Ale's voice, reminding me about the next stage of the alchemy process, which he told me about before – *dissolution*.

"This is where we take the ashes from calcination and dissolve it in water. Think of it as taking a plunge into your subconscious where you may have hidden parts of yourself in order for your ego to create an image of who it wants to be identified with. But those parts of you are necessary, and you must honor them instead of reject them. All your faults, imperfections and past experiences that you may have buried are part of who you are. In this stage, give yourself permission to let go of old structures and perceptions of yourself that have held you for so long, and take the opportunity to know who you truly are."

Chapter 13

Shame

I had been thinking about the Russian nesting dolls – the matryoshka, which is a tiny piece of wood living in progressively bigger versions of itself, in the early hours of the morning.

Are we like those dolls? Each of us are made up of expanding layers that neatly fit inside the next bigger one.

Each day we are repeating the same old patterns, while unconsciously living out the same fate. We multiply the pain, blocked emotions, traumas and limitations and without becoming aware of it, store it deep inside. At night we go to sleep and that seals it in.

In the morning we wake up and live that fate again, with the same record player on a loop, playing the same old tune for us that we mechanically accept as a given. We are not awake – we are simply on autopilot.

Can we snap out of it to see that what we are doing is pure insanity? Our eyes are closed to see these patterns of thoughts, feelings and behaviors. We are hostages to this loop. We keep nesting ourselves in continuously bigger versions of our pain, day in and day out, and we don't want to break out of this seemingly comforting and familiar sequence, which we have known and grown accustomed to since birth. And the further away we get from the centerpiece (seed), the more we suffer.

Until... we become aware. That's when we open our eyes and realize that it's time to go back to the center. That's when the work of peeling those compounded layers back and away, one by one, shedding our old blockages and patterns can start. It can be a hard and painful process without an end for the whole lifetime. But there's no way around it, except right through it.

By now, with all the work Nayanna had me doing each day, I had become very aware of this process and the emotions that needed to be released so that I could stop the compounding of my pain and the hardening of my ego. But still, there was much work to be done. I had succeeded in letting go of feelings of guilt I had harbored for years about disappointing my mother, and most recently the guilt of not doing enough to make my marriage work. But what about shame?

Nayanna had mentioned earlier that guilt and shame, while often confused for the same thing, are actually quite different emotions. While guilt is typically focused on one's behavior, shame is focused on a sense of oneself. If I had done something I perceived as "wrong," I could feel bad about my action, yet still have respect for myself. But shame is a deeper, more universal and primal human emotion that can arise without any action on our part, and if not addressed in time, can lead to loss of self-respect.

I began to wonder how shame developed; if it wasn't caused by our actions. Scanning my memory folders, I searched for the feelings of shame which could give me the answer. A few instances from my past came back in the search results.

It was years ago when I was in my twenties. My second boyfriend, a seemingly well-educated young man who studied in the same college as me, had this impression that women's menstruation contained impurities and toxic bacteria, which the body was cleansing itself of on a monthly basis. He had "mansplained" it to me while I was on the last few days of my period, complaining that he "could get an infection from the bacteria in the blood" and that we should delay having sex until I was "back to normal."

Being that I hadn't fully understood what menstrual blood was composed of, I was left with a sense of being unclean and somehow defective. A few years later when I learned more about women's anatomy, I was surprised to find out that period blood is a combination of vaginal fluid and uterine lining that sheds when the egg doesn't get fertilized; and is actually a very nutrient-rich fluid that can even be used to fertilize house plants. Then it occurred to me that if we both didn't know this, then undoubtedly the majority of the world, especially in developing countries, would believe in the myths and spread that misinformation too.

One of my friends, who immigrated with her family from a small village in Nepal, told me that in her culture when a young woman gets her first period, she is not to be touched by any men in her family and has to spend a week staying in a different house. My friend recalled the dreadful feeling of being treated like an animal, being kept in a small corner of a room, not being allowed to share food or even plates with the rest of the family.

Women being shamed for the most natural and life-giving process spanned history, and I was certain that every woman at some point in her life has had some shame relating to her anatomy or sexuality.

There was another time I felt shame and it happened at the beginning of my relationship with Dave. He had invited me to try a popular new restaurant that was famed for its experimental cuisine called Canvas. Each dish was more bizarre than the last. One in particular that stood out was fennel foam soup with edible flowers and ant eggs. Being an adventurous type, I tried all dishes, except that one and I refused to eat it. Dave thought that the dish was a stroke of creative genius and sneered at my inability to appreciate it. For our next date we agreed that I would pick the restaurant. He insisted I invite my parents since he wanted to meet them. I chose a Chinese buffet-style diner called Mandarin, because it brought back warm feelings of our family dinners when we had just arrived in the US as new immigrants. It was a simpler life for us back then – we didn't have much money or affinity for fine dining, but this was where I formed my most cherished teenage memories. We'd enjoy a big selection of food we've never had before, laugh at family jokes, and bond over this precious time in our lives – just the three of us in the great land of possibilities. I hadn't been to this restaurant in many years, but there was a sense of nostalgia and wanting to reconnect with my parents that made me want to eat there again. And I wanted Dave to be part of these memories. But instead of being flattered that I wanted to include him in our old family tradition, he was repulsed at our lack of sophistication and said he will never agree to eating there again. From then on, his not-so-affectionate nickname for me became "Mandarin" whenever he wanted to push my buttons, and he wouldn't let me forget how he was "forced to eat at a place like that." I felt ashamed and never went back there.

I should've noticed this as a sign that he didn't love me for who I was. Status and class are so important to him. He always considered himself a connoisseur of the finer things in life, and I wasn't ever going to be good enough for him.

Good enough! What does that even mean?

When I say I'm not good enough, what am I really saying? That I'm not good enough in the eyes of others? Or in my own?

I sensed that shame came from a lack of loving myself in a non-judgmental unconditional way – the way I desired to be loved. It may have begun as conditioning from my environment when I was told I was a low-class immigrant by kids in my school, and it stuck with me. The same way as a child who believes his parent or teacher hearing he is "stupid" or "slow" and makes it his reality even as an adult.

But on a deeper level, I was beginning to see that shame originates from the illusion that "I" am separate from life – from everyone and everything. Reinforced by the ego, the belief that I, as an individual, am totally cut off from everything on the outside of myself, comes with a sense of emptiness, incompleteness, and fragmentation. Searching and grasping for things and people that would bring about fulfillment and wholeness proves to be futile. The "not good enough" syndrome sets in.

I've often caught myself thinking that if I don't measure up to some concept of success that I've decided upon in my mind, whether it'd be the number on a weight scale, in a bank account, or on social media – I am not enough.

But now I was becoming more and more aware of my need to people please, particularly my mother. Ever since I could remember, everything I did, every accomplishment I had made, and each prize I won, came with the thought: "I hope this makes her proud of me!"

Although my mom was strict and domineering over my education and intellectual development in childhood, I knew she had good intentions. She lacked that kind of attention from her own mother growing up and believed that being a well-rounded woman with refined worldly skills was the key to self-confidence and self-worth – and to marrying well. Based on this belief, she had me on a full-time schedule of extra-curricular activities that took up all my free time – English lessons, gymnastics, piano and chess. In addition, I was expected to do well in school, and had I brought home a low grade, I received a severe punishment. My mother's wrath fell upon me in varied ways, from being forced to eat some food that I despised to an occasional slap.

I felt her desperation to see me perform well academically and athletically because of how much she wanted me to have as many opportunities as possible to leave Russia. She believed that she was giving me the means to travel outside of this country where I didn't have much of a future, and which oppressed its people for so many generations, including her own family. Of course, under these circumstances, she was probably right, and I complied, doing everything she asked of me, even though these were not the things that I wanted to do myself.

Still, I recall the feeling of shame and self-pity while getting "the belt" or a whack across the face when I crossed her patience boundary. My cheeks would flush red and I could feel the hollow feeling of "not enough-ness" spread through the body.

So here I was, getting to the bottom of my capricious sense of self. The lines between what I wanted or believed and what my mother wanted or believed were blurry. Yes, she gave me a sense of pride for being a cultured woman who could dazzle people at a dinner party, but everything comes with a price. And that price was that I didn't know who I was at my core and what I stood for.

My will power and autonomy had been stripped off, and my dependence on my family for security and approval had me safely tethered to what was considered "appropriate and safe." I was living by their standards of success, deriving a false sense of accomplishment when I reached those standards, yet never attaining a sense of wholeness – of "enough-ness."

I must break free from this way of living. I am a grown woman, capable of making my own smart choices and being comfortable with my own decisions.

~

Nayanna and I decided to sleep in after the festivities of the previous night, and to meet up for a late breakfast. I was excited to share with her all of my insights that I had had in the course of less than a day, expecting to get validation for all the inner work I was doing.

Is that just me trying to get approval again?

Nayanna listened intently to everything I was saying and when I finished, remained quiet.

"Congratulations on such deep self-awareness," she finally said dryly. "Do you expect a gold medal for that?"

"I thought that you'd be proud of how much your teachings have had an impact on me!" I was taken aback by her indifference. "Isn't this what mentors are supposed to feel when their students make progress?"

"You don't need to concern yourself with what I am supposed to be feeling. And whether or not I'm proud of you, does not reflect on your level of progress. You need to decide what constitutes progress for you."

"Alright, but do you agree that I should break free of my mother's control and go find my own sense of self?"

"Sure, if that's what you think you need to do. But the bigger question is... are you actually going to do it? It's one thing to become aware, but it's not until you make an *intention* that anything is going to happen."

"What do you mean by intention?"

"It is sort of like a contract between you and 'your higher self,'" Nayanna made a gesture with her finger pointing up, "that you are ready to make a commitment. Whether that commitment is to change a thought pattern, a behavior or habit, or to make a transformation of some kind.

"I mentioned earlier that you are now on a massive journey of self-transformation, and the first step of that journey is *awareness*, do you remember?"

"Yes, and I think I've done well on that part. I am constantly observing my thoughts and feelings."

"Great! I see that and I am going to give you the validation you crave for doing a fine job in that. Now, we've arrived at the second step of that process – *Intention*. Without intention, awareness doesn't mean much. You are going to have to desire the change and set your sights on it. We always have a choice, don't we? What we choose to do with the cards we've been dealt. I am sure you already know that."

"Of course! I've always given myself the option to reframe it or leave it."

"Yes, but you haven't done that with awareness of who you were doing it for. Now, who is going to be calling the shots on your life decisions?"

"I will!" I answered with conviction.

"That's my girl!" It was nice to hear Nayanna's praise, but I no longer let it affect how I felt about myself. Having a strong sense of self and conviction of my beliefs was enough.

"I can see how this dependence on my mom trickled over into my relationship with Dave. I became dependent on him for so many things. I wanted him to love me and be proud of me. But I wasn't too concerned if I was proud of myself. Plus, I think the lack of my own willpower to do things that my mom wanted left me with the inability to see things through to the end. That's why I started and stopped so many hobbies and projects that I loved.

"I remember learning in Bali that willpower, discipline and sense of self are related to the solar plexus chakra. And that the physiological systems associated with it are digestive and metabolic. Now it kind of makes sense why my digestion was always a bit wonky. Sometimes I couldn't digest food and had a sluggish metabolism, other times I'd have too much acid in the stomach which gave me gastritis. There's definitely some solar plexus imbalance going on."

"Look at you! Analyzing your chakra imbalances like a pro! Now, let's talk about how you can bring that balance with activating and cooling your *manipura* chakra when you notice it swinging too far to either side.

"Have you heard of Kapalabhati pranayama?"

"Yes! Isn't that the 'breath of fire'? Krishnaraj showed it to us, and I tried it a few times."

"Actually, the correct translation of Kapalabhati is 'shining skull' or 'shining forehead' because it clears the mind by increasing blood flow to the prefrontal part of the brain." Nayanna pointed at her forehead. "But it also is a great way to ignite fire in your solar plexus and activate a sluggish third chakra. Why didn't you continue this in your daily practice after Bali?"

"Not sure. I know the benefits of it, but I just couldn't find the self-discipline. Oh, wow... how paradoxical! The thing I need the most is actually the hardest for me to do!"

Nayanna laughed at my epiphany and then confirmed it, "Yes, exactly! You need to find that discipline to increase your discipline. But you'll see how much easier it's going to get when you make it part of your morning alchemy practice. Let's try it together. Just do as much as you can."

We walked over to a small outdoor space behind the hotel and sat on the grass in cross-legged position. With Nayanna leading the way, we did three rounds of Kapalabhati breathing with short meditation breaks in between each round. Besides the immediate effects of energizing the body, I also noticed how decluttered my mind became. It felt like a light had been switched on in my head and I could see everything without confusion and overwhelm. I understood why it was named the "shinning skull" now.

"In general, solar plexus chakra is controlled by working with temperatures. Steam or sauna, and sun exposure can help you activate it. Taking a cold shower or plunge can help you bring balance if it's overactive. There's also breathwork, called 'Sheetali pranayama' or 'cooling breath,' to calm down an overactive solar plexus, as when you feel the painful effects of acidity due to stress and being over-worked."

After the breath work we went to have lunch, since we had missed breakfast at the hotel, which was a good thing because most pranayama techniques were recommended to be performed on an empty stomach. There was a quaint traditional restaurant a few blocks over in the old part of the city that served arepas – grilled corn flour dough pancakes with various fillings – a local dish which was a signature of Colombian food culture.

"What is the one thing you've always wanted to do but never allowed yourself to even consider doing for fear of your mother's judgment?" Nayanna asked unexpectedly while we were eating.

I thought about it for a brief moment and then cautiously answered, "I've always wanted to get a tattoo. When I was a model, our agents advised us against it to make sure we'd get more bookings, so I didn't. But for the past few years, I've been really thinking about it since I'm not modeling much anymore."

"And why didn't you do it?"

"Oh well... my mom wouldn't let me. I know how silly this sounds – I am an adult! But I know how she feels about them. She thinks that the only people who get them are criminals or otherwise society's outcasts. She wouldn't hear of it to have her daughter walking around with a tattoo!"

"And how do you feel about people with tattoos?"

"I don't mind tattoos in general – some are really beautifully done. It's everyone's personal choice to decide what to do with their bodies. Of course, some designs are not very appealing to me, and the location on the body is important."

"So, if you were to get one, have you thought about where and what you'd choose?"

"I think it would have to be a place that's not too obvious, because I'm worried I will get sick of looking at it myself. But it also needs to be somewhere that I can see it if I do want to look at it – not the back of the neck or lower back. That's really just for other people to appreciate. And... it has to be meaningful!"

"Finish your food and let's go then!" Nayanna had a vibrant sparkle in her eyes. "We are both going to get tattoos now!"

I almost choked on my yuca fries, "What? Now? Um... okay, yeah, I suppose we can?" I was giggling nervously trying to convince myself mentally to seize the moment.

This is it! Time to step into my power and solidify my autonomous self at last!

If I don't, I'll be continuing to let society and other people define me. I need to set my boundaries and intentions on how I will live my life.

Nayanna had the location of a tattoo parlor pinned on her phone and the taxi was speeding along the narrow streets towards it.

Oh, God, my mother is going to freak out when she sees me with a tattoo! Am I really going to go against her? Wow, this is so unlike me!

Wonder if it's going to look trashy?

Nayanna, who was always so perceptive of my auric field, interrupted my internal anguish, "Notice your preconceived notions of a person with a tattoo and ask yourself where these came from. Sure, in your parents' time, the only people they knew who had them were mafia and ex-cons. Of course they have a negative association with it. What is your own association with tattoos?"

I didn't have many, except maybe with people who considered themselves artists and creatives, and usually those who didn't have corporate jobs. Alejandro had a few tattoos, which I found aesthetically pleasing and didn't think they made him look like he belonged to a gang, despite what the background noise of my upbringing was mumbling.

I'm going to look like such a hippie!

Wait, who cares about these labels? I'm not doing this to fit any identity – this is going to be just for me.

"Remember, you decide on your own values and choose which ones serve you best. Make your decision and be comfortable with it. Hesitating and being half-way sure is not *intentional*. Only you know when something feels right or not."

I was certain that this decision was all mine and the feeling associated to it nestled comfortably in my gut.

Let this tattoo be a symbol of my intention to always act on my own values, desires and dreams!

We arrived at the shop and the tattoo artist gave me a few photo books to leaf through to see which design I wanted. Nothing stood out to me as unique or meaningful. I wanted something that would be a reminder to myself about something important.

Should I get a mandala? Those are pretty... and symbolic of the universe. But they only look good at the back of the neck, and I wouldn't be able to see it there.

Maybe a bird on my collarbone – the symbol of freedom? Nah, wouldn't want to be a copycat of my friends.

An infinity knot on the ankle? But what does that really represent to me?

Then I thought about what I had most recently been working through in my solar plexus chakra – the sense of self and wholeness which of course was expressed in the love I felt for myself.

Love for self... Self-love.

Immediately, I knew what my tattoo would be. I described what I wanted to the artist and she found a few examples of the script to choose from. She printed out a stencil sticker to mark on my skin and began her work.

It didn't take long to finish and didn't hurt much because it was a small tattoo with one word in a dainty line. I got up from the table and hurried over to the mirror. Turning to the side and lifting up my arm, I looked at the word "Love" on my left ribcage at the level of the solar plexus reflected in the mirror from the backwards image I had the artist ink into my skin. You could only decipher the word by looking at it in reverse. It would be just for me, to look at in the mirror after a shower or before getting dressed. It would serve as a reminder to always love myself and others.

Nayanna ended up getting a symbol of the Inca moon goddess – Mama Quilla, on her left shoulder, which was normally depicted as a silver disk with a human face wearing the moon as a crown. She said she chose her because this goddess, being the regulator of the moon's cycles, was regarded as a symbol of female empowerment and as the protector of married women, and that's who Nayanna was in service to in her healing work. It was a beautiful tattoo that suited her perfectly.

"Excuse me," a woman next to us addressed Nayanna, interrupting our discussion, "I couldn't help but overhear... you work with married women?"

The gorgeous middle-aged woman getting a tattoo next to Nayanna had medium-length wavy dark hair, large hazel doe eyes framed by long feathery eyelashes and neatly combed thick eyebrows, and full lips. She was impeccably styled in chic clothes, shoes and matching delicate jewelry, and it was evident that she came from the upper echelons of society.

Nayanna and the woman, who introduced herself as Angelina, were drawn into a conversation about the different healing modalities that were available for couples whose relationship needed an overhaul. It turned out that she and her husband were traveling on their private yacht around the Caribbean islands. Their two children, who'd grown up and moved away from their permanent home in northern Italy, were studying at Cambridge. The couple took the opportunity to revive their marriage and reignite the fire that had been slowly waning over the past twenty-plus years. Angelina had been looking for alternative couple's therapy, having exhausted all traditional psychotherapy routes. She and her husband, Fabiano, wanted to give their marriage one final chance.

I was listening quietly as she confided in Nayanna about her desperation of saving what was left of the relationship. Angelina mentioned that the night before, at the very same carnival party that we had attended, she met a woman dressed in a silver costume that looked like the moon goddess, Mama Quilla, which she noticed Nayanna getting a tattoo of. And since she was a big believer in signs, she took this coincidence to mean that Nayanna was someone she needed to seek help from.

As the artist worked to finish Nayanna's tattoo, Angelina inquired where we were heading next. We told her our plans for crossing over to Central America, and her eyes immediately lit up. She offered us a ride to Puerto Limon, Costa Rica, on their boat, which would be a perfect opportunity for Nayanna to work her magic on healing the relationship, if she would agree. Angelina proposed a generous compensation, but Nayanna declined, saying that it was enough to be receiving transportation as payment for her services.

Angelina gave us the name of her yacht, The Echidna, and told us where to meet her the next morning for a prompt departure at eight o'clock. As we were about to leave, I asked about the meaning of her tattoo that she was getting on the back of her shoulder. I could see the outline of a female's top half on the design but the bottom part hadn't been done yet.

"For me, this immortal and ageless creature from Greek mythology, which happens to be who we named our boat after, is a symbol of fierceness and beauty.

"She is half woman and half serpent."

Chapter 14

Inner Child

I once went to a numerologist named Sylvia, whom Alejandro recommended to me, and had my Life Path number read. In the study of Numerology, your Life Path number is a significant indicator of who you are at your core and the lessons you are here to work through in this lifetime in order to become who you are meant to be as your highest, most authentic incarnation. It can be calculated by adding each digit of your full birthdate until you get a total sum between 1 and 9, or the Master Numbers 11, 22 or 33.

For example, if your birthday is 07-23-1995, you would calculate it as follows:

Month: 0 + 7 = 7
Date: 2 + 3 = 5
Year: 1+9+9+5 = 24
24 is reduced to 2 + 4 = 6
Add it all up: 7 + 5 + 6 = 18
18 is reduced to 1 + 8 = 9

That makes your Life Path number to be 9.

When looking up what your number means, you'll discover that it's revealing your own unique set of positive and negative traits, values that are most important to you, and how you tend to deal with, or react to, life's challenges. This number is not meant to be your fate, but instead as a guidance system on how you can step into your natural gifts and talents and make the most out of opportunities that come your way. Life, as it often does, presents us with many chances for taking our given path, but it's up to us which side of the road we choose to walk on in each situation, and what lessons to learn from each experience.

My Life Path number, as it turned out, was 5. Sylvia explained to me that people on this life path are here to work through issues of freedom through discipline, and because of the particular combination of my numbers, 23/5 (2 + 3 = 5), I was also here to find a balance between dependence and independence.

The freedom part rang so true for me since the moment she said it. I craved freedom since a young age, and when straddled into a routine, I quickly became bored with whatever it was that I was doing. Adventure always called after my soul. It was becoming more obvious to me now on this trip that the humdrum routine of having an office job was not sustainable for me in the long run. I needed to be given the freedom to express my talents and make my own decisions about what to do on a daily basis. But as I could also see, discipline was going to be my biggest challenge to achieve the freedom I craved. I set my intention on doing my breathwork and alchemy practices every day from then on.

After having done so much introspection, it was becoming clearer that I've been swinging to both sides of the extremes between dependence and independence. There was certainly a lack of balance in this part of my life. In childhood, I'd wish that my parents were less controlling and had given me more freedom, yet I was afraid to stray too far on my own and clung to them for support. I didn't like to be alone at home, or to play by myself, craving the presence of a friend or my parents. In adolescence, I would never go to the movie theater alone, or eat by myself at a restaurant, always seeking company.

Same thing happened when I got older and began to date. If I was single, I'd yearn for connection with another person and for a feeling of belonging with someone. But if I was in a committed relationship, I felt trapped by the boundaries of monogamy. It was a recurring theme with me – never being totally satisfied with either option for long. I wanted to share my life and all its amazing experiences with another person, but I couldn't seem to get beyond the initial stage of a relationship to maintain the same excitement I had started with.

When we arrived at the marina, Angelina, dressed in a white flowing full-length beach kimono, greeted us aboard The Echidna – an impressive Italian luxury double-decker 50 ft Azimut yacht. Soon after, we were sailing towards Puerto Limon, Costa Rica. It felt so good to be around water after a long time on the road through the mountains and jungles, and my heart was singing with joy and freedom at the sight of the open sea. It would take us two days of cruising at 30 knots to cross 447 nautical miles with one overnight stop.

Getting to know Fabiano and Angelina was a treat. The couple exuded warmth and generosity. They both had an unquenchable thirst for adventure and exploring everything life has to offer. Fabiano, a tall and lean Italian man with a full head of mostly silver hair, was slightly older than his wife. He was always playing music through the speakers and loved to dance, glass of wine in hand, even when no one wanted to join him. They made a good match – both fit and looking great for their age, successful, well-educated and financially free. It was hard to not want to be like them one day, when I'd reach that age. They seemed to be "living the dream," as most people would describe it, but their marital problems were sweltering just under the surface of their picture-perfect life.

Nayanna spent a few hours a day working with Fabiano and Angelina individually, and while one of them was in the session with her, the other would take the opportunity to vent their frustrations out with me, even though I didn't show any interest in getting involved. I listened out of courtesy, of course, and although I couldn't offer much help, I found it to be very educational for myself.

From what I was hearing from Fabiano, Angelina was too involved with her art-lovers community and preferred to spend more time going to theater and exhibitions than being with him. Angelina, on the other hand claimed that she was being smothered by Fabiano's neediness and wanted him to find a hobby that he could do without her.

Fabiano was the caretaker in their couple's dynamic, always taking responsibility for Angelina's behavior and emotions, especially when she drank too much. Both of them loved to drink, but Fabiano seemed to be more functional and less dependent on alcohol. He had tried to influence Angelina, convincing her to change her ways and be the kind of woman he wanted her to be – a compliant, soft-spoken, homebody who put him and the kids as her priority. This is the kind of woman his mother was, and he needed to receive love from a woman in this way. But Angelina was quite the opposite, and although at the beginning that's what attracted him to his wife, he ended up chasing her affection and forgetting himself in the process for the majority of their twenty-seven years of marriage. There was infidelity from both sides, each one saying that they simply couldn't get what they needed from the other.

Although I couldn't offer much advice, I calculated both of their life path numbers using their birthdays and read out their individual descriptions from a numerology website in hopes of providing some clarity of their unique traits. Angelina's lifepath number was 1, which made her rebelliously independent, authoritative and ambitious. This made it difficult for her to be cooperative in romantic or business relationships. She even alleged herself that being unattached provided her with more freedom to move on her goals. Fabiano's lifepath number was 2, which was the exact opposite of his wife in terms of cooperation and romance, and his main priority in life was building and sustaining a romantic relationship. As with other people on the same life path, Fabiano's desire to make strong bonds and take care of others' needs first made him a bit passive and people pleasing. The more I understood their individual life path numbers and heard their stories, it became clear that they were stuck in a push-pull pattern with each other that was hard to break out of.

When we docked at the marina in Puerto Limon, the work Nayanna was doing had only scratched the surface of the underlying issues of their codependent relationship. So, she suggested they join us to travel to our next destination – Masaya, Nicaragua, famed for the active volcano and its neighboring crystalline crater lake which were considered the highlights of the region.

As we made our way north towards Nicaragua by a hired minivan with driver, the natural beauty of Costa Rica had me infatuated with this Central American country. The nature looked almost pre-historic, with some plant leaves the size of umbrellas, and many varieties of which I had never seen before anywhere else on the planet. Fabiano was knowledgeably sharing various facts about Costa Rica with us, and we learned that the country, considered to be very ecologically clean, ranked as one of the highest in the world for its "green" efforts and sustainability. Producing nearly 98% of its electricity from renewable resources, it was also mostly free of deforestation with a quarter of the country's land having been turned into protected parks and reserves. It was easy to see why the people would always greet each other with the national slogan – *Pura vida!*

I had plenty of time to ponder my own issues of codependency as the car zoomed us along on the Corridor Noratlantico – the national primary road, which provided us with astonishing views of rainforests, national parks and rivers. Being so focused on making the relationship with Dave work at all cost, I had lost a part of myself to it. The things that were so important to me before I got married became part of my past self – playing badminton with my friends every weekend, for example. But I gave that up because he didn't like badminton and wanted to spend his weekends sailing or playing guitar with the band he had formed with his friends. And as a good wife, I chose to be with him, slowly forgetting what made me happy.

I also stopped going to the spiritual community gatherings, which Alejandro was always inviting me to join, where they'd have group meditations, day-breaker parties and various types of workshops from visiting and local healers. I knew that Dave was a bit jealous of my bond with Ale, though he had never admitted it. Ale was the polar inverse, the anti-Dave. And he didn't like that "hippie" trait that he thought Ale accentuated in me.

I always felt that there was a mutual distrust between Dave and me, which began developing shortly after we got married. After the thrill of the chase wore off with me, he reverted to his playboy habits, and no matter how much he tried to hide it, I saw the look in his eyes every time he admired beautiful women when we went to fashion shows and parties together. I didn't think I was giving him any reason to doubt me, but he did anyway, possibly projecting his own weakness onto me. That's why for the majority of our marriage he didn't want me traveling or going anywhere alone so he could keep me in his radar. And I in turn would go with him to give myself a sense of security, knowing where he was most of the time. But eventually, we realized that neither of us were enjoying each other's company, and we started to drift apart, spending less and less time together, just us two. In those last few months, when we could barely find anything to talk about or even be in the same room, was my moment of weakness when I had that affair. I had given up on our relationship before it was officially over, and I haven't forgiven myself for it since then.

Emotionally, I had forgotten to take care of myself as well. Dave didn't like to talk about feelings, and every time I'd bring up the issue of our apparent disconnect, he'd brush it off, saying that everything was fine in his opinion. I craved a deeper connection in our relationship – the kind of intimacy that filled up the emptiness inside – to be "seen" for simply being myself. It reminded me of the kind of longing I'd had in my childhood, wanting to be seen by my mother for the child I was. Not just being praised for getting a perfect grade or winning a gymnastics medal, but appreciated for who I was in my essence, stripped from all the titles. She was hyper-focused on getting things done for me as a mother, always making sure I was taken care of in a tiger-mom kind of way. But she couldn't simply enjoy me as a child, impatiently waiting for each milestone of my development. She'd say things like, "Oh how I wish you'd graduate already, so I can finally breathe easy!" It seemed like she was in a rush to see me grow up. As much as I appreciated her actions, I sensed her worries and fears. It clouded her vision of me and she couldn't allow herself to just "be" there with me, in total presence and complete acceptance. The "doing" and "being" are equally important, and I understood now that every child yearns for both from her parents – to be acknowledged for her soul, for her light and for the miracle that she is.

By the time we arrived at our rest stop in Nicaragua, it was late and all four of us were exhausted from the whole day of travel. Nayanna and I were sharing a guest room that Angelina and Fabiano rented for us in Granada on the shore of Lake Nicaragua. The owner of the old colonial building where we would stay for a few days told us a bit of history about this historic city that was established by Spanish conquistador Francisco Hernandez de Cordoba, who named it after the Spanish city of the same name. The rich cultural heritage and architectural façade had an Andalusian appearance influenced by that region in Spain. I had traveled through Andalusia with Dave a few years back and being here fueled my memories of him. I began to reminisce about our good days, when we first started dating, and the adventures we took together. This city was so charming, and I wished I wasn't there as a single woman. I decided to go for a walk to take in the sights of the Moorish-style buildings lit up by soft spotlights in the night.

I'll definitely come here on a romantic getaway one day! I made a silent promise to myself for when I would eventually find my next love.

I am not meant to be single; I just know it. I have so much passion to give another person! Is it wrong to want to share it with someone?

When I got back to the room, Nayanna had already showered and was reading in bed. I asked her if she had a life partner.

"Not at the moment, but to be completely honest, I am totally okay with being alone for the rest of my life."

"Really? You don't want to share your life and all of your love with someone?"

"I have a lot of people around me who I can share everything with. I've been with a few really great men… and one woman. In fact, we still keep in touch and we love each other deeply. But my work is my priority over any relationships. It wouldn't be fair to any of my partners because I've dedicated my life to serving others.

"The way I see it, a relationship is simply an added bonus – a cherry on top of a scrumptious cake that is your life. If it doesn't add that extra value to a life that you are already happily living, then there's no point being in one. Up till now no other person has been that cherry for me, and that is okay because I am totally content with being on my own. I don't need anyone to give me what I can most certainly give to myself."

"And what is it that you give to yourself?"

"Everything! I give myself total love. The term self-love gets thrown around much too casually these days, but few people actually know what it means. Remember the first cornerstone of divine love for self?"

"Self-awareness. How many cornerstones are there again?"

"There are three. I'm taking my time revealing them to you, because I want you to fully embrace each one before taking on the next. You've done a phenomenal job with your self-awareness from what I see: noticing the background noise in your mind; asking yourself the right questions to find the root cause; discovering the blockages that used to keep you trapped in repeating patterns. And you are observing your thoughts and emotions as they arise with presence and mindfulness. Now it's time to make space for new energies to replace the old ones you have no more use for with *self-care* – the second cornerstone."

"Ooh, I am the queen of self-care! You should see my bathtub ritual, and I'm at the gym minimum three times a week."

"Self-care is not just physical, and it's not about face masks and a toned body. Besides the physical, which you are already practicing with all the fitness, nutrition, and grooming, there are three other types of self-care. *Emotional*, which includes tuning into your creativity, passions, sexuality and self-expression. It's also about being able to fulfill your need to connect to others through shared experiences and be of service to humanity. *Mental*, where you set your boundaries and values that you choose to live by. Learning to say no and stop people-pleasing is part of that type of self-care. *Energetic* self-care reinforces your spiritual connection to the higher realms in order to realize your oneness to everything in the universe. It helps you balance your energies through meditation, prayer, gratitude and various healing techniques. And with all of these, you need consistency and commitment, and taking accountability for yourself – no one is going to do it for you."

"When you say sexuality as part of my emotional self-care, do you mean being responsible for my own orgasm?"

"It's not just about how often you give yourself sexual pleasure. It's about understanding what fuels your desire and what makes you turn on. Asking yourself 'when do I feel sexy most?' and 'what awakens my inner goddess?' That way the responsibility stays with you, and not with your partner to make you satisfied. Most people in long-term committed relationships blame the other person for not giving them what they want. It's not about the other person at all. It's always about *you!* Each person needs to know what turns them on and that takes some inner work."

"So that inner work applies to mental and energetic self-care as well? How do I include mental self-care in my daily practice?"

"The best way I've discovered so far is by journaling and stream of consciousness logging. The first one is more of a structured approach where you can answer some questions every morning in your writing session, for example:

What are my values and priorities and how can I live in line with them today?

What can I give of myself to others and what are my boundaries that I won't allow to be crossed?

What can I say yes to, and what can I say no to today?

"Stream of consciousness is a great way to get out what's in your mind on to paper and acknowledge those thoughts and emotions, thereby releasing them. You can write about your frustrations and grievances, wishes and hopes about things from the past, present or future. You can write your regrets, but also things you are grateful for. It really can be about anything you are feeling or thinking at the moment. Let it flow and don't stop to think about it too much. What you'll find is that solutions for your problems will appear right there as you are writing, or maybe a bit later, but most importantly you will gain a lot of clarity – internally and externally."

"And energetic self-care is my meditation and mindfulness practice?"

"Yes, and so much more! It's really something only you can decide how to work into your own connection to God – to the Divine, and meditation and breathwork are a big part of it. But it's your job to answer the questions that make you yearn to find out the truth: 'What is the meaning of life?' 'What is my purpose here in this lifetime?' 'Who am I as consciousness?' No one can answer these questions for you, and that is what spirituality truly is – making your own interpretation of what it means to be human."

Nayanna was silent for a few moments, and as I considered what she had said, I clearly saw how for the majority of my adult life I had placed a lot of the responsibility on other people in all aspects of myself. I gave away my power and my autonomy, and entrusted my well-being to family, friends, partners and even spiritual teachers.

"I'm going to show you a beautiful technique for getting back to yourself and reclaiming that sense of self. It's an inner child meditation."

Nayanna had me close my eyes and lie down for this meditation to facilitate relaxation and healing. As with the other few times, she guided me to connect with my breath and body. Then she asked me to scan my body up and down, side to side, and front to back, and to find my center – the point somewhere between the chest and the stomach.

"Now imagine that in this point, in your center, you see a child – the little girl version of you. Any age between about two and six.

"Notice how innocent and pure this child is. This child is precious and made of love. Observe all the details of this child – the color of her hair and eyes, her soft tender skin – see how beautiful she is. You recognize yourself in this child and you know she is you. Look deeply into her eyes and acknowledge the purity and infinity you see there. You see the whole universe in her eyes with nothing but love coming through. This child has no hate, no fear and no vengeance – she is pure love. Can you appreciate her for all she is on the inside and outside?"

I silently answered "yes," and let Nayanna continue.

"Now express your appreciation and gratitude for this child. Tell her how beautiful she is. Say the following words to her out loud or internally: *You are beautiful. You are pure. You are powerful. You are limitless. You are amazing.*

"Express everything you have in your heart for this child and tell her she is deeply loved. Say the following words to her: *You are loved. You are protected. You are cared for. You are safe.*

"Keep looking at the child and continue praising her: *You are perfect as you are. You are complete. You are whole. You are enough.* Reassure this beautiful child that you love her deeply and completely. Tell her that you will always be there for her and promise that you'll never neglect her needs. Give her your word that you will always acknowledge and take care of her."

I repeated all the words Nayanna was saying to the little self, whose innocent eyes I was imagining looking in, silently, in my mind. There was so much love I felt for her – for myself.

"Look at the child radiating joy and happiness – beaming with a gorgeous wide smile. She hears you, appreciates you, and loves you back. She knows you are connected. She feels safe, protected, loved and whole. Feel the joy in your heart for the knowledge that your inner child is happy. Give her a big hug and reassure her that you are always together and that the love between you will always flow."

I imagined caressing my little self with tenderness and compassion, which felt comforting and as if it was everything that I could ever want or need.

After a few minutes of silence, Nayanna concluded the meditation.

"When you are ready, come back to the center of your body and your breath. Recognize that every breath nourishes you and your inner child. Be grateful for that, and take a few deep conscious breaths, filling yourself up with loving energy on each inhale. Release any tension or fears with each exhale.

Observe your body again and become aware of each part of it and all its senses."

Nayanna turned off the lights and invited me to continue relaxing. Without realizing it, I had entered into a deep theta brainwave state and soon fell into a deep sleep.

My serpentine spirit guide, Naga, came to visit me in the early hours of the morning as I was just about to wake up. She showed me a vision of the beast from my Ayahuasca session and my inner child in a standoff. The creature was roaring fiercely, hurling threats and insults at the child, who stood bravely and calmly head on to the beast, transmuting each attack into pure love. Through the child, I understood that the beast is lashing out in vulnerability, pain and weakness, and saw through this violence, choosing to love the beast instead of fighting it.

There was a loving presence of a multitude of material and ethereal beings all around me, surrounding me with their support, comfort and love. They were my angels and spirit guides, perhaps my ancestors or my soul family. At that moment I knew that I am never alone and acknowledged the beings with gratitude. Then, I watched my child-self transforming into an adult – my present-day self – standing tall and fearless in the face of any challenge or nightmare, real or imagined. I finally grasped my true value and self-worth. And at last, I accepted myself on my own, without a partner or lover, fully stepping into my independence and sovereignty. I saw myself as a whole, no longer as an unfinished counterpart to a whole, but a complete self-contained piece.

Nayanna's words about a relationship being like the cherry atop a cake took on a deeper meaning, and I decided in that instant that I would only choose to be with a man if I wasn't relying on him to make me happy. As long as I had a deep connection to myself with true self-love and complete acceptance, the love of a man would serve as an extra blessing, but nothing more.

Naga, acknowledging the conviction of my intention, manifested a background of bright yellow fire all around, representing my own internal fire of will power, confidence and personal growth. A volcano erupted with all its glorious magnitude, and sizzling hot lava sensually glided down the sides, showing me just how beautiful and graceful the strength of a woman can be. Presenting me with my gift – a stunning yellow crystal for the solar plexus chakra, Naga blessed me with her benevolence and disappeared into the fire.

When I awoke, everything around me once again had a kind of freshness as though I was seeing it through the eyes of a newborn. The comfort and fullness inside were clearly palpable in a pleasant sensation in my center – where my sense of self resides. I was whole and contented.

After I got up and began practicing my morning alchemy rituals, Nayanna showed me some more movements for stimulating the manipura chakra and nurturing my inner child.

~

Inner Child Morning Alchemy Exercise as taught to me by Nayanna

Standing up, begin shaking and bouncing in place for a few minutes to activate the vibration and energy flow in the body. You can do little jumps or jog in place but try to shake and use every part of your body.

Next, start twisting at the waist and flinging your arms side to side. Any type of twisting poses or movements are an effective way of helping release stagnant energies and performing this simple move daily is a perfect energetic hygiene ritual. You can do 15–20 swings to each side.

Fold your hands into fists and use them to lightly tap around the hips and pelvis, gradually moving down both sides of the legs and back up a few rounds, then tapping around the belly, lower back and sides of the body.

Continue tapping at all the chakra points on the front of the body, then moving down the arms towards the wrists and back up, and finally tapping very lightly with only the knuckles around the neck, head and face.

Sit down or keep standing with your eyes closed and quietly observe the sensation after this exercise, which is going to make you feel incredibly energized; you will feel a massive shift in your auric field.

The last part is optional, but nice. Give yourself a generous foot massage, then wrap your arms around your sides and give yourself a big hug, while squeezing the opposite arms up and down.

You can use this ritual daily as an easy way to express self-love while reconnecting to your inner child.

~

As I was taking my morning shower, Ale's words, talking about alchemy were floating around my mind, as I remembered the next stage of the alchemy science – *separation*, where the alchemist separates and filters the result of the previous stage. When we talked on the phone the previous day, he shared with me that old habits, emotional patterns, painful memories and worn out narratives that my mind was constantly playing, could now be separated from my sense of self. But not all of it needed to be rejected, and it was at this stage when we had a chance to sift through all the materials to see what needed to be kept and what needed to be shed.

"You are now ready to filter through what has been dissolved and see which parts of you that you previously deemed useless are actually important to help you grow and evolve. These parts are what build your resilience and add depth to who you are.

Don't be so hasty to get rid of them and ask yourself how you can use them to bring value and inspiration for yourself and other people. At the same time, take the parts that no longer serve you and are ready to be let go, and make a decision to discard them once and for all."

Chapter 15

Loneliness

Fabiano and Angelina invited us on a guided tour of Granada which gave us a chance to hear more about the history of colonization in the city.

In the afternoon we drove to the nearby village, Masaya, just 10 miles away from Granada. Noting the coincidence of working through my manipura chakra, which is connected to the fire element, with our visit to the Masaya volcano, I was reassured once again that I was on the right path.

We visited a local artisan market to shop for traditional handicrafts and to try some Nicaraguan food, saving our visit to the volcano for last, as it was most impressive to see it in the nighttime. The weather allowed for a magnificent sight of magma spitting, gurgling and hissing as we peered over the railing into the volcano. I observed how incredibly alive I've been feeling the whole day, and seeing the fire element in action here was reflecting the internal revival of my prana, which was now playfully engaging my energy field.

What a difference between how I feel here and back home! I was always so drained there, even on weekends.

"It may be just the excitement of travel and adventure, but I think all the work I've been doing here with you is having a huge impact on my energy levels," I told Nayanna.

"Of course, novelty, curiosity and mystery are the main ingredients in desire. That's why you feel so alive when you fall in love – when you are touched by Eros, the romantic love as it's called in Greek philosophy. The amount of energy you have is so immense, you feel almost superhuman! You don't even want to sleep! It's the same ingredients for the love you have for life – the universal selfless love of Agape. You ignite the spark of that love when you visit new places, connect with different people and expand your consciousness through new experiences."

"Are you saying that when I go home and fall back into my regular life, I'll lose that spark? Isn't there some way to maintain it?"

"There's something I want you to realize about life force energy – prana. It is not generated by your body like in a power plant. It is conducted through you from the unlimited source that is available in abundance all around you. Look and see how much of that prana there is on earth alone. It's in everything – literally everything. It's in the volcano and the waterfall. It's in the oceans and mountains. It's in the trees, and earth, and air. The whole universe is run on this incredible power and we have direct access to it with the energetic tools, some of which you now have at your disposal. That's what ancient practices of Kundalini, Tai Chi, Qigong, Tantra and many others have been teaching us for centuries.

"The key is to utilize these methods on a consistent basis and take full responsibility for charging yourself up with prana, which is unique to you, as everyone has their own techniques that work for them. But no one is going to do it for you, and if you start to feel lethargic, it is up to you if you want to stay in that state or change it.

"I've been working with Angelina and Fabiano to help them fill their own cups and learn to be self-sustained the same way you have been doing. But the biggest challenge is still ahead. It's a matter of the heart," Nayanna touched her hand to her chest with a somewhat melancholy look.

"Well, I think it's safe to say I've passed my heart opening with Madre Ayahuasca. That was one hell of a cleansing!"

"It sure was, but it usually doesn't take just one ceremony to fully break your heart open. And life has a way of showing us if we need more work. You will know the lessons when they come because they will jolt you to the core. But it'll all be worth it, you'll see."

Before I could say anything else, Fabiano and Angelina came over and shared an idea about going to visit an orphanage to make a donation since it was on their bucket list for this trip. Nayanna said it was a great way to express generosity which is a language of the heart, and said she knew one in the town of La Esperanza, Honduras, which was going to be our next destination.

~

Where is God?

I was somewhere in the middle of a very realistic and vivid dream, but I knew I was dreaming. Although it all felt so real, I was in control of my actions within this alternate reality. I was in a dark forest – a dense, thick jungle – looking for God.

There was no path and I had to push myself through the rough bushes and long grass, fighting against an invisible force that made it so difficult to move my arms and legs. I was searching for a path, which I had been walking on when it suddenly disappeared, and I didn't know how to get back on it. I was lost in the darkness and the dangers of the nighttime jungle were creeping all around me. Sweat was trickling down the sides of my face and I could hear the sound of my own breathing, labored and shallow. There was an all-consuming gnawing feeling of emptiness spreading through my chest that felt like a black hole. It was loneliness – the collective global epidemic.

Where do you even begin to look for God in that great vastness of infinity out there? I'm so alone out there... and in here... a small, insignificant "me" against the infinite.

How can one compete with that unfathomable space?

That feeling of irrelevance and smallness, against the limitlessness of the universe is enough to put the most empowered person into an existential crisis.

No one is on the inside here with me except... me.

And the only companion I have is that mental voice, which is following me like a shadow on the ground, and which parrots everything I think back to me.

It's nearly maddening to keep listening to it, whenever I try to observe it.

Who is that voice? Is it the ego? Or Jung's shadow self? Or the Ahamkara from Vedic teachings, which Krishnaraj had talked about?

But who am I if I'm not the voice?

I cannot grasp this concept, and I can't seem to find this "real me" who is observing the voice. If the real "me" is something I can understand with my mind, then isn't it just another construct of the mind?

I was drowning in an endless vortex of my consciousness, fighting with the ego to try to find the "real self," while in the dream world I continued to search for the path as I tore my way through the jungle.

Suddenly, I heard a vicious animal growling and attacking its prey, which shrieked in fear and pain, and I woke up with a gasp.

It was so startling to be jolted out of sleep in such a punishing way and it took me a few moments to realize it was all a dream. I touched my forehead. It was moist with sweat.

Wow, the mind sure is powerful! It can make the body believe something is happening even when in reality it's not.

We had a long day of travel ahead, so I quickly showered, dressed and packed all my belongings into a small suitcase. I have been enjoying traveling with less stuff, as I had only packed enough for a week when I left home. There was no need to think much about what I was going to wear each day because there was only a small selection of clothes that were clean at any given point. It felt liberating to have less on my mind. I now understood why some people lived minimalist lifestyles – the more you own, the more it weighs you down, figuratively and literally. I considered getting rid of a big part of my belongings back home upon my return.

Time to make space for new energy!

We took off as a group from Granada and continued our journey northbound towards Honduras. The drive to La Esperanza, a small city in the heart of the country, took us the whole day, partially passing along the Río Goascorán – a river snaking through the country and bordering El Salvador on the other side.

During the drive, Angelina and I got to talking about her progress and insights from the work she was doing with Nayanna. She revealed a rather unconventional method which Nayanna was using to help bring her and her husband to a mutual understanding and compassion for one another – MDMA therapy. Apparently, this pure version of the substance, which is commonly called "Ecstasy" as a street drug used by ravers and party-goers has been recently approved for research by governments in several countries to study its effectiveness in treating PTSD (Post-traumatic Stress Disorder) and other mental health issues. According to Nayanna, on an energetic-emotional level it also had a unique ability to break down walls between people and open the heart chakra. Under her supervision, Angelina and Fabiano both ingested a clinically-approved dose of MDMA, and after about 45 minutes started to feel its effects – increased physical sensitivity, tightness of the jaw, dilated pupils, an elevated emotional state, and a feeling of oneness with everything and everyone. By guiding the couple with questions and prompts to have an open conversation, Nayanna skillfully navigated to the core of their problem. Angelina admitted that over the years their resentment for each other had built up to a point where neither one of them would yield to their partner. The mistakes and hurt they've been harboring inside were eating away at their relationship. Forgiveness felt foreign and impossible. And when they were finally able to see each other from the dimension of unconditional love, which the MDMA facilitated, the shell of their individual egos cracked open and they witnessed a type of re-birthing of themselves and met each other's inner child. While integrating the experience on the following day with Nayanna's guidance, Angelina told me that it was the first time in decades that she talked to her husband with the kind of loving compassion as when they first fell in love. It was a new way of looking at themselves and one another that helped them move past old grudges and make a choice to live in honesty and kindness from then on.

When we arrived, Nayanna briefed us on the plans for the next day. We would start off by visiting an orphanage to spend half a day with the children, followed by a cacao ceremony and ecstatic dance in the second part of the day. I was excited for all three activities that were awaiting us.

The children at the orphanage were beautiful! From the moment we stepped through the gates, they ran to us, wrapping their arms around our legs and climbing up to give us hugs and kisses. I could see how much love these children had inside of them!

I held hands with one of the young girls named Lola for the entire tour of the grounds – she wouldn't leave my side, and by the end of our visit we had made quite a connection. Lola's mother had given birth to her in poverty, and the father left them. When Lola turned three, her mother, realizing she couldn't take care of her alone, decided it would be best to leave her child in the care of the people at the orphanage. Lola had only met her mother four times in the past five years since she'd been living here. Despite her arduous life journey, the girl had a brilliant smile and eyes that gleamed with lively playful energy.

The children dressed up for our visit in traditional Honduran costumes – girls in wide-rimmed blue and white skirts sewn in horizontal stripes and ruffle-collar shirts in the same color scheme; boys wore white pants and shirts that were accentuated by red scarves on their necks and wide-brimmed hats. They appeared to be of various ethnicities that reflected the demographics of the population in La Esperanza, which consisted mostly of the Lenca Tribe indigenous people and Mestizo (a mix of Indigenous and European heritage). We were told that although the original language had been lost, the Lenca people still held on to their religious and cultural practices such as traditional textiles and pottery production, and dances. We were entertained by the children's dance performance in a special welcome ceremony.

While Fabiano and Angelina discussed what help was needed by the foundation that they could provide for them, I spent time playing with the children, seeing their bedrooms, which were shared amongst at least five kids per room, and helping out in the kitchen to prepare lunch. The kids were excited to be having *balaedas*, a traditional Honduran dish consisting of flour tortillas filled with refried beans, hard cheese and cream.

I was enjoying my time spent with the children, but the sensation of emptiness that I'd experienced in my dream that morning was still there and was growing in intensity. I tried to ignore it and turned my attention on the kids to give them as much of my attention as possible.

Isn't there more I can do for them?

As we were saying tearful goodbyes, I couldn't stop feeling like my visit there was not enough, and I was overwhelmed by the desire to do more to contribute, although I didn't know what that could be. We bought some handicrafts that were made by the older children from the onsite shop and signed our best wishes in the guest book, which already had our photos glued on to the empty pages. I made a silent vow to come back and visit when I'd get another chance and made a promise to Lola that I'll never forget her.

Nayanna noticed the impact this visit had made on me. As we were driving off, she told me that what these kids need more than anything is our unconditional love, and that even if we cannot be with them every day, we can send that love through our hearts and keep them in our prayers daily.

"Compassion and empathy are not the same. While empathy makes you feel the pain and hardship of another person, it is the willingness to help and maintain your high vibration that will ultimately be the energy that everyone can benefit from – and that is what compassion is." Nayanna's comforting words helped me get through the pain of leaving the orphanage, and to create more space for love to flow to the children by wishing them to be safe and happy.

"Now, let's go open our hearts some more with sacred cacao. Have any of you tried it?"

Fabiano and Angelina shook their heads no, and I said that I had signed up to an online cacao meditation session but couldn't attend it since I decided to come on this trip. This was the perfect way to make up for it – to do it in person, in a place that boasted to grow some of the best cacao beans in the world.

"Drinking cacao in ceremonial settings has been part of the Mayan civilization since as early as 1500 BC," explained Nayanna. "Here in Honduras, as well as in other parts of Central America, the Mayans had a large presence in their time, and they considered cacao as a drink to connect to each other as well as to support the departed on their journey to the afterlife. Tribal leaders drank it when they came together to facilitate cooperation and friendship.

"I drink it to open my heart, release what may be blocking it and receive insights for deeper understanding of myself and the world. During the ceremony, there are elements of movement and dance, social connection by sharing, and meditation or visualization."

I was getting increasingly excited, especially about the dance part. Nayanna continued:

"Your blood circulation will increase by up to forty percent and you will feel a kind of 'heating' on the inside. That's why we dance – to spend the energy, which the cacao activates inside as a fire that will burn away old stagnant energies that no longer serve you. You may feel comforted and supported emotionally, and you may once again reconnect to your inner child, who will communicate with you what you didn't realize you needed. Listen to her. And if you feel the need to share, there will be an opportunity for that in the circle when the time comes."

We arrived at the location of the ceremony which was in an old house in a remote area just outside of town, overlooking a lake fittingly called Laguna Madre Vieja.

Alma, a currandera in her seventies, was Nayanna's long-time friend who she considered as a "soul sister," and has been working with this sacred plant for over forty years. She welcomed us in and promptly escorted us up the stairs to the covered rooftop, where about ten other people had already gathered for the ritual. The space was prepared with candles and bowls of burning herbs. She served each person a cup of the cacao, which was prepared by combining the stone-ground beans with boiling water and her secret ingredients to sweeten the taste.

"This sacred plant medicine is used by shamans until today to connect to the spirit of Mama Cacao," Alma was saying as we sat around her in a semi-circle with cups of her offering grasped between our hands, "and to allow this feminine energy to manifest itself through the person drinking it. It is an ancient ritual to honor the elements of nature and to create harmony between all living beings. It is often called the medicine of the heart as Mamacita Cacao vibrates on the frequency of unconditional love, kindness, compassion, gratitude and joy. You may experience her energy as a gentle motherly touch. Allow her to open your heart and let her become what you need in the moment, whether it be your teacher, healer, guide or friend."

Then she instructed us to mix the contents of our cups with wooden spoons while setting our intentions. As we did so, Alma began singing to the spirit of cacao to activate them:

"Limpia limpia energia...

Con la luz, con amor...

Limpia limpia medicina..."

As hard as I tried, I couldn't figure out my intention, so I quietly asked Nayanna if she had any advice on how to set one.

"Whenever I'm not sure of what I want to achieve in a ceremony, I simply say the following:

I hereby open the sacred space to receive the blessings of the spirit [of Cacao].

Teach me what I need to learn;

Show me what I need to see;

Heal what needs to be restored.

"Then I open myself up to receive whatever needs to come through."

Alma finished her song and asked us to bring the cups to our hearts and internally repeat our intentions. I said the words recommended by Nayanna and began connecting with my breath. We were then invited to drink the cacao slowly, savoring the rich bitter taste, which was not at all unpleasant but not so easy to consume in such a raw form.

As the music for the ecstatic dance began to play, Alma broadcasted the final instructions to the group:

"Remember, the sacred spirit of cacao can only meet you half-way, and you need to come the other half to meet with her. Let go of judgments and resentments. Let go of expectations and entitlements. Let go of anything that stands in the way of being able to give and receive pure love."

I tried to relax into the moment and tried to let the music flow through me, just like I did at the carnival party in Cartagena.

The deep beats, eclectic instruments, and exotic vocals played through the speaker were inviting and I tried to awaken my inner goddess to come and play. But she was in no mood.

By now the cacao took an effect on my physical body and I noticed an increased heartbeat and tremors, which always happened when I ingested high doses of caffeine. Emotionally, I was feeling on edge too. It was as though I was a musical instrument and everything around me was playing the wrong notes on my insides.

As the music picked up its pace so did my agitation. I was noticing every little thing that felt wrong or out of place, and it was disturbing me deeply. The heat, the smell of sweat that filled the small space, the uneven pace of the music that kept knocking me off my rhythm. I felt awkward and graceless. I watched as some of the people around me started making very strange dance moves. Some were acting like animals, others were twirling in place as if in some trance, and a few were sitting on the floor and swinging wildly from side to side.

The rules of ecstatic dance were as follows: 1. No talking. 2. Respect each other's personal space and do not interact without consent. 3. Forget the rules of conventional dance and move freely without restriction or judgment. I took it to mean that we were meant to be doing whatever we want as long as it didn't interfere with anyone else. One young man, with a shaved head, wearing loose-fitting linen shorts, was acting more erratic than anyone else. He was screaming, laughing, bouncing against the floor and twisting himself into convoluted poses. No one seemed to pay him any attention and continued doing their own thing, as though his behavior was totally normal. But I couldn't let my guard down and kept a safe distance, avoiding eye contact with him.

This is so dumb! What kind of normal person would come to this? These people must be a bit too "out there." I am not like them!

Watching Nayanna, Angelina and Fabiano, who seemed to be totally in the zone, I felt like the odd one out. Nothing was making sense to me. I even hated the clothes that I was wearing, which I had carefully planned for this occasion and thought were perfect for that "hippie" side of myself – a Boho-print floor-length skirt and crochet crop top.

I look ridiculous! Did I really think this is me? I'm not this girl and will never be like these pretentious groupies!

I tried to focus on the music and my own dance moves, but my mind kept ranting in animosity.

Why are we doing this? Is this really necessary?

I don't think I need to push myself out of my boundaries this far.

I could've gone home by now and saved myself this insane spectacle!

A woman in her late forties dressed in tight leggings and loose top, rolled out a yoga mat and, positioning herself on all fours, began to wail loudly and writhe to the music. It looked like she was in between having an orgasm and going through exorcism. I imagined that in her regular life she was a businesswoman, judging by her glasses and short bob hairstyle.

How would her colleagues feel if they saw her doing this?

What about all these other people? Everyone here must have a job or a place in society they position themselves in, so how can they allow themselves to act like this?

I was getting repulsed by everything and everyone, including myself.

I hate this! I can't stand being around all these smelly people who have nothing better to do!

The yawning suction in my chest, which had been growing since morning, was becoming an unbearable sensation. I felt isolated from everyone there. They were in their own worlds, and I was in mine. The space between myself and everyone else was widening and engulfing everything around into itself. I couldn't connect to anyone, and there was a deep yearning to be part of something, to belong somewhere, and to be seen, acknowledged and appreciated by someone. But everyone was consumed in their own world. I felt lonely and disconnected.

I've never felt so alone in my entire life, right there in the middle of the dance floor full of people.

A voice, which I could now distinguish from my ego's usual monologue, came through as that familiar "inner knowing."

We can surround ourselves physically with people to not feel lonely, but on the inside, we are alone. Alone in the space of nothingness...

We can't stand that feeling of emptiness. We are afraid of being sucked into this void because it would surely mean the end of "me" – a death of the self.

We are afraid of dying. For death is a void we cannot comprehend.

So, to quell the discomfort and pacify the fear, we do the only thing we can.

We build a framework of boundaries and structures to keep from falling into the great abyss. We create a barrier made of an identity between us and the void and keep busy with it.

We grow that identity and continue adding to it: name, gender, nationality, personality traits, likes and dislikes, opinions, beliefs, affiliations with groups of people, and so on. All of this, in an effort to have something to grasp on to, to belong somewhere, to understand who "I" am.

Because if not for this identity – who am I? If we strip it all away, what is left?

Nothing! How can "I" be nothing? That's a scary and uncomfortable idea!

That's why the ego builds and cares for this identity and keeps so focused on all of "me" and all of "my" stuff.

It's easier to deal with the terrifying uncertainty of what's beyond the barrier when we have something to distract ourselves with, and to not think about it temporarily. But it remains a certainty we cannot escape.

The DJ who was in charge of the music, changed the tempo to something that I couldn't comprehend at all – an incoherent combination of industrial house mixed with animal sounds. This was a level of obscurity and bizarreness that I wasn't prepared to take any longer. I erratically stumbled through the dance space towards the stairs and ran down into the house to get away from it all.

Sitting in a dimly lit room, my mind took me to a dark dimension, where I've always avoided going. It was showing me memories of all the wrongs I've ever done, the mistakes I've made, and the people I've hurt. I remembered all the times that I had been selfish, jealous, possessive and entitled. There were flashbacks to my teenage years when I hated my parents for not allowing me to go to a concert with my friends. The time when I was resentful and jealous of a coworker when she had gotten promoted ahead of me. Every instance when I lied in order to protect my ego from being criticized or rejected. The times when I put my own needs ahead of my friends who really needed my help. Every condescending and judgmental thought I've had about how I was better than someone. And how I neglected to acknowledge the feelings of every boyfriend whenever there was a disagreement, because I thought my feelings mattered more.

I was staring straight into my darkness, my demons, my shadows. It was a dreadful sight, and I desperately wanted to look away, to run away, to be freed from this unbearable self-loathing. Yet there was nowhere to go. I had to face up to everything… but I didn't know what would happen if I did.

In a desperate attempt to find consolation and distract myself from admitting my own "ugliness," I reached for my phone. Elephant-sized tears splattered on the screen as I scrambled to search for a flight back home from the nearest airport.

I am going to be alone forever. Who would love someone who doesn't know how to love others?

I don't deserve to be loved, anyway! What a stupid idea this was to go looking for this temple that promises true love!

There's no such thing as true love, anyway – it's a lie! And even if it were true, I wouldn't be the one who gets to have it.

Love is for those who are pure. And I'm anything but that – I have so much darkness inside.

Nayanna came down looking for me and found me sitting on the floor, weeping uncontrollably. She sat next to me and we stayed in silence for a few minutes.

"You want to go home... I understand," she said pointing at my phone which had the flight selected and ready to be booked.

"This turned out to be harder than I thought," I choked out through quiet sobs. "I just don't think this method of healing is for me. You said it yourself, there are many other ways to find the same truth. I'll just go home where I belong and where I understand who I am. All of these people... they are here for their own reasons, and they all want healing. But I'm not like them. I can't do the things they do. I hope you understand, Nayanna. I just want to be with my family and friends now. They are not perfect, but I know how to deal with them, and they know how to deal with me. I'll get by..."

"I won't try to stop you. It is your decision and whatever you want to do is fine by me. Don't worry, I won't hold it against you. Let me take you back to the hotel, please, so you don't have to be alone, and you can grab the taxi to the airport tomorrow."

We gathered our things and Nayanna went to inform Fabiano and Angelina that we'd be leaving. They insisted we take the driver and asked to send him back to collect them later. I would say goodbye to them in the morning.

As the car pulled away from the house, I couldn't help but feel like I had failed my mission.

Well, this wouldn't be the first time I failed at something.

Off I go to lick my wounds and try to piece myself back together again.

Part 3

The Epiphany

Chapter 16

Breath of Love

There once was a king who built a palace of mirrors. He placed a beautiful red rose in the center of the main room, and the mirrors multiplied the image of this one flower all around. He then let a pigeon fly freely around the room. The pigeon, attracted to the beauty of the roses he saw in the mirrors, flew into the walls and hurt himself in trying to touch them. His desire for the roses was so strong that he kept chasing the images reflected in the mirrors with all his might, breaking his beak each time, only finding pain instead of the happiness he craved. Finally, when he had no more strength, he gave up his desire and collapsed in exhaustion, falling right on the real rose, attaining true happiness at last.

This was a story that Krishnaraj told in one of his meditation sessions in Ubud. He explained that "your mind is like the pigeon, always searching for something to land on to find ultimate joy, satisfaction, and contentment. Only you never find it because the desire makes you blind to the truth – that what you seek is already within reach. All you have to do is awaken to the reality and stop searching for it on the outside."

"If the mind is like the pigeon," I asked Krishnaraj, "then what does the rose represent?"

"The real rose – the one and only flower in the center of the room, is your true self – the *atman*. Not the mirages of the many roses that are reflected by the mirrors. Those reflections are like the false persona or illusory self, known as *jiva* in ancient Vedic texts, and it is the byproduct of *ahamkara*, which is the ego self."

I often reflected on this story and it helped me to make sense of who I was whenever the question arose about my identity.

But on that day, as I was more confused and lost in knowing who I am and what I am doing with my life, this story only took me further from the truth. After all, the rose was simply a metaphor, and in order to recognize the essence of who I really am, it was not possible to use my mind.

I sat with Nayanna in the back of the car as it took us towards the hotel, where I would pack up my things and book the flight home. Watching life unfolding in front of me on the streets of La Esperanza, a town in one of the poorest countries in the world, I ironically felt hopeless for the future of the world (Esperanza means "hope" translated from Spanish). The homes we passed by were small and shabby, and the roads were cracked. The men and women were dressed in very simple clothes and many of them didn't have shoes. My heart was crying for the sadness, desolation, and poverty that was the reality for billions of people in the world.

But all of a sudden, as I looked into the people's eyes, I began to notice the same kind of love that I saw in the eyes of the children in the orphanage. Each person we passed had a child inside of them and I saw that child clearly.

Look at that man with a big belly hanging out of his pants and unbuttoned shirt, unshaved and smoking a cigarette – he once was that beautiful child, just like the boys I met today.

And that old woman with heavy undereye bags and messy hair, hunched over from years of hard work – she was once like Lola – innocent and pure. They grew up, but their child is still within.

I could notice that the beauty, innocence and purity was still there in every single person.

We think of a baby or a little kid as a delicate flower. Precious – like a diamond. We see his true essence and we love him with all our heart.

But the moment he becomes an adult, suddenly, we stop seeing him for that preciousness, which never went away, but somehow, we became blind to.

We put up walls around our hearts, and our minds create a story – a judgment about this person, who just a few years before we considered to be pure love.

I told Nayanna my realization, and how terrible I felt for judging people instead of loving them.

"Of course, you judge people. If you said you never judged anyone, I'd tell you that you are a liar! That's just part of being human in this world. We evolved due to our ability to judge everything to ensure our survival. It's a normal process of the mind, and you probably wouldn't be alive today if you didn't use it that way. You judge a person coming towards you on the street and decide to cross to the other side if he seems potentially dangerous. The same way as you judged the screaming guy in the ecstatic dance when you moved away from him," Nayanna pointed out with a giggle.

"And that is okay, as long as you are aware that you are judging. That's the key to waking up – realizing that you do judge but forgiving yourself for it and giving unconditional love to yourself and to the person you judged."

"That's what I find the hardest," I complained, "Facing my own darkness. Tonight, I was in shock when I remembered how terribly I've acted in the past with pretty much every person who matters to me. And even how awful I was being to those people in the dance back there. I couldn't relate to them, and my mind was saying really horrible things about them. I just can't justify it – I don't deserve to be loved!"

"You know what you had back there? A catharsis! It's another type of purging – a release of repressed emotions, leading to a sense of relief or big realization. And that's exactly what you needed to experience as part of your healing and growth.

"Some people experience a catharsis through ecstatic dance, and they let it out by screaming, crying or laughing. It's very healing and cleansing, but you don't need to do it like that if that's not your style. Everyone has their own way. And maybe one day, you'll experience it like that too. Tonight, all your negative emotions that had been stuck for years without awareness came out and you didn't know how to deal with the outpour. You chose to run away, instead of facing up to it and simply forgiving yourself for the past."

"Where does this aversion and rage come from? I was surprised at how much of it I had in me!"

"All forms of hatred are simply a projection of that part of yourself that you haven't accepted. You haven't accepted yourself for your darkness as well as your light, for all of the bad and good that are both present in you. And instead of doing the hard work to integrate all its parts, the ego finds a scapegoat to spill that darkness externally, onto the world. Again, it comes back to awareness and acceptance, while being willing to change, and setting your intention on improving."

We had arrived back at the hotel and Nayanna said that she had one final exercise to teach me before I left, which would help me in my spiritual growth.

"Since we couldn't finish the cacao ceremony, it's a great time to do this exercise, which will culminate the process that we started with this sacred plant medicine. I call it *The Seed* meditation."

We sat down on the floor of our shared room facing each other. As in previous exercises, Nayanna had me close my eyes and begin to breathe consciously, observing each inhale and exhale and the effects it had on the body. After becoming aware of my whole body, part by part, she once again asked me to scan it down to up, right side to left side, and front to back.

"See if you can land on a central point of your body and become aware of the deep inner space you hold in that center.

"If you were a piece of fruit with a seed inside, where would that seed be? Locate that area and tune into the sensation of its depth and spaciousness. Once you find it, you will know right away, because it'll feel very familiar, homey, and comforting – as if you've come to your cozy warm house after a long day out. Have you found it?"

"Yes, it's somewhere right in between my solar plexus and the heart, very deep inside of me."

"Alright, you've located your seed. How does it feel to find it?"

"As you said, it feels like I've come home and found that comfort and familiarity. A place where I can kick up my feet and drop every care in the world, and simply be myself."

"That's it! This is the spot from where you feel your emotions – the place from where you send and receive love, and where your compassion comes from. You've known yourself to reside here for as long as you can remember, right?"

"Yes, this is the place where I can say my authentic 'self' lives."

"Notice how this place has no boundaries, labels, names, time or limits. Feel how eternal, boundless and formless it is. It has a kind of transcendental quality, doesn't it?"

I nodded and fell deeper into my internal space, relishing in how comforting it was to be in a place where I didn't need to pretend to be anyone else, other than who I was, stripped of any label I, or anyone else, could stick on me.

"As you inhale, imagine the stream of air flowing through your nose, down your throat and into your lungs. As the air reaches down, expand that space inside of you. Breathe into the space, clearing all that doesn't belong there. Exhale from that space and allow yourself to relax deeper. Sink deeper into that comfort and familiarity, and expel that which restricts you from being yourself, out through your nose.

"Breath is the bridge between your body and your soul – between the physical self and the ethereal self. Breathe, and notice that connection. To breathe is to live. Breath happens involuntarily, naturally, without involving your mind.

"Breath doesn't only happen if your financial situation is stable, or if you have a loving partner, or if you are happy with your life conditions. We all breathe with equal persistence and consistency – it does not depend on our status or state of being. As long as you are breathing, you are alive."

I had never thought about breath in this way – as the most fundamental part of being alive. It was the most basic of necessities, without which we couldn't live for even a few minutes. Yet we consistently take it for granted and don't acknowledge it as much as it deserves to be.

"Now start tuning into the channel of *gratitude* for this breath and for being alive. Breathe, and take pleasure from the act of breathing and having life. Breathe, and realize that each inhale and exhale is a gift, a blessing, and a miracle. Whenever something happens outside of your control that you don't like, just remember that you can breathe through all the negative emotions and thoughts and be grateful for this gift of life."

I was truly beginning to realize how incredibly blessed I was – not because of any life circumstance that I found favorable, but simply for the pleasure and honor of being alive. Each breath I was taking was a small gift of life that I received humbly and graciously. I've never experienced breathing in such a way before. These were the sweetest and deepest breaths I've ever taken, and through them, I could feel the connection between my outer and inner worlds. Through the breath I could travel to the far reaches of the external universe, because it was the same space as my internal universe.

"Now, tune into the channel of *hope*. Hope resides in the heart, and as long as your heart is beating you can have hope. As long as you can feel your heart, your breath, your body and all its senses, it is your confirmation that you are on your path – the one that's leading you to your ultimate destination. Visualize that beautiful place with a path leading towards the mountains with the sun setting behind them, which you went to on our first visualization together. Have trust that this is your right path, and that it's in the highest good of yourself and the universe that you are walking on it. You can't make the wrong decision or take the wrong detour, because ultimately, it will all lead you back here to this path. Have trust in that."

Finding hope in my heart made me smile and I sunk deeper into the "seed" space inside.

"It's time to tune into the channel of *compassion* – for yourself and every person you've ever met and will meet on your path. Understand that each person who has hurt you did so because of their own pain. The way they acted was the only way they knew how to, with their own level of awareness and within their own abilities in dealing with that situation. And equally understand that every time you've acted with anything but love, it was your own unawareness and ability at that moment. Be compassionate for yourself for the pain that you've been in, that made you project it onto others."

Nayanna's words had hit me straight in the heart-space. I realized that there was no point in blaming myself or others for our emotions. Emotion is the voice of the soul.

"Visualize your inner circle of family and friends. Send them your compassion, see them as their little selves – as children, and love them with all your heart. Visualize the wider circle of your friends and acquaintances. Send them your compassion, see them as children, and love them with all your heart. Visualize the next wider circle of people in your life whom you know but don't know that well – neighbors, coworkers, friends of friends. Send them your compassion, see them as children, and love them with all your heart. Visualize every so-called archenemy – ex-friend or ex-boyfriend, person you dislike, and anyone who you felt disrespected, hurt or betrayed you. Send them your compassion, see them as children, and love them with all your heart. Visualize strangers and people of the world – the whole human race on our shared home Planet Earth. Send them your compassion, see them as children, and love them with all your heart."

I used my best visualization skills to picture the continuously expanding circles of people in my life and sent out my love to them in a form of an electromagnetic wave, from my heart to theirs.

"And with that compassion, tune into the channel of *forgiveness*. Forgive all those people from your nearest to widest circles. Drop all the resentments, animosities, guilt-trips, blames, aversions, and all anger, hatred, and pride. Think of all the people you would like to forgive, one by one. Look into their eyes and tell them you forgive them. See how they accept your compassion and forgiveness and watch how the external hard shell of their egos melts away, revealing their own 'seed' of love."

I imagined standing in front of my parents and realized that I had been harboring some resentment for my emotional blockages and blaming them for affecting my chakras in the ways they have during my child years. Compassion overtook me as I saw my mother and father as little kids, who had their own emotional traumas and dysfunctions from their childhoods. They did the best they possibly could, considering their individual upbringing and mentality as the result of their own programming and baggage of their parents.

How could I ever hold any bitterness for these beautiful, innocent, pure beings?

They gave me life and everything else that they could have.

Whatever mistakes they made, was simply because of their fears.

But without them, I wouldn't be the person I am today, and for that I am eternally grateful to both of them.

Nayanna told me to send my love and compassion to each person by visualizing myself radiating a beautiful healing light towards them.

I looked into the eyes of my mother and father and told them that I forgive and love them deeply. I watched both of my parents smiling back at me with love streaming between our hearts in a brilliant green light.

Then I visualized Dave, and with a bit of trepidation, I approached him and looked into his eyes, not really sure of what I would see there. His inner child was in there too, of course, and he looked as lovely and pure as any child. My heart gave way to compassion for this little boy, who was dealing with life the best way he knew how. I saw the ego that tried to build itself up around his true essence in order to protect itself for fear of being rejected and feeling insignificant. I understood that our fights and problems came down to his insecurities and desires to be the best at everything, the same way that I tried to hide behind mine.

I forgive you Dave, and hope you forgive me.

I imagined giving him a long hug, and with it sent the love from my heart to his in a radiant beam of green light.

I told Nayanna that I was visualizing a green light coming from my heart.

"Yes, that's the color of the *anahata* chakra. Don't forget to forgive yourself. Send some of that gorgeous green light to yourself. What do you want to say to yourself – say it now."

The words I began to speak were not of my earthly self, but coming through me from a higher self:

"I forgive myself for all the things I couldn't do or that I wish I would have done differently.

"I forgive myself for not always being truthful to myself and others.

"I forgive myself for all the people I couldn't help as much as I wanted to help.

"I forgive myself for not being perfect, or not seeing how perfect I am in my imperfection.

"I forgive myself for the pain that I caused others as it was my own pain that I wanted to release onto the world.

"I trust that I am on the right path and am being helped and guided every step of my way."

"Amen," Nayanna spoke after a few moments of silence, "Gratitude, hope, compassion and forgiveness – these are such gorgeous emotions that vibrate on the frequency of unconditional love – a very high frequency of an open heart chakra. You have tuned into each one of them and experienced what it is like to give it and receive it. This is what it means to be living out of creation – out of the heart, instead of living out of survival from the lower three chakras, which unfortunately is how most of the world lives. The only thing left to experience is *humility*."

"Humility as in not thinking too highly of myself?"

"As in seeing yourself as an integral part of God, but still being humbled in awe of the greatness that God is. To not give credit to yourself for your intellect, kindness, wisdom and beauty, but to know these are divine qualities that are channeled through you from the Great Divine. Knowing yourself as creator, but also as the created, and to ask for guidance, blessings and mercy for your time here in this incarnation from forces working in higher dimensions and frequencies."

"I think that's why, when pushed to a place of total desperation, even an atheist can pray." I pondered out loud and then admitted, "I've always been skeptical about the notions of God and prayer, but I found myself with that humility in my darkest hours, and I prayed so hard!"

"Right, so maybe now you won't have to be pushed to rock bottom to find that humility. You can pray anytime. And prayer doesn't have to come from the Bible or the Koran – you can write your own, as you just so eloquently did with the forgiveness speech.

"There's a great quote by Meister Eckhart: 'If the only prayer you said was, thank you, that would be enough.'

"Simply saying 'Thank You' and giving your most genuine smile, opens your heart chakra. That's how easy it can be to pray – you can try it now and see!"

We both closed our eyes again and I smiled softly, tuning into the humility channel by giving gratitude to the higher powers for my body and mind, for all my blessings, for my loved ones and for being able to have this human experience.

"To wrap up the cacao ceremony, let's visualize a fire burning in the middle, between us. Take whatever you want to let go of – fear, grief, cravings, doubt, stress, pain, conflict, negativity, suffering – whatever it is that you don't need, and throw it in the fire. Imagine each thing as an object with a form or shape and watch the fire consuming it. Watch as the fire transmutes it back to its original state, which is simply energy, and ask the higher powers to take this energy from you, where it will be merged with the divine light, and where it will no longer be the darkness that it once was.

"Repeat the following words mentally or out loud,

"I am loving awareness.

"My light overturns the darkness.

"I am the vessel through which Unconditional Love flows into this world."

I repeated each sentence out loud. As I did so, I began to have visions, like the ones I've been seeing in my dreams, only this time I was fully awake. Green misty air was shimmering across the screen of my closed eyelids. It was bright and beautiful. It was flowing in and out of me connecting the two sides of the universe together through my breath.

"Let's thank Mama Cacao, the earth, our spirit guides, angels and masters who have been with us tonight," Nayanna offered.

As I gave my final words of gratitude, Naga appeared in my vision and revealed to me her next gift – a green jewel of the heart chakra and the unconditional love it represents. I accepted the sparkling green crystal, bowing deeply to Naga.

And with that, my strong sense of "inner knowing" came through again, and at once I understood who I really was.

"I" wasn't anything that I could ever comprehend with my mind.

It's a feeling, rather than understanding.

Who "I" am is simply the "feeling" of Unconditional Love.

~

"Ale, I've never felt so much love – it's so pure, so beautiful, so warm!" I spoke softly into the phone tucked between my ear and the pillow. "My heart is wide open and this love feels like waves of crystal clear water washing over this deep space in my chest that doesn't seem to have a boundary."

"Mmm..." I heard a sleepy murmur of Ale's voice on the line. "You are finally seeing yourself for who you truly are, the way I had always seen you. Now you are in the next alchemy stage – *conjunction*. As a spiritual alchemist this is where you begin to form a new substance from the separated elements, which you chose to keep."

Ale kept talking for a while and I fell asleep to the sound of his voice, being caressed from the inside by waves of love.

Chapter 17

Mantra

A sound of guitar accompanied by a woman's voice outside my window, penetrated my awareness in the early hours of the morning, gently coaxing me awake. It was such a harmonious way to wake up, and before I even opened my eyes, the corners of my lips curled up into a soft smile. I focused my attention only on the sound and lingered in the "now" for a few blissful moments. The angelic voice singing in Spanish was strumming on my heart strings.

"Pacha mama, pacha mama,
Pacha mama, madre tierra;
Virikuta virikuta virikuta
Grande espírito;
Taita Inti, Taita Inti, Taita Inti
Grande espírito;
Gracias, Pacha mama..."

There is so much beauty and enchantment in this world. The voice, the guitar, this comfy bed, being able to breathe and wake up like this – everything is pure magic!

I realized that smiling continuously for even just a few minutes ignited a chain reaction of positive thoughts and emotions, simply because it was impossible to hold a negative thought in that state. I tried to think about something unpleasant or sad, but couldn't, as long as I kept my most genuine smile on my face. I made a note to do this kind of "smile meditation" every morning, as it was the perfect way to tune myself into the frequency of unconditional love and start the day on the right note.

I got out of bed and went over to the window to see who was playing and singing. It was Fabiano on the guitar and Angelina singing, while Nayanna sat next to them with her eyes closed, lost in the music and smiling softly. I slipped on a bathrobe and went outside to join them.

When the song was finished, we all sat in silence for a while, relishing the perfection of the moment. Finally, Angelina informed us that they would be parting ways with Nayanna and me from today, and heading back to their yacht. The couple expressed their deepest appreciation for having crossed paths with us. I asked them about the rest of the cacao ceremony the night before, and they said it was exactly what both of them needed to open their hearts towards each other. Fabiano admitted that he had never danced in such a raw animalistic way as he did that night, which made him more confident in verbalizing his feelings in their relationship. Angelina said she had a moment of clarity after the sharing circle that made her realize why she had been so distant from her husband, and that she saw right through her own ego, which was running the show for so many years.

We said our goodbyes and I went back to the room with Nayanna.

"What about you? Am I going to say goodbye to you today too?" she asked me.

"Well, I thought I had made up my mind last night and nothing was going to change it. But then I called Alejandro, and he reminded me of how close I am to re-integrating myself, and I realized that quitting now would be like throwing away pure gold!

"I am so at peace with myself now, in every aspect of my being. You could say I even made friends with my ego, instead of constantly rejecting it. It's like I got a glimpse into my true essence, which has nothing to do with what I can think of myself."

Nayanna nodded knowingly.

"Also, hearing the music this morning moved me somehow. The song spoke to my heart in a way that calmed my worries and made me hopeful about everything ahead. I think that if I don't give myself a chance to experience whatever it is that's waiting for me at the end of our journey, I will always wonder about it for the rest of my life. You only live once, right?"

"Well, sure... on this earth, in this incarnation," Nayanna chuckled. "Are you willing to do anything it takes to heal yourself for the sake of your soul, your ancestors and any potential future children and grandchildren?"

"Absolutely! I don't want to leave this mission half-way. I need to complete what I had started. Let's keep going, shall we?"

"There's no stopping us! And yes, songs tend to have that calming, reassuring effect, if they are sung from the heart, and in the right moment for the person who needs to hear it. Sound, in general, has a lot more influence on us than you realize."

"How do you mean?"

"I will tell you on the way. Let's pack and head out. We've got a lot of road to cover over the next few days towards the next stop. You are going to love this place we are going to in Guatemala!"

We got on a bus and traveled for six hours to cross over the border towards a small town called Rio Hondo, which means "deep river" in translation. It was mostly made up of farmlands that grew a variety of fruit like mangos, limes, and avocados, and was known for its river after which it was named. Nayanna said we would stay for a few days at Esperanza de Vida, a large Christian humanitarian community center which included a retirement home, an orphanage, and a hospital. The outreach program run by Nayanna's friend welcomed volunteers from all over the world who came to serve the children and senior citizens of Guatemala and support the mission of this organization. From the moment we arrived, I knew I wasn't going to want to leave anytime soon. The place was nestled amongst a backdrop of rolling green hills bursting with rich vegetation and animal life.

Nayanna took me to a nearby river every morning where we performed some of the alchemy practices, and she taught me a few more breathwork techniques which were new to me. One of them was the Bhramari pranayama, or the *hummingbee breath*.

~

Humming Bee breath as taught to me by Nayanna

This technique from the Hatha Yoga practice works really well to quell an overactive or anxious mind by activating the parasympathetic nervous system, which governs relaxation, rest and digestive functions of the body. It reduces the effects of stress, anxiety, anger, brings down blood pressure and balances the heart and throat chakras.

To perform this pranayama, sit in an upright position and close your eyes (this should never be done lying down).

Block your ears with your index fingers by placing them on the cartilage part of your ears and pressing them in.

Take a deep breath, inhaling through the nose, and on the exhale make a humming sound like a bee with your mouth closed, for the entire length of the exhale.

Repeat 5 to 7 times, or for about five minutes.

~

After our morning sessions, we spent the rest of the day helping out in the kitchen to prepare food and spending time with children and elderly residents of the retirement community. The days were so fulfilling that a week went by in what seemed like an instant.

I woke up every day full of purpose and energy, even though I was only getting about six hours of sleep every night and couldn't wait to spend the day being of service to those who needed support. Nayanna got me into the habit of waking up at 4 a.m. and we were out the door to get to our meditation spots near the river before 5 a.m. She said that waking up early and meditating with the rising sun was an especially potent energetic time of the day, same as the sunset. She explained that we benefit greatly from utilizing the shift of the earth between nighttime and daytime, as the energy present at those times helps us tune into the highest possible frequencies. I remembered a similar explanation about why monks wake up to meditate between 3 and 4 a.m., which Krishnaraj gave us in one of his lectures. There is something special in the early hours of the morning that allows for maximum connection to the divine, which in turn helps us to receive more downloads – divine wisdom and intelligence from the entire universe which is held within the Akashic records. He briefly mentioned that Akashic records can be thought of as a giant database of information that spans all dimensions and realities, and translated from Sanskrit means "sky" or "atmosphere." Believed by theosophists as a library, which "holds all," it exists in the non-physical, but rather the mental plane, and is encoded with information from all the past, present and future realities. Every thought, word, emotion, intent, event and action, as well as information about when your soul was created, how many lives you've lived, and all the possible future lives you will have, is contained in the Akashic records. All the knowledge of the Universe and even beyond is said to be held in this one giant source of collective consciousness, from which many great thinkers claim they receive divine inspiration and wisdom.

The other positive effect of all this energy work I was doing, was that my immunity seemed to have improved significantly. Ever since I was a child, I've had chronic throat infections, that led to the removal of my tonsils, but even after that, I still continued to have frequent illnesses which were severe enough to need antibiotics several times a year. I knew of the harmful side effects of antibiotics but ended up taking them because I wanted to recover faster to get back to my busy life. It didn't take much for me to get a sore throat – a stressful period at work, a bad night of sleep, being exposed to cold weather or someone who was sick – immediately after which I could feel the bacteria spreading and I'd be down for a week or more of bedrest. Yet here I was, being around many sick people and children, sleeping very little, dipping into the chilly water every morning in the river, and I felt stronger than ever.

"How can my immune system be so weak when I'm back home, but here I haven't once gotten sick with a sore throat or anything else?" I asked Nayanna on the last day of our stay after the morning alchemy session.

"Many reasons I can think of. For one, you are feeling so much drive for what you are doing here, which is serving other people. Your presence is so needed here and serves a greater purpose, so the universe conspires to help you in your mission by paving the way for you to keep doing more. It's simply the law of energy exchange at work. You give your energy, time and love, and you get it all back in vitality, health and fulfillment."

"Is that why there's an expression that once you find your passion, you'll never work another day in your life, since you'll be loving what you do so much, it won't feel like work?"

"I see passion and purpose as two different things. Passion for your hobbies, work or favorite music, just like romantic passion, tends to fade over time. You are passionate about something one day, then you evolve and become passionate about something else. Passion channels the energy inwards and serves only yourself. When you channel that energy outwards and focus on serving other people, you know you've found your purpose. Life then, becomes more meaningful to you because you are not just fulfilling your own needs but the needs of others who rely on your time, expertise, or help. The idea is to take your passion and turn it into a purpose – that's when you'll never work another day in your life!"

"That's so true, I've been passionate about so many things – music, nutrition, fitness, travel blogging – but these were just activities I liked to do for myself, and I haven't found a way to turn them into a purpose that provides value to others. I've seen people who did manage to do that – all these incredible DJs, bloggers, nutritionists and fitness coaches who make it their purpose to serve others with their work, and they do it so effortlessly and happily."

"Yes, there are as many ways to serve humanity and our earth, as there are people in the world. You have your own unique set of gifts, abilities and natural talents, so don't waste much longer before you put them to use for the greater good.

"The other reason you've been feeling so strong and energetic is because your chakras are open and operating optimally to allow the prana to flow unobstructed up and down the main energy channel – from root to crown and back down. It's the combination of the exercises you've been doing, which incorporate three main elements of prana flow: movement, breath, and sound. Notice how all the practices I've introduced to you have those elements embedded into them. It is through performing activities that incorporate physical movement, breathwork, and some form of chanting or sound vibration on a daily basis that we keep the energy channel clear of emotional and energetic junk."

"I see how movement and breathwork helps to let go of blocked energies. But how does sound fit into this process?"

"Sound is actually a very powerful piece of this trifecta, because it makes up the building blocks of everything in existence – all matter."

"Matter is made up of sound?" I raised my eyebrow in surprise.

"Essentially, yes. Quantum physics, as opposed to Newtonian physics has uncovered the spiritual element of science and we now know that molecules and atoms are not at all solid materials that make up everything we can touch and sense. As we move in closer to see what is inside on the quantum level, matter begins to reveal itself as a field of energy, which is a cluster of oscillating neutrons, protons and electrons that create waves of energy around the nucleus. Inside the atom it is mostly just empty space and vibration of the circulating particles that are made up of energy vortices – there's no matter in there at all."

"Yes, and sound is also a vibration. So, what is the body made of then? Just emptiness and rhythm? Sounds like on the subatomic level we are nothing but a dance of energy!"

"Beautifully said! And now you can see how sound vibrations help us in the healing process by affecting the subtle energy body. Your thoughts are energy, your feelings are energy. The words you speak are made up of energy. The material world is actually an illusion. The whole universe is not split up into matter and energy – everything is made out of energy. And all the energy fields interact with one another and have an effect on one another. The power of sound, especially through healing music, sound bowls, instruments and sacred chants, like mantras of the East has been harnessed for thousands of years. Sound can influence your own vibration in positive or negative ways."

"How do mantras work? I've heard Krishnaraj chanting in the mornings... he would repeat a mantra 108 times."

"It is said that the ancient sages of India and Tibet downloaded the information sent to them from the Divine source on how to heal, transform and manifest things into reality, and they in turn recorded it as secret formulas to be passed down from generation to generation, and they called it *mantra*. In Sanskrit, it can be translated as "divine speech" and there are mantras for all kinds of circumstances and events. They can help you calm down anger, cope with illness or even facilitate physical healing, bring clarity or insight to a difficult situation, give you the energy to take action on solving a problem, tune into the frequency of money or material gains, or bring harmony and balance to a relationship you are in.

"That's why in yoga practice there is an important element of chanting. A simple 'Ohm' sound can help restore balance to all of your chakras and tune you into the frequency of all creation, as it is considered to be the primordial sound of the Universe."

"Do you mean the Ohm chant we do at the beginning and end of the practice, like this...? Ooooohhhhmmmmm...." I dragged out the syllable.

"It is actually a combination of vowels that make up that sound – A – U – M, each one representing a number of sacred trinities. Most common one being the creation, preservation and destruction – or liberation.

"In Vedic cosmology, it is believed that the universe came into being through God's divine speech, and that power is referred to as Saraswati – the Word, from which everything in the universe manifests into existence.

"And it wasn't only in the East that the power of vowels was said to be sacred. In the Kabbalah the sounds of O, A, E, I, U are regarded as divine. In Sufism there is also a connection between sound and manifestation as a divine creation. Even in the book of Genesis it is said that the beginning of everything came when God spoke, 'Let there be light...' from which we can derive that before light, there was speech."

"Wow, I had no idea how powerful sound is! Which mantras do you recommend I use for balancing my throat chakra? With all the infections I am always getting back home, I feel like I could use some subtle healing there."

"In yoga the sound for the throat is 'Hahm,' and there are certainly specific mantras associated with effective communication and authentic self-expression, which are related to the *vishuddha* chakra. However, before going down that route, perhaps we can explore the root cause of this issue, on a psychological level? Why don't you take some time over the next few days and contemplate on your ability to express your needs since your childhood, and whether or not you've used your voice to communicate clearly what is inside of you? We will come back to that once you've gained some insights. For now, I'd like to share with you a water ritual you can start doing daily to exercise your throat chakra. Together with water, our speech can be amplified, creating tremendous power that we, as humans have at our disposal."

~

Water ritual/Shower mantra as taught to me by Nayanna

Every time you shower, or even if you bathe yourself in a pool or any natural body of water, before you finish, say the following words,

Let the water wash away all judgments and preconceptions I have about myself and others.

As the water runs off, only Love remains.

The next line in this prayer is your intention on what you are going to do to create positive change in your life. Feel free to add in your own words here. For example,

I intend to be healthy and energetic, grateful and happy, kind and generous, present and aware.

And the last line in this prayer is going to be about faith – having trust that you are being protected and provided for, by the unseen energies. Feel free to add whatever words you wish. I like to say,

I have faith that I'll be safe, protected, loved, healthy and abundant. So shall it be.

Finish it up with a moment of gratitude by saying *Namaste, Amen* or just *Thank You* out loud, or simply by feeling it.

Chapter 18

Karma

We arrived at our next stop on the journey towards the temple – a village on the shore of majestic Lake Atitlán – San Marcos La Laguna in western Guatemala. The location was mind-bogglingly beautiful. Nayanna booked a shared room for us at an ecological resort, situated on the side of a mountain overlooking volcanos and the lake itself. There were spiritual activities happening on a daily basis, including sound baths, yoga, ecstatic dance, cacao ceremonies, and various arts and music events. This was truly a place of transformational healing! Nayanna and I attended practically every session that was offered on our five-day stay.

In between all the sound healings, meditations and dances, I had given a lot of thought about the origin of my throat chakra problem. While I could see that I had trouble expressing my wishes since childhood, I couldn't quite figure out why that was the case.

Recalling the times when I'd go to a toy store with my parents as a kid, I wouldn't ask for something I had really wanted. Looking at the display counter with a small selection of toys and trinkets for children, I would silently wish that my mom could read my mind and know exactly what I liked. But I couldn't speak a word and kept my desire to myself, quietly longing for that item I had my eye on.

Why didn't I just ask for it if I wanted something so badly? My parents wouldn't have said "no" to me. Even if they didn't buy it right away, they would've probably ended up surprising me with it later as a gift.

When I got older, my inability to ask for things and express my desires affected my romantic relationships. I couldn't ever ask a man to pay for the date and always pulled out my wallet to offer sharing the bill. And most of the time, the men would let me, knowing that I made enough money. Although I'd tell myself that I'm proud to be an independent woman who takes on the responsibility to pay my own way, deep down I felt resentment for these men who didn't want to step up and take care of me the way my father did with my mother. Even with Dave, who had the money to afford it, I couldn't bring myself to ask him to buy anything for me, and most of what I owned, I had paid for myself.

Many things are still like that in Russia and Eastern Europe or this is the way it used to be when women didn't work, but I certainly don't want to be considered a stereotypical gold-digger.

If I don't let a man pay for me, I reserve the right for equal power, so I won't have to give up my freedom, and he won't think he can control me – or worse, use me for sex.

But in the bedroom, I wasn't that empowered. I've had trouble voicing my desires and needs to any man I've ever been intimate with. Reflecting on all my past sexual encounters, I had never left feeling completely satisfied, always wishing my partner would magically turn on his telepathy mode and come through for me in the end. But when that didn't happen, I would pretend that it was enough for me and grudgingly let it slide.

I decided to talk about this one evening in a community sharing circle, in the hopes of gaining some clarity as to why I kept holding out on speaking what's on my mind. It felt like a very safe and comforting space to share amongst fellow adventure travelers and people on the quest for self-transformation, so I allowed myself to speak freely and show my vulnerability. After listening to my story, some of the women in the circle sympathized with my issue and expressed having gone through similar experiences. One woman, Brigit, shared about her inability to receive compliments, praise, and gifts, and how she discovered the culprit of this through a therapy called *past-life regression*. It turned out that in one of her previous lives, Brigit was a peasant girl in England, orphaned from an early age and growing up in extreme poverty. She was constantly shunned by society, and the people around her would always call her by derogatory names. Never having received a kind word, she believed she was worthless. Brigit's therapist explained that her inability to receive kindness through words and actions was because of the karmic debt that hadn't been worked off in that lifeline and which was still present in this lifeline. Karmic debt, as she described it, is a spiritual energy law of cause and effect that is an accumulation of a person's past actions, feelings and circumstances that spans lifetimes. According to Brigit's healer, in the Vedas karmic debt can be either positive or negative, but either one would keep a person stuck in the wheel of reincarnation – or *samsara*, until they "work off" the remaining debt and only then be able to transcend the physical plane into higher realms as a soul. Brigit explained that her healer used the same method for calculating her life path number to see her karmic debt number, which showed up as 16 – relating to past and current life repeated cycles of toxic relationship patterns. Brigit's insight after discovering this was that her purpose on earth or at least one of the reasons she reincarnated here in her present life, was to give her soul the opportunity to work off this debt through honesty and loyalty, so she could break the old cycle and stop making the same mistakes in love in order to move on to the next stage of her soul's evolutionary journey.

I quickly wrote out my birth date and birth year numbers on a piece of paper to see if I had 16 and discovered that I didn't have any of the four karmic debt numbers – 13, 14, 16, or 19. I wondered why my soul came back to live through another human life cycle if I didn't have anything to release from the past. After the circle sharing, I asked Nayanna if she thought I should do a past life regression for better self-awareness.

"I don't see why not, if you find the right healer who is qualified at hypnosis and working with your subconscious mind. But before you do that, don't forget that you are lucky enough to still have access to your living ancestors. Why don't you ask your parents and grandparents about their own issues related to speaking truthfully and self-expression? I bet you'll discover plenty of insights from just one conversation. That may shed some light on your own issues that are passed down to you by generational trauma."

"What is generational trauma exactly? Does it affect a person the same way, like karmic debt from past lives?"

"No, karmic debt is something your soul retains like knowledge, that cannot be seen or studied by science because it is not a material substance. Generational trauma, however, can actually be passed down in genes and there is a field of science on this phenomenon called *epigenetics*. Traumas and stressful environments can affect the genome's structure, and just like with hereditary illnesses, this altered or weakened DNA can be passed down from parent to child. A lot of this is still theoretical. There haven't been too many extensive studies to prove that generational trauma is responsible for people who suffer from anxiety, depression and PTSD, or that children of parents who went through extreme suffering are surely going to inherit the same genetic patterns. But there are clear examples of certain populations of people who seem to be more affected by mental distress and issues like those who have historically been subjected to systemic racism and oppression, hate crimes, war, natural disasters, or domestic abuse."

"Could a compromised immune system be a result of generational trauma?"

"Yes, and as experts are learning more about how trauma affects the genome, there is some evidence that prolonged exposure to stress may affect the DNA and lead to autoimmune diseases or increased susceptibility for illness."

I was curious to find out more about what my parents and grandparents went through in their childhood and adult life, growing up in the Soviet Union, and how it may have affected them.

That night I called my parents. My mother picked up the phone and was eager to hear how my travels had been going. I briefly updated her on the details of my trip and asked her to tell me about the oppression she'd experienced living under the communist regime. She told me that although in her time it wasn't nearly as harsh as what her parents and grandparents had to endure, it was still a time of massive restriction on what they were allowed to talk about. She recalled stories of her grandparents who had been reported to the government by envious neighbors for having accumulated slightly more wealth than the rest of the community, and being branded as "kulaks," had been stripped of all their material possessions and sent away to Siberia to live in hard labor working camps knowns as Gulags. Back in those days, even a single word uttered against the political party could land you in one of those camps.

My father, overhearing the conversation with my mom, joined in on the call. He said that in their early twenties, they had to be careful who they spoke with about their political opinions. Although there wasn't a threat of being sent away anymore, being shunned by society and losing your job was a common occurrence, had the government caught wind of any back talk against them. Radio channels and any form of written media from the West was strictly prohibited, and people had to rely on underground networks to gather independent information about what was happening outside of the USSR. He recalled a story from his adolescence when on June 2, 1962, in the city of Novocherkassk just a few miles from where he lived at the time, soviet forces opened fire on civilians including children during a peaceful labor strike, killing and injuring hundreds, imprisoning and sentencing to death many of the survivors. The news was not reported and covered up with lies and manipulation. No one was allowed to talk about this massacre, and my father said that it was a tough pill to swallow.

Keeping silent for the sake of surviving.

That certainly must have put a strain on the throat chakra of the people in those times. Perhaps this is the generational trauma Nayanna was referring to that was passed down to me from everything my parents and their ancestors had been through.

I told Mom and Dad how grateful I was for their strength, and said that there was one more thing I needed to tell them.

"I just want to ask for your forgiveness."

"Forgiveness? For what, darling?"

I could hear the worry in my mom's voice.

"Over the past few weeks, I've been discovering a lot about myself – becoming aware of my recurring life patterns and shadows. I have to admit that for many years I've held a bit of blame over you both for these weaknesses. I won't go into the details of the issues I've uncovered in myself now, but maybe one day I will tell you."

"We always did the best we could." My mother answered softly. "I know we are not perfect."

"Well, this is actually what became very clear to me… your personal journeys have taken you to be who you are as parents – the best possible parents that you can be. Everything you are and everything you've done to raise me, has been your divine mission and act of unconditional love, even if I didn't see it at the time. So I'd like to ask for your forgiveness for not being aware of that earlier."

"There's nothing to forgive, sweetie, you've been a great daughter. We are two of the luckiest parents in the world to have you!" My mother gushed. My father nodded from the back. He wasn't much for sentimentalities and expressing his love in words.

"As Nayanna had explained to me, and what I choose to believe is true, is that all souls make a contract with one another to be each other's teachers, no matter how cruel or tough their teachings may be. Because the only constant of a soul's plan is the unconditional love with which they operate. There is no doubt in my mind that I had chosen you as my parents... way before I was born!"

"You know we don't believe in all these soul and energy things," my mother giggled, "but we are so very proud of you!"

"And I am proud of who I turned out to be, because of you both!"

We continued chatting for another hour, reminiscing and laughing about our most memorable family moments and how naïve we used to be in our early days as immigrants while adapting to a new world, making mistakes, and learning to speak English.

I thought about all the challenges my parents had presented me with and how each one was actually a blessing in another form. They taught me with every hug, as well as with every spank, with every kind word, as well as with every reprimand. I was blessed with all that they've been able to give me, and with everything they couldn't.

"Thank you for my life and for loving me for all my flaws and imperfections. I couldn't have asked for better parents!" I tenderly said before ending our call.

I wondered why I had never talked so openly with my parents before, seeing how good it felt to speak from the heart.

Dave and I never spoke to each other like that either. I can't blame him for that if I didn't really try to open up first.

I need to speak to him now. He needs to know everything, even if there's no way back for us.

Picking up my phone to make a call, my breath got caught up as I saw Dave's photo pop up on the screen. He was calling me for the first time in over a month!

Chapter 19

Intuition

Letting the phone vibrate in my hand a few seconds before picking up, I stared at the screen in disbelief at the timing of his call.

Why is he calling me? Does he know I've been away? He wouldn't have known about my absence and where I am now.

"Hi..." I finally answered, "I didn't expect to hear from you."

"Hi," Dave's voice sounded stiff and somewhat different than how I remembered it. "I had been meaning to call you for a few days now. I wasn't sure you'd want to speak with me."

Time had done its job well to estrange a person who had once been so close and familiar.

"I know it's been a while but I'm glad you did. There's so much that's happened since we last saw each other. You wouldn't believe where I am!"

I told Dave briefly about my trip to Peru, the ayahuasca experience and the decision to extend my travels, crossing thousands of miles from one continent to another and ending up in Guatemala. He listened patiently and then wanted to know who I was traveling with. I told him about Nayanna and my spiritual healing that she was helping me through.

"I've been on a bit of a spiritual journey myself," Dave said, catching me off guard since he'd never been the type to follow that path. "I even spoke to a psychic last week, imagine that!"

"That doesn't sound like you at all! You never believed in psychics and always laughed at people who did. What changed?"

"Well, life can push you towards things you'd never thought you would do, and loneliness can make you believe what you swore you'd never believe in."

"*You* – lonely? What about all your friends and family?"

"There's been this empty feeling inside that I can't seem to fill. I think what's missing is a deeper connection – the kind we had once, do you remember?"

"I'm curious to hear what the psychic said," I changed the subject to avoid talking about our past.

"He said that we still have a chance – you and me. We can have a family soon if we give it another shot. He saw us with a baby next year. Can you picture it? Us, as parents? We can be a family!" Dave paused for a moment and then in an almost whisper added, "I haven't stopped loving you. Is there any spark of hope left in you, or am I crazy?"

Wow, this is not the same person I once knew! Is he seriously telling me he wants to have a baby because a psychic told him?

I managed to regain my composure after being taken by surprise and calmly answered:

"Dave, are you certain that this isn't just some insecurity of yours about failing at our relationship and being seen as someone who can't keep his personal life in order? I've been through that – trust me, I hated that feeling. But trying to save something that clearly wasn't working by starting a family is not a good idea. I'm not in a place for that, and I don't think you are either."

"Maybe you're right. I just don't want to give up like this!"

"I've just barely regained my balance, and I want to keep evolving. But I'm worried that getting back together is going to jeopardize all the work I've been doing. And look, I wasn't honest with you at the end... you deserve to know the full story...

"I had an affair a few weeks before we split up."

These words came out so suddenly that it even surprised me that I said them. I waited for Dave's response – I had no expectations about how he'd react.

After a bit of silence, he finally spoke cautiously.

"Thank you for being honest. I was going to tell you as well, but you said it first. I had a couple of affairs myself throughout our relationship. But they were just flings that didn't mean a thing to me. You were the one I always wanted to be with!"

I was not upset hearing his awkward confession, and strangely felt tranquil inside.

"Well at least we are both honest now." I could clearly see now that my intuition had been right and that it had always spoken to me through this quiet, peaceful sense of knowing.

It's the mind that gets agitated, but intuition stays calm. Ego talks, while the true self just listens.

Dave started to try and convince me to come back home and see how we can work out our issues, but I needed to tell him something more important.

"This empty feeling you mentioned... does it feel like a sucking black hole that draws everything in and makes you feel isolated and disconnected from the world?"

"Yes! You feel it too, don't you? It's a sign that we need each other. I've never felt like this before, and I don't think I could go on another day without you in my life!"

"It's not me that you crave, Dave. That emptiness is not going to be filled by us getting back together. Actually, I don't think you can fill up that hole with any other relationship or experience. That emptiness is there as a signal that you are ready for growth and leveling up. Yes, it hurts, and it's supposed to. That's how the universe shows you that you have veered off the path and is trying to wake you up so that you take the opportunity to find your way back."

"Back to what?"

"Back to yourself. And who you really are on the inside. It's something you've forgotten, just like I have. But when you do the inner work and remember, it'll all be worth the pain and discomfort, I promise you. I have experienced it myself these past few weeks, and I can tell you that finding the path back has been tough. But I've never felt more fulfilled and alive! I wish the same for you... because I do love you."

"So, you still love me! Then there is a chance we could get back together if I promise to do my inner work?"

"I don't know what's in the future for us. I only know one thing – when we both are self-sustained and not seeking to fill what's missing from one another, that's when we have a chance at something real between us. I'm doing everything I can to get there, but I can only do my own work. So if it's meant to be, by the time I finish my trip and come back home, we will meet again as two autonomous selves and see what happens."

This was clearly not what Dave had expected to hear from me. I, myself, was surprised at what I was saying. The "old me" would've been tempted to run back into the familiar. And I had to admit that a part of me was pleased to have him wanting me back.

Am I making a huge mistake here? He's not a bad person and he seems to want to change.

Maybe I should give him a bit of hope to keep this thing warm while I figure it all out. I wouldn't want to regret this later.

I was aware of the voice in my head and that it was driven by one particular emotion – the fear of being alone and never being able to find someone "as good" as Dave.

For all his faults, I surely could do much worse – it's a rough place out there being single. And I am not getting any younger.

Yet behind all that chatter there was a simple awareness that I needed to finish this journey I had started, and to not rush into making any decisions until I complete my mission.

"Before I go, can I just tell you one more thing?" I sighed with release, feeling the lightness in my heart space for having spoken so freely and honestly. "I am grateful to you for being my teacher on this journey to find out who I am."

"You're already who you are. I don't think you needed to go so far and do all this crazy stuff to find yourself. Could've saved yourself a lot of time and money."

Dave dryly suggested we meet up when I get back, hastily ending the call before I got a chance to say goodbye.

I sat on my bed for a few minutes staring at the phone, trying to process what had just happened. My mind was still full of commentary, but it was late, so I turned off the lights to get ready to sleep. I planned to call Alejandro the next day to discuss this new development.

Suddenly, the phone pinged and I noticed a message from Ale, checking in on me. I answered back saying I wanted to talk. He called me immediately.

"It's so late; why aren't you sleeping?" he gently inquired.

"I could ask you the same thing." I smiled for his genuine concern, mentally thanking my lucky stars for placing Ale in my life and wondering if the timing of his call held a synchronistic meaning.

"Something was telling me you need me right now. Is everything okay?"

I told him about Dave's surprising reappearance in my life, and his even more surprising request to get back together. It seemed strangely coincidental that Dave was calling me now, at this stage of my healing journey.

"Well, it could mean that you are actually ready for this test."

"What do you mean – a test?"

"At this stage of the alchemical process, it's all about testing the new substance to not only ensure its quality but also to make it stronger. This is where in the science, bacteria and other micro-organisms are introduced into the substance, to initiate the process of *fermentation*. And just like any type of fermentation in food, for example, to make a fine delicacy, in life any form of suffering and hardship makes a person more resilient and that more indestructible."

"Do you really believe that this phone call from Dave was my test to see if I would buckle under the temptation to run back to him, instead of going forward with my transformation?"

"Maybe... who knows? What's important is that you observe how all this made you feel and what new insights come up now, as opposed to how you would've reacted in the past. And then, of course, realizing how all of your work can be integrated into the new self."

I acknowledged the progress I'd made with my newfound ability to stay grounded despite such an unnerving situation, and to be aware of the ego's attempt to take me out of the present moment.

"Do you believe we are a soul family, Ale? I get this feeling like our souls planned to help each other in this lifetime, long before we were both born."

"There are no accidents in this world. We met and became friends for a reason."

An overwhelming wave of affection for this man, who had been such a strong pillar of emotional support for me over the past several years, washed over me. I wanted to tell him how I felt but doubt about his reciprocal feelings stopped me. Instead, I asked him how the date which he had a few weeks back had gone. He told me he'd been seeing this woman a few times and it was going well – they had a "great connection." My ego felt slightly wounded, as the potential of us being more than just friends got pushed back, out of reach. I knew that I loved Ale, because all of me was buzzing with a desire to know him deeper and to take care of him. So if we were not meant for each other as lovers, didn't matter to me, because it was the kind of "real" love that extended beyond possession and attachment. I'd be happy to see him thriving, healthy and in love, even if it was with another woman.

"I love you, Ale," I finally allowed myself to say, and that felt enough.

"I love you back."

I fell asleep shortly after our call, content with the unconditional love I managed to express for Alejandro. I dreamed of him as a famous musician, performing a guitar solo on stage, and myself, watching him from the crowd, admiring his talent and beauty. Unexpectedly, I saw him crumble down and I was swiftly at his side, holding him in my arms. He was bleeding. Had he been shot? I didn't know, but all I wanted was to protect him, to keep him safe. So, I just held him close to my heart and prayed hard that he would be okay.

As that part of the dream dissolved into the background, I was submerged into a beautiful dreamscape of turquoise light, iridescent with diamond-like quality. The light was soft and healing, and I was swirling around in it like an acro-dancer suspended in the air. I was free to fly in any direction and express myself through the most sophisticated and elaborate movements that were possible for the human body. I was singing in the full range of octaves that were available, showcasing my vocal talents, which I suddenly possessed in this dream state. And I was painting the sky like a canvas with each stroke of my arms and legs in vibrant colors as I danced around.

The colorful strokes I left in the sky transformed into a familiar figure – it was Naga. She swayed side to side in her snake-like fashion in front of me, darting her fuchsia tongue, and extended a sparkling light-blue crystal to me as a gift for finding and using my voice. I thanked her and accepted the precious gem, tucking it deep inside myself with great care, alongside the other four gems I had previously collected.

Chapter 20

Kundalini Rising

Nayanna informed me that we were just days away from our destination. The final part of our journey would take us over the border to Mexico's Chiapas region, known for its archeological parks and magnificent natural wonders. I couldn't help but question the significance of Dave's call while being so close to the temple that promised true love to anyone who reached it. I was still having mixed feelings about him.

He says he wants to change... should I give him another chance?

Every morning, I performed my alchemy ritual, choosing the activities based on what I wanted to achieve that day. If I needed a bit more masculine energy, I did the Warrior One movement. If I wanted to tune into my creative flow and let the Inner Goddess play, I would perform the Warrior Two ecstatic dance, which I became quite comfortable with after spending a week at Eagle's Nest, dancing nearly every day at sunset. I continued to activate my chakras through movement, breath and sound daily, and recited the water ritual mantra every time I showered.

Upon our arrival to the lodge in Palenque, Mexico, I was ready to go to the temple, which was about an hour and a half hike away from the Misol-Ha waterfall. Nayanna suggested that we take a day to rest and charge ourselves up with fresh energy from the surrounding nature. The next morning, we drove twelve miles south towards the waterfall.

It was everything one would hope a waterfall to be – water cascading over a hundred feet down into a clear round pool you can swim in, and a roomy cave behind the falls where you could sit and meditate for hours while being coaxed by the soothing sounds. It was hard not to fall in love with this magical place!

Nayanna had much to share with me as we sat down in front of the turquoise pool.

"You are nearing the end of your self-transformation journey. Do you remember the first two steps of the process and the cornerstones of self-love that we've covered so far?"

"Yes, the first two steps for self-transformation are *awareness* and *intention*. And the first two cornerstones of self-love are *self-awareness* and *self-care*."

"Good! And so far, you've put into practice all of these as well as the next step and cornerstone, which I will share with you now. I've been watching you commit to your intentions with daily consistent rituals. That is the third step, and one where many people give up because it is not easy. *Action!* Without action on your intentions, you simply won't make any progress. You must prove your worthiness to achieve the transformation you desire by showing up and doing what you promised to do.

"Whatever healing or change of habit or mindset you wish to create, won't happen by only thinking about it. The universe favors doers, not talkers. In fact, one of my life philosophies is – *action is the best form of prayer*. It's an act of love that creates magic and transforms evil to good, as I'm sure you've heard from all those fairytales in your childhood."

"That's so true!" I agreed, remembering all my favorite stories that my mother and grandmother used to read to me. "An act of true love has been the cornerstone of so many stories. And isn't that why there's an expression, 'actions speak louder than words'?"

"Precisely. Love is a dynamic force. It's a choice, not an emotion. It's an action, not a feeling. Expressing love comes through your actions.

"And with that, you arrive at the third cornerstone of self-love – *Self-Development*. By following your curiosities and passions, and by taking consistent daily moves on your intentions, you work on becoming the next best version of yourself. We can't be content in a static state as human beings. While at our core, we are stillness and presence, it is the drive to evolve that is the purpose of the "one" consciousness. Without that drive there wouldn't be a physical universe. The dance of Shiva and Shakti. The universe is said to have come into existence out of the desire to move forward and experience everything possible by the Great Mind.

"And here we are, almost at the end of the journey and you've learned to master so many aspects of yourself, with just one more step to go in this process. I will share it with you tomorrow before you go to the temple."

"I am going to hike over there alone?" I asked, not able to hide the anxiety in my voice.

"Don't worry, all you have to do is just walk on the path which I'll show you. You won't miss it. This is considered a sacred ritual that one must experience on her own. I've heard how exceptionally profound it is from the people I've sent there, as it was for me on my first visit."

"So did you find your true love after you went there?"

"Of course," Nayanna smirked, "Just like the legend promised. Now I'd like to show you another exercise that you will find very helpful on your walk, and hopefully in your life. This exercise is meant to develop your visualization ability while strengthening your mental resilience. It has been practiced in many forms of marital arts, but also has been used in Yoga and Qi Gong. I call it *sit in a chair, hug a tree* pose. It requires concentration and at the same time letting go of things that your mind doesn't need. I'll give you ten minutes to stay in this posture, so get ready for a bit of discomfort. But you can do it, no doubt!"

~

"Sit in a chair, hug a tree" Qi Gong exercise as taught to me by Nayanna

Open your feet wide and squat half-way down as if you are sitting on an imaginary chair, and open your arms in front of you as if hugging a huge tree trunk. Close your eyes and recreate the image of a waterfall, or any other scene or object, in as much detail as possible. This will exercise the third eye chakra with the power of imagination and visual memory. Observe your thoughts and listen for what kinds of words are coming through for the duration of the exercise.

As you stay there, remember two things – concentrate your attention on the vision you're holding, and relax the rest of your mind when unnecessary thoughts try to derail you. If it helps, imagine that you are sitting in a room with only one chair. As you are the only person in the room, you take your place as the occupier of this space. If anyone walks in and sees you there, they understand that the room is occupied, and they have to leave. Similarly, you must stay alert by taking up all the space inside your mind with your awareness. You are that awareness that sits in the center of your mind, and any thoughts that try to come in will see that the space is occupied and will have no choice but to get out.

After a designated amount of time, which can be anywhere between two to ten minutes, release your body into a child's pose.

~

I could sense my inner warrior stepping up at the half-way mark of the exercise. At five minutes into it, which seemed like eternity, I pressed on despite the involuntary trembling in my arms and legs and the screaming mind that was telling me to give up. I even managed to smile softly as I accepted the moment for what it was, to find joy of the present moment even through the pain.

At the full ten-minute mark, as Nayanna called time, I happily collapsed onto the mat.

"That was impressive to see you smiling through the most difficult part at the end," Nayanna offered her praise. "What you've done there with that smile was actually the last step in the four-step transformation process – *Surrender*. This word gets misinterpreted as giving up, but in fact it's one of the hardest things to do in life – to accept with gratitude things that are out of our control and surrender to the flow of life, instead of resisting or fighting against the current of the flow."

"That's exactly what I did there as my body was shaking uncontrollably. I just let it shake, instead of fighting to stop it or let my mind take me out of the pose because of it. Once I accepted the pain, discomfort and shaking, it was like I've crossed some kind of threshold into a new dimension, where I was peaceful and even enjoyed the sensations. That was incredibly empowering!"

"I'm glad you found it beneficial. This can help you in so many ways in life, especially in challenging or dangerous moments when your mind tries to trick you into believing the worst-case scenario. Keep the focus on your vision – use the power of your third eye to create a solution and best outcome and stay attentive in occupying the room of your mental space, keeping every negative thought out. Take up all the space with your most beautiful dreams, your higher purpose, the reason why you are doing it, and awareness of your unlimited potential. Leave no room for anything else."

"Our potential as humans truly is unlimited. If I could hold that pose for ten minutes, I could probably handle a lot of things that life throws at me. Is there anything I can do to help me activate the third eye chakra more, besides this pose?"

"The *ajna* chakra, as all other chakras that correspond to a specific organ in the physical body, is connected to the pineal gland – a small pine cone-shaped part of the brain, known to be in charge of our intuition, wisdom, and consciousness."

I recalled reading about the pineal gland when I was researching plant medicines and DMT receptors in the brain and remembered that its main purpose is to process information about the light/dark cycles from the environment and to produce and release melatonin to help us regulate our sleep/wake cycles.

"Did you know that children's pineal glands are soft and tender but as we grow up they tend to harden as calcification occurs?"

"No, I didn't. What is calcification and is that a bad thing?"

"It's bad from the perspective of keeping your third eye open. As we get older, and if we don't exercise the third eye chakra consistently, the gland becomes hard and loses a part of its function, which helps us to connect to the divine consciousness. Children are much more connected than adults to the metaphysical dimensions through their heightened perception of energy and their imagination. If we continue to stay sensitive and open to these subtle energies as we grow up, the pineal gland helps us perceive more than just our five senses. We can continue to use intuition and even develop extrasensory abilities."

"How do we make sure that calcification doesn't occur and is there anything we can do to exercise this chakra?"

"One of the ways is through the visualization exercises, like the 'sit in a chair, hug a tree' pose you just did. But the most effective method is to continuously send energy that you absorb from the ground with your root chakra towards the third eye, which is a Kundalini practice, and there are many variations that have been taught by different disciplines. I know you practice yoga and you've had some teachings you received in Bali. Have you tried any Kundalini raising exercises?"

I told Nayanna about some breathwork techniques Krishnaraj had introduced us to, and how I used to experiment with an altered state of consciousness as a kid with my friends that seemed to mirror these patterns of breath and movement.

"Oh, good, you are familiar with the concept. Well, when you perform any of these practices like Uddiyana Bandha Kriya, you are pulling up the energy as if drinking it through a straw from your root chakra and sending it upwards to the middle of your head with the breath. You then retain the breath and hold that energy at the top, feeding your pineal gland with it, while utilizing the *bandhas*, or locks, at the base, middle and throat level to prevent that energy from escaping. Let's try it now together."

We performed the process three times, and after the last one a rush of energy shot through the body up towards the head, making me slightly dizzy. Sitting in front of the waterfall with eyes closed, I let the sounds and other sense perceptions drop me deeply into the present moment. I could feel notes of love in everything around me, from the jungle's hypnotic orchestra to a gentle breeze of wind that kissed my skin. I was in Love. Not with anything or anyone. In Love as a state of being.

"Open your eyes and look around you. Connect to everything here through your senses.

"Listen to the sounds, and the silence between them. That's the stillness, peace and harmony that you are made of.

"See the vibrant colors, patterns and abundance of plants and animal life. That's the abundance you are made of.

"Breathe in the fresh air and aroma of the flowers. That is the sense of joy and happiness you are made of.

"Touch the wood, rock, earth and water to experience the well-being and health all around. That's the well-being you are made of.

"Taste the fruits and waters of nature and experience the Love of the universe that you are made of."

I was in a state of deep awareness and serenity where time became irrelevant. There were no limits to who I perceived myself to be – pure consciousness without any inhibitions.

Nayanna broke the silence and explained that this breath technique increases blood circulation in the body and the brain and stimulates the vagus nerve at the base of the skull, which toggles between the sympathetic and parasympathetic nervous systems. The former activates the "fight or flight" response, and the latter is responsible for the "rest and digest" mode of the body.

"This is why you feel so calm and balanced after. As little as three to five repetitions of Uddiyana Bhanda per day can work wonders on your nervous system and support your holistic well-being. Even your periods will be lighter and less painful if you do this often."

"I'm certainly adding this to my morning alchemy practice. It feels amazing!

"You mentioned intuition as one of the characteristics of the third eye chakra. But I recall you saying that intuition is something that is more of a gut feeling that lies in the sacral chakra. How do I work on developing my intuition more?"

"There are two kinds of intuition – one is more visceral and physical, when your body responds to vibrations whether they are positive or negative. This is the one that comes from the sacral chakra and you may experience it as hair standing up at the back of your neck, goosebumps, butterflies in the stomach, or simply that animal instinct that tells you something is not right. The third eye intuition, on the other hand, is the kind of intuitive sense you get as you grow spiritually and begin to foresee events before they happen. You start reading the metaphysical signals on a subtle energy level and you may even begin to see auras of others.

"The most important thing to do is stay aware of the signals your body is sending you and try to communicate with it. Us, women, are especially connected to our intuition and it tends to develop with time as we learn from mistakes and experiences."

I considered what Nayanna had said and made a mental note to watch for these intuitive signals.

"Alright, that's all for now. Let's go back and rest for tomorrow. We will come back here in the morning and I'll send you off to the temple."

That night, as I was getting ready for bed, I found it hard to settle down. My body was still vibrating with all the prana I had collected during the waterfall visit. I closed my eyes and began to visualize myself walking through the jungle on the path to the sacred temple.

Finally, as I drifted into a deep meditative state, the jungle scene dissipated and the background turned into an indigo sky with millions of sparkling stars. Suddenly, the stars began to fall over me like raindrops. As I looked closer at them, I realized that these were not stars – they were shimmering gemstones shaped like tiny prisms. I marveled at the interplay of rainbow colors that the prisms were projecting as they caught the light.

I was expecting Naga to appear with my gift, but instead, I saw two snakes slinking into my vision, one from the left the other from the right. The pair of serpents met in the middle and began to coil around a staff in opposite directions, intersecting at five points as they climbed up. Once they reached the top, the pair locked eyes with one another and large wings sprouted up behind them at the end of the staff. I recognized this symbol as the *caduceus* – or the staff of Hermes from Greek mythology, believed in ancient times to have the capacity to restore vital energy and bring people back from the dead. But the significance of seeing this symbol now in my vision was lost on me.

A deep blue crystal materialized at the top of the staff, and the two snakes presented it to me as my sixth gift for the opening of my third eye chakra. Taking my prize, I thanked my new friends, and asked them to pass on my gratitude to Naga. I wondered if she'd visit me again.

In the morning, as I recalled the dream, Ale's words about the second to last stage of alchemy – *distillation*, came to mind. He had insinuated that it was here, where the solution the alchemist is left with is boiled and condensed in order to increase the purity of the substance, that presented us the final opportunity to purify the spirit and transcend the ego.

"This is where the new self, one that is not shackled by any construct or destructive elements of ego, begins to emerge. But this is not the stage to sit back and relax. Instead, continue watering the sprout with spiritual rituals that will strengthen it and help it grow. Meditate, introspect and always keep asking the question, 'who am I?'"

I remembered the caduceus symbol from my dream and how the two snakes intertwined at five points along the staff – the five chakra points that I've worked on healing along the main energy channel that runs up the spine – to meet at the third eye and sprout wings behind them.

Perhaps that's what the two snakes in my dream symbolized... the creation of a new "me."

Chapter 21

The Secret of Divine Power

I was sitting next to a tranquil, pristine lake – perfect in its purity and stillness. The water was so clear and blue it was tempting to get in for a refreshing dip. But the serenity of the scene, like a sleeping child, couldn't possibly be disturbed, so I admired it from the side.

I had been walking on the path instructed to me by Nayanna for over an hour, and I should've already reached the temple. Instead, I came to this lake and it left me in a disoriented and confused state.

Should I keep walking, or go back and try a different route? Maybe I took the wrong way?

I had to make a quick decision, but first I needed to rest and drink some water from the bottle I had in my backpack. It was still early, and I had plenty of daylight to go, but I could already feel a slight tinge of anxiety beginning to intrude into the room of my mind.

The day had begun with excitement for finally going to the destination I had set my intention on so many weeks prior. That morning, Nayanna took me to the waterfall where we did our morning alchemy practice and breathwork exercises, activating the chakras and raising up Kundalini energy. I had felt focused with a full reserve of fresh energy running through my body, as I set off on the trek towards the temple.

But here I was in the middle of the jungle, with exhaustion and mental confusion starting to set in. I made the call to go back and try a different path I had seen earlier. I had hesitated to take it and was now regretting that decision.

I just have to follow my intuition and surely it won't lead me the wrong way.

I walked back quarter of a mile to where the road split off into two paths and chose the one I had wanted to take in the first place.

Nayanna's directions were fairly straightforward: walk west on the main path without veering off on to any smaller ones and look for a pyramid structure that's different than the other Mayan temples. I had seen several temples at Palenque Park near which our lodge was located, so I had an idea of what these pyramids looked like.

"When you reach the sacred temple, you'll know it," she told me, "Just keep looking for signs that won't leave you second-guessing yourself."

Being geographically challenged, I had always had trouble with directions and orienting myself spatially. I was now well into the second hour of the hike but the road just kept taking me deeper into the jungle, with no temple nor any signs on the way. With each passing minute I was getting more doubtful, questioning whether or not I was on the right path.

Soon, the vegetation became denser, and it was increasingly difficult to walk through it without moving giant plant leaves out of the way. Anxious thoughts were wrestling their way in, making it harder to breathe deeply. Fatigue was seizing my muscles. I heard rustling in the bushes to my right and froze momentarily, trying to identify the source of the creepy sound.

That could be a snake there! A poisonous one!

Aided by a release of adrenaline that shot up through my body, I sprinted ahead on rubbery legs, not paying attention to where I was going. I just wanted to put some distance between myself and whatever was in the bushes. The amygdala part of the brain activated the flight response, overtaking the prefrontal cortex. There was no more logical reasoning or critical thinking as I was left to operate on pure instinct. I ran like a frantic gazelle spooked by a cheetah.

A few moments later I found myself in a clearing with scattered boulders, and I collapsed down on one to catch my breath and recalibrate. Realizing that I had completely lost track of the path, made me hyperventilate, and I thought I was about to pass out. All of my senses heightened as the body's sympathetic nervous system activated its response. I wanted to lie down to release the pressure in my aching legs. But I was too scared to move – I was in freeze mode.

Find your breath. Exhale fully and inhale deeply, slowly. Feel your hands and each finger. You are okay as long as you are breathing.

I tried to talk myself out of the panic attack I was having. But it was no use. Instead of the logical part of the brain leading the way and thinking rationally about possible options of getting myself out of there, the emotional part was front and center, churning out every possible worst-case scenario.

What if I get attacked by a wild animal? Are there panthers here?

I'm almost out of water! How long can I last without it?

It's possible that I won't make it out before dark, and then I'd have to spend the night in the open jungle!

What if I run into rapists?

I couldn't control my paranoia anymore. Every possibility seemed dangerous and potentially deadly. Looking at my phone, I noticed that three hours had already passed by since I began my trek. There was no signal. I felt fragile and vulnerable like a tiny, insignificant bug that could be crushed between two fingers so easily and wiped off the face of the earth in a second.

The dark thoughts kept getting more gruesome by the second. I was already imagining my parents having to fly to Mexico to retrieve my body to bring it back home for a proper funeral. I flashed forward on to a scene with all my friends gathered together, telling their favorite stories about me and crying over their loss.

Whoa, the mind really does get ahead of what's happening so fast!

I became aware of how the projections of my mind were taking me into the future – out of the present moment.

It's not going to help me out of this mess if I continue thinking about something that hasn't even occurred yet and getting all psyched out!

I need to be alert about what I allow into my mind. What can I think of that can help me get grounded?

I closed my eyes and immediately an image of Alejandro popped up, his sweet smile and deep brown eyes looking lovingly at me. I visualized all of his features to the smallest detail, the way Nayanna had taught me to do in the exercise the previous day. I observed his short thick facial hair above the lips and along the jawline, and a distinctive constellation of freckles under his right cheekbone. I admired his beautiful wide-set large eyes with long black eyelashes and prominent masculine nose. Picturing the stubble on his neck and chest, which was adorned with his favorite gold chain with the ankh symbol pendant dangling from it, I gasped in surprise.

Wait... I have it with me! He gave it to me to keep me safe!

I touched my fingers to the pendant on my chest to make sure it was there, suddenly remembering a conversation with Nayanna at the waterfall earlier that morning. I had asked her whether she really believed in the magic of the sacred temple, or if it was simply something she used to give people hope for finding their true love.

Nayanna pointed to the ankh pendant around my neck and said,

"Any object is meaningless until we assign a meaning to it. This pendant you wear is just an object – a small amount of metal wrapped into a shape, hung on a string for decorative purposes. It is also a symbol that carries cultural significance and represents something to a large group of people. And it is also something meaningful to you for personal reasons.

"What does this symbol represent to you? Why do you wear it?"

I told her that it was something that my best friend gave me to help me on the journey of self-discovery, and it held a two-fold meaning. One being the symbol of eternal life that is believed to bring vitality and balance, and the other, that it was a gift from a dear friend, who loved and believed in me. It was special because I loved and respected Alejandro.

"Yes, so you see, without the meaning that you assigned to it, this object would be useless. Just like a flame, a wick, and some wax – on their own they don't constitute much value for us. But put them together and they make up a candle – an object that is useful and also has meaning for us."

I understood what Nayanna was saying and agreed about assigning a meaning to images of deities, just like people do for a cross, or a painting or sculpture of their God. I had a whole bunch of them on my altar at home. But I still didn't get why she was telling me all this.

"My point with all this, my dear, is that without a conscious mind, a mind that chooses to believe in something magical, there is no magic to be found. If you believe that wearing this symbol or having an icon on your desk will bring you luck, prosperity, protection and health, it is your mind that makes it so, not the actual object itself. So, it's your belief that makes the magic happen! And who is responsible for that belief?" Nayanna paused slightly and then concluded,

"The all-powerful, all-knowing, all-loving YOU!"

I considered what she was saying and then asked her about the meaning we assign for numbers, and how special sequences like 1111; 2222; 3333; and my own angel number – 34, applied here as symbols.

"In exactly the same way," Nayanna answered. "Mathematics is one of the languages of the Universe. It holds so many secrets of life within its mysterious, yet familiar patterns that are prevalent throughout nature and the cosmos. The Fibonacci sequence, for example, is found in everything from a seashell, sunflower, and pinecone to the spirals of the galaxy, and even in parts of the human body. The number 34, by the way, is part of that sequence: 0, 1, 1, 2, 3, 5, 8, 13, 21, 34, 55, 89, 144... and so on."

"So what does the number 34 mean?"

"Learning, growth, expansion... actually, whatever you want it to mean to you. Use it in the same way as the ankh – as a symbol of empowerment, love, strength or anything else you want it to mean. Call upon it in your visualization, remember what it stands for, and invoke the healing, protective, transformative qualities of it to help you channel the love that can transmute any darkness."

As I finished my flashback to Nayanna's words, I suddenly felt very clear-headed, and everything that Ale had said to me at the restaurant about humans as "divine beings" made perfect sense. The power of our belief IS the divine, magic power that gives us the energy to dream, imagine and create. We are the creators who can conceive a new life, build a spaceship, write a book, find a cure, and do so many other incredible things that humans are capable of. If we are made in the image of the creator, as some religious texts assert, then by extension, we are the divine creators ourselves.

This changes everything!

I am not a little spec of insignificant dust in the vast infinite universe.

I AM the universe.

I am not a tiny creature that inhabits the earth.

I AM the earth.

The real "I" is infinitely capable of miracles!

This was equally empowering and humbling. Right then, I had no more doubts that I was in charge of my destiny. I was no longer feeling like a victim of circumstances as I became aware of the incredible power I held within, using my mind as a tool to access it. The visualization exercise helped to ground me in the moment, and the ankh symbol reinforced my belief that I am always guided and protected.

I visualized my angel number and the ankh symbol to find the courage and balance they represented for me and set a clear intention to get out of this predicament. Taking a deep breath and reaching inwards to find my inner warrior, I felt this masculine energy presence as a strong valiant force inside. I imagined myself as a Mayan warrior dressed in ceremonial battle gear, holding a shield and a spear as a weapon. Repeating the Warrior One movement from the morning alchemy ritual a few times, I tuned into the masculine part of myself that I needed in that moment. Gaining more stability and strength in my legs now, I stood up and looked around, scanning the area for possible clues on where the road could be. Realizing that the only way to help myself was to keep moving, instead of staying frozen in fear, I let my warrior sense propel me forward towards the edge of the clearing where I noticed the leaves were bent to the ground.

This is where I had come in and stepped on the leaves. This must be the way back!

Pushing my way through without hesitation, I followed the crushed plants and broken branches for about a hundred yards until I saw the path from which I'd veered off. A massive sense of relief flooded in for saving myself. I decided to head back to the waterfall, where I would be able to call for a car to take me back to the lodge. The temple would have to wait another day as my main priority at this point was a safe return.

When I arrived on the main path that would lead me back to the waterfall, I looked at the fork in the road and wondered whether the first path that I took, which led me towards the lake was actually the right one all along. I didn't want to test fate and risk getting lost again, so I started making my way back when I heard voices and laughter coming from that direction. I was startled to realize they were men's voices speaking in Spanish.

Oh no, this is what I was afraid of – being alone in the woods and possibly running into rapists!

Although I could hear my mind amp up the paranoid thoughts, I remained calm and present, fueled by my inner warrior. I realized that there was no point in imagining something dangerous, which was only a slight possibility. As the men approached, I was alert but composed, which gave me the best chance for dealing with the situation, instead of reacting out of the emotion of fear.

There were four of them and they appeared to be locals, dressed in clothing splattered with paint and carrying buckets and supplies. When they spotted me, the men stopped talking amongst themselves and locked their eyes on me. I confidently made eye contact with each man individually and said "Hola!" to them with a polite nod. I didn't know their intentions, but I wanted to assert my confidence and project positive vibrations towards them. My gut instinct was not telling me to run, and I decided to trust it. The men greeted me back and flashed me their biggest smiles.

"Habla Español, señorita?" the youngest one of them asked me. I was amazed at his striking resemblance to Alejandro. He was roughly the same age as him, with a medium build and a slightly darker complexion, but with the same dramatic dark eyes, which held the same type of intensity and kindness when I locked in on them. He had curly black bushy hair that looked like it hadn't been brushed in years. Although he didn't look in the least bit threatening, there was enough mysteriousness about him that kept me on guard. It was the same mysteriousness, which I found captivating in Ale, and which I always found attractive in men.

"Not well. Un poquito..." I tried to collect all my Spanish words, and when the man saw me struggling, he began to speak in heavily accented English.

"That's alright, if it's easier we can speak in English. My name is Ángel [Anh-hel]."

I introduced myself and felt compelled to continue talking to him. He appeared to have a mixed heritage – a mestizo, which was a large representation of the population here. His features were pleasing to my eye, revealing a native Chiapa background, similar to that of the locals I'd met over the past few days: deep-set eyes, high cheekbones and full lips.

He asked me some questions about the weather and people in my country, and I started to feel more at ease. The other three men, who didn't speak English were looking at us with fascination. Although I wanted to get back to the lodge quickly, there was a curiosity to know how far I was from the sacred temple. My guard had come down and suddenly, I sensed the female presence of my Warrior Two who was ready to be vulnerable and find the courage to ask for help.

"You are from around here, right?" I asked Ángel. "I'm sure you know about the sacred temple that pilgrims come to. Is it far from here?"

"Ah yes, of course, el Templo de Amor. It's a bit more than half-an-hour walk this way," he pointed to the path that I had originally taken but returned from. "You are going to the temple now?"

I told Ángel about my detour and getting lost for a while. My inner goddess was awake and speaking to me as my intuition.

Ask him to take you there! He is your sign that Nayanna told you to look out for.

I could tell the difference now between my thoughts and intuitive feeling. It was calm and easy, rather than erratic and urgent. I didn't intend to put him out of his way, but the thought of walking in the jungle alone and possibly getting lost again was out of the question.

There must be a reason why this man who reminds me so much of Ale appeared, especially after visualizing him so intensely. The power of manifestation!

By chance, I glanced at the bucket of paint in Ángel's hand and noticed a number printed on it. It was a series of zeros followed by the number I had grown to regard as my angel sign – 34. Barely able to contain an excited yelp, I pointed at the bucket and started rambling about how special and meaningful this was to me. Ángel was amused at my elation about a bucket with some numbers and jokingly offered it to me as a gift.

Angel number with a man named Ángel! *This has to be a sign to follow!*

"Would it be terribly inconvenient for you to take me to the temple? I am such a dimwit about directions, I could certainly use a guide in these jungles."

"I am happy to take you. You can tell me more about your country and I can practice my English with you."

Ángel gave his bucket to one of the men and briefly told him what was going on. He then turned to me and said that the village they were walking to is not very far on the other path, and he'd return there after taking me to the temple. The other three men took off in one direction and we went in the other.

The scattered rays of the setting sun were playing with the surrounding nature, making it all aglow with golden shimmery earth tones. The air was warm with only a slight humidity and felt like silk brushing against my bare arms and legs. Ángel was a great companion on the long walk and I learned a lot from him about traditions of the local tribes. He wanted to know more about life in a big city and I told him how "trapped" I've been feeling there lately with an overload of consumption and lack of nature. He said that he sometimes felt a similar restriction living in a small village and wanted to experience more freedom and anonymity that a large metropolis offered. I chuckled internally at the irony of human nature – never fully satisfied with our given conditions and always imagining that it's better somewhere else. Being "here" but wanting to be "there."

However, in this moment, I didn't want to be anywhere else but right where I was. It all somehow felt as though pieces of a giant jigsaw puzzle were finally put together in their right place, creating the finished picture that I had been working on for so long. I had a birds-eye view of my life, as if I zoomed out over it and could at last make sense of everything in my past, present and future. Life seemed to make sense, like never before.

My inner goddess was content at having done her job well in convincing me to ask for help, and she was now enjoying being at ease in a secure presence of masculine energy. I was beginning to understand what Nayanna had said to me back in Peru about intuition finding its own way to communicate with each person. My intuition, as I clearly grasped now, was speaking to me through my inner goddess.

I reflected on the times when I had felt attraction, and other times, repulsion for men in work or personal situations, and how foretelling it actually was for the outcomes of these relationships. The men that I found unappealing and sexually repulsive, always ended up being bad for me in one way or another. I recalled one of Dave's colleagues, Thomas, whom I decided to partner up with in a side business, who jostled me out of a large sum of money. If I had only paid attention to the signs that he wasn't a good person to get involved with in business, I would've saved myself a lot of trouble. From the moment I met Thomas, I had this unexplained repugnance for him. He wasn't a bad-looking guy, and many of my friends found him quite attractive, but I never did. The signals that my intuition was sending me back then were clear now, but I had shut myself off to them at the time, thinking that the fact that I found his appearance unappealing had nothing to do with his trustworthiness. I couldn't justify judging someone on such superficial factors as looks and told myself to focus on his business expertise and other skills. Yet somewhere deep down, my intuition was telling me he wasn't someone to be trusted, and that wasn't the only time it proved to be right. I felt the same kind of aversion towards an acquaintance who offered to be the designated driver for my friends and me at a party a few years ago, and then crashed into a tree while intoxicated, injuring three people including myself.

That female sense is hardly ever wrong, and I was learning how to communicate with mine.

Feeling comfortable with Ángel, someone who I certainly found pleasant-looking and who reminded me so much of Ale, I leaned into my woman's instinct and allowed him to lead me deeper into the jungle.

We passed the same lake which I had walked up to earlier, and I laughed when I realized that I was on the right path from the very beginning. Ángel pointed ahead and said that we are nearly at the temple.

This is it! Three weeks of travel to get here – I'm so close!

The long hours on the road, the moments of catharsis and emotional turbulence, the fears and doubts that stood in the way of getting here, were all massive challenges that I've had to overcome, and I acknowledged them as essential pieces of the puzzle. Without these hurdles, the road to reach the sacred temple wouldn't have been so meaningful and transformative.

Up ahead, about a hundred feet away, camouflaged by the jungle, I noticed a structure unlike any I've seen in Mexico from my research on Mayan architecture. The sun was casting its long brilliant rays just above it, making it appear dark and mysterious. As we moved closer, it revealed more of its magnificence and I was rendered speechless the moment we arrived at its base. This temple was quite different from the typical scaled staircase pyramids with a flat top that I was expecting to find. It looked more like an Egyptian pyramid with smooth sides that connected to a sharp point at the top. The other distinction was its color. While most Mayan temples were a gray or brown shade of rock, this one was almost entirely covered in moss and vines creating an earthy-green lush façade.

"Bienvenidos, señorita! El Templo de Amor!" Ángel announced, proudly presenting the temple.

"I feel like I've traveled back in time! This is straight out of a fantasy novel!" I gushed as we walked around the perimeter. It was as tall as a two-story house and had a small arch-shaped opening on one side. Ángel said that I could go inside if I wasn't afraid of the dark, but it seemed too spooky, so I asked him to help me take a photo in front of it instead.

As I was posing for the camera, I detected some movement out of the corner of my eye. Glancing over my shoulder, I froze in horror.

Watching a dark, long weaving form slithering along the side of the temple sent a zap of electric-like shock through my entire body.

The serpentine shape looked distinctly like a cobra with a signature hood around its head.

Chapter 22

The Prism

"Oh my God, it's a snake!" I yelped as I jerked towards Ángel, who was standing farther away with my phone to capture the entire temple in the frame. "I think it was a cobra, those are poisonous!"

"Cobra? There are no cobras in Mexico. It must be a different kind of snake. Can you show me where you saw it?"

I walked cautiously back to the wall, hiding behind Ángel and pointed to where I had seen the snake.

"I don't see it," Ángel said, straining to catch a glimpse of the reptile in the dim light of dusk, "Maybe it was a shadow or something?"

But I could see it clearly in the same spot, and I suddenly felt a presence of a benevolent female companion that had been with me all along on this journey.

It's Naga!

I didn't question whether she was a phantom of my imagination or had appeared there in physical form by some magic – it didn't matter to me either way. She stopped moving and locked eyes with me. Immediately, I knew that she meant me no harm and was here to see my journey through to the end. I sensed that she wanted me to follow her, and I watched as she crawled inside the temple through the opening in the wall.

Ángel was still peering into the space around the wall, trying to locate the snake. I took a deep breath and allowed my body to relax. I was not afraid, and found myself calm and determined, knowing that I needed to finish what I had started. There was a final piece of the puzzle that was waiting for me inside and I could feel its calling to be found.

There is no point in coming all this way and not taking the final step. I'm coming, Naga!

"You are right," I told Ángel, "it must have been just a trick of my eyes. Would you mind waiting here for a few minutes while I go inside and have a silent moment to myself?"

He replied with a nod and handed my phone back to me so I could use the flashlight setting to illuminate the dark interior of the temple.

Taking a deep breath, I walked in through the doorway slowly, shining the light on the walls and floors and observing what I could see as I passed through the narrow corridor. The atmosphere was slightly more humid and cooler than outside, and smelled earthy and fresh despite the dark closed space that it was. The surface of the floor and walls revealed the smooth gray rock that the temple was composed of and had large patches of moss carpeting it, giving the corridor an inviting feel. An invisible force kept pulling me forward, deeper inside the structure, and I continued walking, letting my intuition guide me even though a faint echo of my mind was sending alarm signals to turn around and walk back out. I focused on my breath and physical senses, which kept my fears and hesitations muffled and distant. I was using my mind as a tool to help me move forward to achieve what I had set my intention on, instead of letting it control me and allowing it to make me run away or freeze in fear. I felt in complete control of my reactions and internal state, like an expert equestrian wielding the reins to maneuver her horse as she needed.

Just a few more steps. Keep the steady pace and just breathe. You are almost there.

I didn't worry about what was waiting for me inside, and simply focused on the process of getting there.

After a dozen more feet, I had arrived at the end of the corridor and panned the flashlight over the frame of the doorway and directly inside the opening. It appeared safe to walk in, so I stepped over the threshold and found myself in a spacious chamber with a small hole right above the center which streamed in a faded light from the top of the pyramid onto a pile of neatly arranged flat-top rocks on the floor. It wasn't bright enough to illuminate my surroundings, but the flashlight was strong enough to see into each corner of the room which appeared to be empty.

Naga was nowhere to be seen. I was alone in this enigmatic space that seemed to separate me from the outside world by a distance far greater than what I had walked to get inside. It was as though I was suspended in space and time and all I wanted to do was dissolve into the vastness, which was all around and within me.

I sat down on the flat rocks in the center and immediately fell into a deep trance-like state. My eyes were closed but I could somehow see the inside of the chamber bathed in a brilliant white light clearly, as if they were open. An unexplained energy began to course through my body, making it feel light and vibrant, like I had felt when I was a child. The boundary between my body and the outside world began dissolving until I couldn't feel the separation of the energy fields that made up everything in existence. I was alert and aware of everything that I was experiencing, but it too, somehow began to blend into the vast ocean of energy that constituted the mental aspect of myself. There wasn't any longer a sense of "me" as an individual person who had a name, identity and personality. Instead, there was a strong conscious presence of a universal "I" that was the only point of awareness that could ever exist. This awareness was reverberating with unfathomable peace, cascading joy, and prolific, abundant love.

"I" floated outside of myself and was now seeing everything, including my body sitting at the center of the temple, as an observer from a higher perspective. As I floated higher, I could see the pyramid where I was actually located, but it looked like a glass prism, which was floating in a vacuum of darkness. My awareness was free to move 360 degrees around the pyramid and observe it from every angle. The two-dimensional geometric shapes that made up the pyramid began to glow on the surface of the glass, revealing four triangles as the sides, and an equilateral rectangle as the base.

The Three cornerstones of Self-love! And the Four Pillars of Self-transformation!

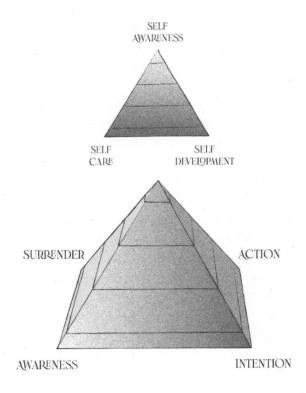

I had a visual representation of what Nayanna had been teaching me through this journey. There was so much divine knowledge contained within the pyramid and its sacred geometry, and I was downloading all of its intelligence, seeing how beautifully it all fitted into my life, and recognizing exactly what I needed to do to live in harmony with the universal laws of the Universe – of God.

A celestial white beam of light entered into the glass prism from the top, coming from an unidentified but evidently infinitely powerful source. It flowed into me from the top of my head, trickling down into the rest of my body, penetrating every cell and infusing me with a sense of holistic well-being. The chakra crystals that I had received from Naga up to this point were all in their place at their respective energy centers, glowing with their most brilliant radiance. A tornado of all of nature's elements, the totality of all species of plants and animals on the planet, light and sound waves of the entire spectrum, and even metaphysical beings like angels and ascended masters swirled around me at warped speed, but I could sense and appreciate the individual energies of each life form.

Naga appeared out of the vortex, looking extra regal with her aura radiating in a violet light, and we exchanged our greetings with one another. She told me that we are connected beyond this lifetime, and that as my spirit guide, I could count on her to be there to help course-correct me should I stray off the path. With that, she dissolved back into the swirling mass of the universe before I could inquire about the final jewel – the one of the crown chakra.

Immediately after Naga's disappearance, the caduceus with two serpents wrapped around it, appeared again, and I was introduced to the two beings as Pingala and Ida. Pingala, the solar, masculine energy, and Ida, the lunar, feminine energy of the Universe. As the polarities merged inside of me to create perfect balance and to connect me to Collective Consciousness, a thousand-petaled pink lotus flower appeared above my head. I watched the petals unfolding to reveal my gift – a violet crystal of the *sahasrara* chakra, signifying spiritual connection with the divine.

Then the beam of light that was streaming from the top through my body began to bend and, just like I had seen in physics experiments where white light diffracts through a glass prism, dispersed into its component colors: red, orange, yellow, green, blue, indigo and violet.

What a beautiful way to show me how each of us can receive the light of divine love and diffract it through the chakras as a rainbow out into the world!

This is exactly what I came here to find!

The true love I came looking for is... the Divine Love!

It's not something that can be given to me, and it doesn't come from outside myself.

It's the love I've had to build inside – my own temple of self-love.

At that moment, I felt like stretching out on the floor into a restorative yoga pose called Supta Baddha Konasana, or the "surrender" pose, which Krishnaraj had taught us in Bali. With my head and chest slightly elevated by the rocks, arms outstretched to the sides, and feet pressed together creating a diamond shape with the legs, this was the physical expression of the energetic state of total surrender that I was experiencing.

I was in complete acceptance of myself and my circumstances, relinquishing all control to the grand Universal order, and allowing life to unfold as it does in its own divine and, sometimes mysterious, way. Releasing all internal resistance for everything which I found unfavorable or unpleasant, I embraced every challenging, painful and regretful event as a blessing. Each moment had always taught me something or otherwise helped me grow, even if the lessons were not so clear at first. I no longer felt that time was my enemy and something that I must fight with, but instead fell into the depth of the present moment, where everything is perfect as it is. It was a massive relief to stop fighting, struggling and paddling against the flow. There was no wanting, chasing, and craving, because everything that I needed – peace, joy, and love – was already within me. I was free to set goals and move towards my next stage of evolution, not out of fear, desperation or external validation that the ego needed to fulfill, but out of my soul's plan, driven by the force of love, for the good of all.

My transformation journey was complete, and the temple securely formed. With awareness still outside of my body, I watched myself levitate off the floor. Then I proceeded to ascend towards the peaked ceiling, and float up and out of the temple to perch on top of it, getting a bird's eye view of the jungle below. The uniform canopy of opulent green treetops spread out as far as I could see in every direction, and out of the thick, lush shrubberies I noticed the tops of other temples peeking out. I could count at least a dozen in my range of view, but I knew there were more out in the distance. On top of each temple there were human silhouettes, all sitting in meditative lotus poses, radiating with bright auras.

Who are these people? How many of them are out there?

I didn't know the answer, but I could sense that this was a tribe of a growing number of people, who have dared to venture into the unknown with a clear purpose: to rise above mere survival, and to heal past and present wounds that prevent them from opening their hearts to live in creation, in harmony with nature, and in peace with each other. Although each path is unique to the individual, all of them lead to the same one universal truth. That truth cannot be described or taught, it needs to be experienced through one's own journey within.

Alejandro's spirit form appeared in front of me, and I suddenly derived a profound understanding from his stories of the Rainbow Warriors Prophecy, and how each of us has the ability to transmute our darkness into light, and channel that light of divine love through the rainbow of our energy centers, to help heal the world.

As more and more of us work on creating internal balance and restore our chakras to their optimal frequencies, we will one day reach critical mass, and join the legendary tribe of these Rainbow Warriors, thereby fulfilling the prophecy and helping humanity move into the next stage of our collective evolution. A higher consciousness of the entire species!

I heard Ale's voice reciting the prophecy as it's been passed down in spiritual circles:

"There will come a day when people of all races, colors, and creeds will put aside their differences. They will come together in love, joining hands in unification, to heal the earth and all Her children. They will move over the earth like a great Whirling Rainbow, bringing peace, understanding and healing everywhere they go. Many creatures thought to be extinct or mythical will resurface at this time; the great trees that perished will return almost overnight. All living things will flourish, drawing sustenance from the breast of our Mother, the earth."

"As for the alchemy process, did I pass the final stage – *coagulation?*" I asked Ale's spirit.

"This stage is about crystalizing into a solid state – a union of your physical and energetic self – of matter and spirit. When 'you' as awareness become self-aware, there is no more distinction between the duality of inner and outer, good and evil, dark and light parts of yourself. You can perceive yourself and everything around you on all levels of consciousness, and each one is simply a reflection of the other."

"So that means that we are all reflections of one another!"

"Precisely! You've passed the final stage!"

Here, above the jungle canopy, the peace, joy and love, which I had been searching for when I first set off on this adventure, was revealed to be my permanent state of being.

It's been within me all along!

Like the sun shining as bright as ever, even on the cloudiest of days.

The sun and the clear blue skies are a constant, just like the light of Divine Love.

And I have access to it in this life and beyond, because... this Divine Love is who I am!

~

The hotel car was speeding towards the airport with Nayanna and me in the backseat. Taking in my last glimpses of the sumptuous forests and rivers we passed along on the wide road, there was a mixture of emotions. I was already beginning to feel nostalgia for the great adventure that I had completed, and the memories of all the experiences I've had and people I had encountered were flipping through my mind like a photo album.

I flashed back on the moment when I came out of the pyramid to find Nayanna waiting for me at the entrance. Ángel had disappeared, and when I asked her about a young man who helped me find the way, she said that there was no one there when she arrived at the temple. She had begun to worry when I hadn't returned to the waterfall before sunset, and proceeded to the temple to find me. Then we walked back together in the dark, arriving safely at the lodge at nighttime.

Had I imagined the whole getting rescued by Ángel scenario? Or was he a guardian angel, who manifested into human form to help me reach the temple?

Maybe he was a real person, and it was all just a beautiful coincidence?

When I asked Nayanna what she thought about it, she gazed away thoughtfully, then grinned and answered that these jungles were known for their magic to those who are open and ready for it.

There was an excitement brewing within, for my newfound insights that I could hardly wait to apply in my daily life.

I'm going to talk to my boss and ask for lighter hours so I can get my eco business going. Mother Earth needs to be loved.

And all children need love too! I should find an orphanage in the city to do some volunteer work with the kids — it's so good for the heart. I might even go back to Nicaragua one day.

And Dave... I am going to see him soon. Who knows? If he's willing to do his inner work, maybe he's got some potential...

Ale... I hope he is happy with his lady. I know I love him, but it's not meant to be. He'll be so proud of me for becoming a true Rainbow Warrior!

Whoever it is that I will eventually be with is going to add extra value to my already rich and beautiful life. I'll never put myself in the background again.

But if I'm meant to be alone for a while... as long as I have my temple of Love, I'll be okay.

Though... I am never really alone. I am always guided and supported by my spirit friends.

There is nothing that I cannot overcome. Everything I can dream of is within reach.

As I was pondering these positive implications of the journey I'd just completed, I recalled the four pillars of alchemy that the author Paolo Coelho had written about in *The Alchemist*:

"One must believe in the Soul of the World."

"One must listen to the voice of the heart."

"One must be faithful to one's dreams, for they both test and reward us."

"One must surrender oneself to the universe."

It seemed to fit in perfectly with the Four Pillars of Self-transformation that Nayanna introduced me to, and which I had seen so clearly in the pyramid.

Believing in the Soul of the World is linked to having the *awareness* of your divine essence as part of a spiritual force, which binds everything and everyone together, governs the order of nature, and speaks to us through mystical signs and coincidences.

Listening to the voice of the heart is your ability to decide what you want to accept as your own truth, and use it to construct your own mental framework to set an *intention* which is right for you, and no one else.

Being faithful to your dreams that test and reward you is the consistent *action* that needs to be taken patiently and devotedly, for it is only those who truly commit to making the change who get to enjoy the fruits of their labor.

And lastly, *surrendering* to the universe is the act of living with non-resistance and non-attachment in order to maintain a high vibration that will keep you firmly on the path towards your ultimate destination.

I shared my revelation with Nayanna and she agreed with the similarity between the four pillars, then added,

"The universe will push you to your breaking point when you are going the wrong way to awaken you, to shake you up, and to get you to notice that what you're doing is not working – that you've strayed off your path. When you become aware and start paying attention to omens and dreams that are placed in your path in a divinely timed manner, that is when you begin the beautiful dance with the universe that will open you up to the blessings of the Great Unknown.

"The moment you see the bad experience or event in your life as a gift, instead of a punishment, and when you pledge to take decisive, courageous action to change your old habits, patterns, and ways of thinking, the universe will help you get back on your path, and it will do everything in your favor, as if having the wind in your back, assisting you every step of the way."

At the airport, as we were saying goodbye, Nayanna embraced me tightly.

"So what do you think, Nayanna, is there hope for humanity? Can we make it as a species to create a future worth living?"

"Indeed, my lovely, one temple of Love at a time!" she grasped me by the shoulders and locked her eyes on mine. "But there's still a great need for work on the individual and collective levels. You've formed your personal temple of Love, but it doesn't stop here. As you build relationships with others, as you start a family, as you reach new professional heights, please don't forget the importance of a solid foundation and the seven jewels which will hold it all in balance, stability and harmony."

I hugged Nayanna warmly and promised to keep in touch with her for guidance on conquering new temples.

Walking through the security checkpoint, my heart was open and full of loving energy, which I energetically sent out to every person I passed. Old structures of my mind have been dismantled, old neural pathways erased, and I was inspired to create the life of my dreams, with new ways of thinking about myself, work, family and love. I no longer derived a sense of self from being a partner to another person, and that was the freedom I had always craved since I was a child.

I was free to make my own happily ever after.

Epilogue

Looking out of the small round window as the plane sliced through the sky, my frequency was set to awe and gratitude. Free of thoughts about future and past, my mind's only job was to imagine the shapes of crisp white clouds as animals or random objects on a cyan blue background. In this subdued mental state, I had so much appreciation for being alive and being able to witness the miracle of life that was unfolding in front of my eyes, thousands of feet up in the air, in the depth of the present moment.

A pilot's voice over the intercom brought me back to the earthly dimension with the announcement of flight time and weather conditions on the way home. I was happy to be coming back, overflowing with a sense of clarity, purpose and self-acceptance.

Eager to tell my stories and share my experiences with anyone who would listen, I turned to the man of Asian descent sitting next to me who appeared to have a pleasantly welcoming and open aura. I asked him whether he was coming back home or traveling out, and he enthusiastically picked up on my invitation for a conversation.

"I'm flying through on the way back home to Thailand," he said with a charming accent. "I just finished my trek through South and Central America. I started in Peru and did the whole tourist thing at the Sacred Valley. But then it turned into more of a spiritual journey," he explained, "Mother Ayahuasca called me and I ended up in the jungle in Iquitos for three weeks doing the full plant medicine dieta. I swear, it was one of the toughest things I've ever done – she showed me who I am… stripped away everything I thought I was. But it opened up my heart big time."

I flashed back on my own ego death and heart opening, giving him a knowing nod and smile.

"Anyway, that just made me want to spread some of that love I found inside," he gestured with his hand to the middle of his chest, "so I went to do some social work for a week at a humanitarian center in Honduras. And just before going back home, I decided to have a bit of fun in Guatemala. Did some shadow work, dancing, cacao – all that hippie New Age stuff."

"An eat-pray-love-party kind of trip?" I teased him and he laughed. "I wonder if we had visited the same places?"

We started sharing our experiences, and it turned out that we had in fact both been at Esperanza de Vida and Lake Atitlán, but missed each other by a matter of days.

After speaking for nearly an hour, I realized I hadn't asked him for his name, so I introduced myself and offered a handshake.

He firmly grasped my hand in return. "Kai," he said simply and his eyes, reminding me of a samurai warrior, gleamed with strength and compassion.

I wondered if this man, who has recently gone through a similar self-transformation journey, was one of the rainbow warriors, one of the tribe members I had seen in my vision sitting atop other temples.

"One temple of Love at a time," I heard Nayanna's voice echoing in my mind.

The plane cruised smoothly, carrying me towards home, and as I closed my eyes, I imagined walking on that winding path leading me to a mountain with the sun shining behind it, having complete faith that the road is leading me exactly where I need to go.

Author's Biography

Natalie Glebova is a best-selling author and mindset & energy coach. Through her own extensive spiritual journey to attain self-love and deeper self-awareness, Natalie started a coaching practice that focuses on energetic aspects of personal development to help her clients become winners in both life and love.

Specializing in using healing and transformational approaches and modalities from all parts of the world, Natalie helps her clients achieve deeper and longer-lasting levels of inner peace and happiness.

You can connect to Natalie through social media:

Instagram: @natalieglebova

Facebook: facebook.com/MissUniverse2005

Website: natalieglebova.com

References

Chapter 1

Spinoza's concepts of "totality of existence" and "substance" as qualities of God.
https://moretothat.com/god/

Chapter 2

Jung, Carl. *Synchronicity: An Acausal Principle*. 2nd edition, 1973

Jung, Carl. *Synchronicity: An Acausal Principle*. 1st edition. Princeton University Press, 1952

Chapter 3

The identity of Eleusinian mysteries in the Greek mystery schools
https://nah.sen.es/vmfiles/abstract/NAHV1N1201328_38EN.pdf

Wasson, Gordon et al. *The Road to Eleusis*, 1978

Psychedelic rituals of the Mayan, Aztec and Incan cultures.
https://akjournals.com/view/journals/2054/3/2/article-p43.xml

Torres, 1996, 2006; Torres & Repke, 2006; Velandia, Galindo, & Mateus, 2008

Chinese traditions recorded the use of hallucinogenic plants.
https://akjournals.com/view/journals/2054/3/2/article-p43.xml

Ancient Egyptian artifacts pointing to a reverence of hallucinogenic mushrooms.
https://www.researchgate.net/publication/7566286_The_entheomycological_origin_of_Egyptian_crowns_and_the_esoteric_underpinnings_of_Egyptian_religion

Berlant, 2005

LSD and psilocybin activate serotonin receptors on brain cells.
https://news.weill.cornell.edu/news/2022/10/psychedelic-drugs-flatten-the-brain's-dynamic-landscape

Dimethyltryptamine (DMT) modulate amounts of serotonin – a neurotransmitter involved in the regulation of mood, appetite, sleep and memory.
https://www.release.org.uk/drugs/dmt/pharmacology
DMT is biosynthesized in the pineal gland in the human brain.
https://www.ncbi.nlm.nih.gov/pmc/articles/PMC6088236/

Chapter 4

The science behind ayahuasca diets https://psychable.com/ayahuasca/the-ayahuasca-diet-what-is-it-and-why-do-it

Shoemaker, Alan. *Ayahuasca Medicine: The Shamanic World of Amazonian Sacred Plant Healing*. Simon and Schuster, 2014

Kounen, Jan, Jeremy Narby, and Vincent Ravalec. *The Psychotropic Mind: The World according to Ayahuasca, Iboga, and Shamanism*, Inner Traditions/Bear & Co, 2009

Chapter 6

A black hybrid beast with characteristics of a demonic creature
Inspired by 2022 Burning Man art installation "Facing The Fearbeast" by artist Tigre Mashaal-Lively with Make Love Visible & Stark Raven Fabrication.

Chapter 7

String theory tells us of ten proposed dimensions with infinite number of realities https://www.smithsonianmag.com/smart-news/our-continued-existence-means-other-dimensions-are-probably-super-tiny-180970487/

Psychedelic substances having a positive effect on neuro-plasticity.
https://www.beckleyfoundation.org/2018/06/13/psychedelics-promote-neural-plasticity/

Chapter 8

Native Americans believed you heal seven generations back and forward.

Hellinger, Bert, and Gunthard Weber et al. *Love's Hidden Symmetry: What Makes Love Work in Relationships.* Zeig Tucker & Theisen Publishers, 1998

Chapter 13

Kapalabhati clears the mind by increasing blood flow to the prefrontal part of the brain.

https://www.researchgate.net/publication/297714501_A_Review_Article_on_Kapalabhati_Pranayama

Chapter 14

Costa Rica produces nearly 98% of its electricity from renewable resources.

https://www.unep.org/news-and-stories/story/costa-rica-living-eden-designing-template-cleaner-carbon-free-world

Chapter 15

Drinking cacao in ceremonial settings has been part of the Mayan civilization since as early as 1500 BC https://www.smithsonianmag.com/history/archaeology-chocolate-180954243/

Chapter 17

The combination of vowels that make up the sound – A – U – M, each one representing a number of sacred trinities.

https://www.hinduamerican.org/blog/5-things-to-know-about-om

Ashley-Farrand, Thomas. *Healing Mantras: Using Sound Affirmations for Personal Power, Creativity, and Healing.* Gateway Books, 2000

Chapter 18

Prolonged exposure to stress may affect the DNA and lead to
   autoimmune diseases or increased susceptibility for illness.
https://www.health.com/condition/ptsd/generational-trauma
Gayani DeSilva, MD.

Chapter 20

The pineal gland's main purpose is to process information about
   the light/dark cycles from the environment.
https://www.ncbi.nlm.nih.gov/books/NBK550972/

O-BOOKS

SPIRITUALITY

O is a symbol of the world, of oneness and unity; this eye represents knowledge and insight. We publish titles on general spirituality and living a spiritual life. We aim to inform and help you on your own journey in this life.
If you have enjoyed this book, why not tell other readers by posting a review on your preferred book site?

Recent bestsellers from O-Books are:

Heart of Tantric Sex
Diana Richardson
Revealing Eastern secrets of deep love and
intimacy to Western couples.
Paperback: 978-1-90381-637-0 ebook: 978-1-84694-637-0

Crystal Prescriptions
The A-Z guide to over 1,200 symptoms and their healing crystals
Judy Hall
The first in the popular series of eight books, this handy
little guide is packed as tight as a pill bottle with
crystal remedies for ailments.
Paperback: 978-1-90504-740-6 ebook: 978-1-84694-629-5

WhatsApps from Heaven
Louise Hamlin

An account of a bereavement and the extraordinary
signs — including WhatsApps — that a retired
law lecturer received from her deceased husband.
Paperback: 978-1-78904-947-3 ebook: 978-1-78904-948-0

The Holistic Guide to Your Health
& Wellbeing Today
Oliver Rolfe

A holistic guide to improving your complete health,
both inside and out.
Paperback: 978-1-78535-392-5 ebook: 978-1-78535-393-2

Cool Sex
Diana Richardson and Wendy Doeleman

For deeply satisfying sex, the real secret is to reduce the heat,
to cool down. Discover the empowerment and fulfilment
of sex with loving mindfulness.
Paperback: 978-1-78904-351-8 ebook: 978-1-78904-352-5

Creating Real Happiness A to Z
Stephani Grace

Creating Real Happiness A to Z will help you understand
the truth that you are not your ego
(conditioned self).
Paperback: 978-1-78904-951-0 ebook: 978-1-78904-952-7

A Colourful Dose of Optimism
Jules Standish
It's time for us to look on the bright side, by boosting
our mood and lifting our spirit, both in
our interiors, as well as in our closet.
Paperback: 978-1-78904-927-5 ebook: 978-1-78904-928-2

Readers of ebooks can buy or view any of these bestsellers by
clicking on the live link in the title. Most titles are published
in paperback and as an ebook. Paperbacks are available in
traditional bookshops. Both print and ebook formats are
available online.

Find more titles and sign up to our readers' newsletter at
www.o-books.com

Follow O-Books on Facebook at **O-Books**

For video content, author interviews and more, please subscribe to our YouTube channel:

O-BOOKS Presents

Follow us on social media for book news, promotions and more:

Facebook: O-Books

Instagram: @o_books_mbs

X: @obooks

Tik Tok: @ObooksMBS

www.o-books.com